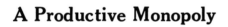
A Productive Monopoly

A Productive
Monopoly

The Effect of Railroad Control on
New England Coastal Steamship Lines,
1870–1916

WILLIAM LEONHARD TAYLOR

BROWN UNIVERSITY PRESS, Providence

International Standard Book Number: 0–87057–123–0
Library of Congress Catalog Card Number: 70–111457
Brown University Press, Providence, Rhode Island 02912
Copyright © 1970 by Brown University. All rights reserved
Published 1970
Printed in the United States of America
By Connecticut Printers, Inc.
On Warren's Olde Style
Bound by Stanhope Bindery
Designed by Richard Hendel

Contents

LIST OF ILLUSTRATIONS ix

LIST OF MAPS xi

PREFACE xiii

1. New England Coastal Lines before 1870 3

The Origins of the Sound Lines 3
Steamship Service in Northern New England 7
Changes among the Sound Lines 10
The Rate War of 1867–69 14

2. Trends and Troubles, 1870–81 17

Developments during the 1870s 17
Changes among the Sound Lines 21
The Lines North of Cape Cod 29
The Rate War of 1877–81 34
The Repercussions of a Collision 40

3. Growth and Consolidation, 1881–99 43

The Steamship Lines in the 1880s 43
    The Establishment of the Interstate
        Commerce Commission 46
    The Impact of the Summer Resort Business 48
    The Growth of the Freight Business 52
The Situation in the 1890s 54
    The Rise of the New Haven Railroad 55
    The Struggle for Dominance in
        Southern New England 57

The Consolidation of the New Haven's Position   62
The Reaction to the New Haven Monopoly   64

4. Technical and Operational Developments,
   1870–1916   68

Technical Developments   68
Steamship Design and Construction,
   1870–1910   69
Propellers and Paddle Wheels   79
The Steam Turbine   81
Improvements in Efficiency   83
The Demand for Speed   84
Improvements in Safety, 1870–1916   85
Operational Developments   88
The Effect of Consolidation   88
Interior Furnishings and Facilities   90
Operating Expenses, 1880–1916   93
Labor on the Coastal Lines   94

5. Rates, Schedules, and Service, 1881–1916   98

Passenger Service   98
The Growth of Tourism   98
Steamship and Railroad Fares   104
The Boat Trains   107
Accommodations and Special Services   109
Freight Service   112
The Rate Structure   113
Freight Rates, 1880–1916   116
The Boat Trains   120
Industries Dependent on the Sound Lines   125
The Importance of the Rail-Water Service   126

6. Terminals and Freight Handling,
   1881–1916   131

Topographical Problems   132

	The Port of New York	132
	New England Ports	141
	Freight Handling	145
	Terminal Operating Costs	150

7. **The New Haven Monopoly, 1899–1907** 153

Competition at Providence 154
Extension of New Haven Control 163
Charles S. Mellen 165
The Formation of the New England
   Navigation Company 166
Competition at Fall River 169
Two More New Haven Acquisitions 173
The Liquidation of the Fighting Lines 175

8. **Challenges to the New Haven Monopoly,
1906–12** 179

Charles W. Morse 180
   The Morse Consolidation 180
   The Battle for Control 184
   The Battle for Patronage 189
   The Collapse of the Morse Consolidation 192
The Metropolitan Steamship Company 193
The Southern New England Railway 198
The Colonial Line 202
Weaknesses of the New Haven Monopoly 203

9. **The Decline of the Coastal Lines, 1912–56** 207

The Investigations of the New Haven Railroad 207
The Dismemberment of the New Haven Monopoly 211
The Investigation of the New Haven Boat Lines 212
The Central Vermont and Maine Central
   Boat Lines 215
The Reorganization of the Eastern Steamship
   Corporation 216

CONTENTS

The Coastal Lines during World War I   217
The Coastal Lines in the 1920s and 1930s   219
Retrenchment and Abandonment   222

APPENDIX A   Tables 1–21   231

APPENDIX B   Organizations and Business Firms
Supporting the Continued Operation of
the New England Steamship Company
by the New York, New Haven &
Hartford Railroad   249

NOTES   253

SOURCES   313

INDEX   317

List of Illustrations

[*Following page 80*]

Old Colony Poster

The *Massachusetts* (*1877*)

The *City of Brockton* (*1886*)

The *Commonwealth* (*1908*)

The *Bunker Hill* (*1907*)

Views of the *Pilgrim* (*1883*)

New York, Providence & Boston Railroad Advertisement

Freight yard of Merchants & Miners Transportation Company, Providence

Piers 18 and 19, Hudson River

Electric Freight Trucks, Pier 14, Hudson River

List of Maps

1. Principal New England Railroads Having
   Connections with Coastal Steamship Lines,
   about 1870   19

2. Routing System of the New York, New Haven &
   Hartford Railroad and the New England Steam-
   ship Company, as Reorganized in 1904   123

3. Port of New York, Manhattan Sector,
   about 1880   133

4. Piers of the New England Coastal Lines in
   Lower Manhattan and Rail Connections, 1916   138

Preface

To THOSE who might think that this is a history of the coastal steamship lines of New England, a word of caution: it is not. It is rather the history of a transportation system serving the economic needs of New England that evolved over a period of half a century. This distinction is not the contradiction in terms that it may seem, for writing of the evolution of the railroad-controlled coastal steamship lines centers on a relatively limited number of lines and only incidentally touches on others. Yet these relatively few routes served every state in New England and provided a service unique in New England transportation.

Much has been written about the coastal steamship lines, but most of it has been of a popular nature and has concentrated on the passenger service they provided. This is understandable, since many still fondly recall the excitement and pleasures of a steamship journey on one of the fine vessels serving the coast of New England. Originally the lines were primarily passenger carriers, but after the Civil War this began to change. As central and southern New England became a leading manufacturing center of high-value goods, ready access to the major markets became necessary. At the same time New York City was triumphing over all her aspiring rivals to become the principal port of the nation and an important manufacturing, marketing, and distributing center for the types of goods produced in New England. As a result a large percentage of New England manufacturers bypassed Boston and shipped their products to New York. For this the coastal steamship lines sailing between New York and ports on Long Island Sound were in no small degree responsible.

Since the earliest days of New England railroading these lines had been controlled by, or had had close relations with, the New England railroads; by 1903 all the lines engaged in through service were owned by railroads. The change in the role of these lines in the years between 1870 and 1916 is what this study describes. I have selected these years because they form a reasonably coherent period in the development of the system. By 1870 the dislocations caused by the Civil War were past, and the lines had taken on the structural form that they retained until World War I. The year 1916 was the last before the United States entered World War I, and it marked the high tide of prosperity for the railroad-controlled lines; thereafter use of the motor truck and automobile and the decline of New England manufacturing altered the role of the rail-water system.

The railroad-controlled steamship lines provide an excellent example of the benefits that can result from a transportation monopoly. The New York, New Haven & Hartford Railroad had many critics, and much of what they said was true. But when these critics urged the separation of the steamship lines from the New Haven, they clearly lacked an understanding of the nature of the system and its service to the region. It was an age of antimonopoly feeling, but fortunately for New England the rail-water system survived its critics and the financial disaster that befell the New Haven Railroad.

My assessment of the value of this system of rail-water transportation and its importance to the New England economy may be questioned because I have not tested the value of the system by economic analysis or measurement. However, comprehensive statistics on the rail-water routes, statistics that can be separated from those of the total operation of the railroads controlling these routes, do not exist; even railroad officials acknowledged that they were unable to separate the two. The statistics that do exist lack a standard base to use in comparing different periods and different railroads with one another or with some standard measure. Moreover, even if it were possible to show statistically that such a system was economically useful or wasteful, a crucial factor would be left out in this kind of impersonal analysis—the attitudes and prejudices of the men who created and used the system. Men do not always recognize the shortcomings of their own time and often prefer to retain what they believe fulfills their needs rather than discard it for some new and untried way that might or might not be more effective. The businessmen and railroad officials considered in this study overwhelmingly preferred the transportation system they had. Little enthusiasm greeted proposals to change it radically. If the transportation system gave these men confidence in their business activities, then, in my opinion, it performed an essential function for New England. I believe that an understanding of such attitudes is far more essential to understanding our past and why America developed as it did than a judgment based on statistics of questionable value.

Those who aided me in this study are many, and I thank each of them. My greatest debt is to the Smithsonian Institution, for a grant that permitted a year's study in the extensive research facilities in Washington, D.C. Howard I. Chapelle of the Smithsonian Institution was a patient teacher and listener to my many questions on steamships and their operation. On matters relating to railroads John H. White, also of the Smithsonian, was most helpful. Others in the Division of Transportation of the Smithsonian Institution were also generous with their time in answering my questions. At the National Archives workers in the Social & Economic Branch and the Records Appraisal Division often went beyond the call of duty in offering advice and making suggestions that made my work easier. I wish particularly to thank Joseph Howerton, Kenneth Hall, and Meyer Fishbein for their assistance.

Dr. Robert Lovett and his staff in the manuscript section at Baker Library, Harvard Business School, were most obliging in meeting cheerfully my requests for the large, cumbersome ledgers and journals of the railroads and steamship companies of New England. They also provided me with information on the location of similar records in other depositories. I wish to thank Mr. Charles R. Shultz of the Marine Historical Association in Mystic, Connecticut, for his suggestions and for the use of the library facilities. The staffs of the Peabody Museum, Salem, Massachusetts, and the New Hampshire Historical Society provided me with considerable information and took time to suggest the names of several people who were familiar with the coastal steamship lines and New England railroads.

For access to the records of Eastern Steamship Lines, Inc., I am grateful to Mr. Charles W. Allen, who took time from a busy schedule to answer my requests regarding the records and to provide me with a place to use them. Mr. Albert J. McLaughlin, former Secretary-Treasurer of Eastern Steamship Lines, sent me records of the company that he had in his possession. Mr. Richard Dole furnished valuable information on the Maine Central steamers, and Martin J. Butler answered several important questions on the New Bedford Line. Much information on the railroad problems of New York City was furnished by John Wadsworth. Finally, Forrest McDonald encouraged me and advised me on problems of research, and his editorial criticisms and suggestions were especially appreciated.

A special note of thanks goes to my wife Joan whose many sacrifices made this work possible.

A Productive
Monopoly

1. New England Coastal Lines before 1870

THE COASTAL steamship lines and the railroads of New England had a long association. The steamers served as the New York connection for many of the early railroads built along the river valleys to the port cities of southern New England. Because it was too expensive to bridge the many rivers that dissected the region, these railroads were not connected until long after the Civil War by a continuous line between Boston and New York along the shore of Long Island Sound. The absence of such a through route assured the dependence of several New England railroads on a steamer connection to New York City.

A brief chronicle of the early history of the New England coastal steamship lines will help in understanding later developments. It would be superfluous for me to recount in detail the evolution of the coastal lines before 1870, for this has been done adequately by others.[1]

The Origins of the Sound Lines

In the early 1800s travel in New England, as elsewhere in the country, was by water whenever feasible, for water routes were normally quicker and less strenuous. With their extensive coastline and many protected harbors, New Englanders did much of their traveling by sea. An itinerary to places like New York City or Boston often involved a land journey to a coastal town, where a ship was boarded for the remainder of the trip. Voyages by sailing vessels were uncertain, but the packets were well patronized.

During the 1820s and 1830s steamboats and then railroads wrought marked changes in travel. Though crude by later standards, they were superior to existing modes of travel. Soon after Robert Fulton perfected the *Clermont,* southern New England reaped the benefits of steamboat service. The reasons for this are apparent. New York was the natural market for Connecticut and was readily accessible by water.

The New Haven Steamboat Company received its charter in 1822, the first company to provide regular service from that port. It became the oldest company in continuous existence, remaining in operation almost to the end of steamer service on Long Island Sound. It began operations many years before any railroads were built, and the thrice-weekly round trips were apparently well patronized. In 1825 daily passenger and freight service was established.[2]

Bridgeport had steamer service by the mid-1830s. When the Housatonic Railroad was completed in 1842 to Massachusetts, the Bridgeport Line became part of a through route to the west. At that time the New York Central Railroad line along the Hudson River had not been constructed. Until the 1850s New York merchants sent goods to Bridgeport by steamer, where they were transferred to the Housatonic Railroad and connecting lines to Pittsfield, Massachusetts. From Pittsfield the shipments moved over the Western Railroad to Albany and points west.[3] Such a circuitous route is evidence that time saved in transit was more important than the distance traveled.

Other steamboat lines to New York operated from Connecticut ports west of Bridgeport, but these lines handled local freight almost exclusively, especially after the construction of the railroads. As a result, they were only a minor factor in the competition for the business between Connecticut and New York City.

By the early 1820s service on the Connecticut River reached the city of Hartford; the Connecticut River Steamboat Company received a charter in 1823. Traffic between Hartford and New York was heavy, and this attracted many steamboat operators. After Fulton's monopoly in New York was broken, the already keen competition on the river increased. When Cornelius Vanderbilt entered the field in the 1830s, the competition became quite heated. Fares were cut, new and faster steamers were constructed, and there was a scramble for business that resulted in reduced revenue for all the lines. In the desire for speed, to attract business, the lines often relegated safety to secondary importance.[4]

Norwich and New London also had steamer connections to New York during this period. The first regular service began in 1817, and various steamboats continued to provide service during the 1820s. Commodore Vanderbilt entered these waters in the late 1830s. Unlike the routes already described, that to Norwich and New London became part of a through route between Boston and New York. In 1840 the Norwich & Worcester Railroad completed its tracks to Norwich, where boats of the Norwich Line connected with the trains until 1843. Because of the difficulties of navigating the Thames River to Norwich, a new rail line was constructed to Allyn's Point, down-river from Norwich. The terminal for the rail-boat connection remained here until it was moved to New London in 1861.[5] Betraying its origins, the line was generally referred to as the "Norwich Line."

To the east, the next port of significance in the coastal service was Stonington. Though never a large commercial center, it was the terminus of the New York, Providence & Boston Railroad, which connected Providence and Stonington, and the steamboats provided the necessary connection to New York. Stonington had one advantage over Providence: it allowed boats to avoid the often stormy water off Point Judith, Rhode Island. When the Stonington route opened in

1837, the steamboats made Stonington just a way station on their journey between Providence and New York, but within about a decade the port was itself a terminal station.[6]

During the 1820s Providence had a decided advantage as the transfer point on the Boston–New York route. The stage ride between Boston and Providence was only about forty miles. In addition, the hazardous trip around Cape Cod was avoided. Regular steamer service to Providence commenced in 1822. As at other New England ports, new lines were continually challenging the established ones, and racing was a common occurrence. The Vanderbilts entered this area too and, as usual, made competition more lively.

The completion of the Boston & Providence Railroad in 1835 ended the stage lines and began a hundred years of rail-water operations. In 1836 the Boston & Providence arranged with Commodore Vanderbilt to operate fast steamboats between Providence and New York to connect with the trains. The new route not only shortened the traveling time, but also made the journey easier and less expensive.[7]

As new rail lines were completed, they brought more business to the steamers. This intensified competition among the ports on Long Island Sound. Citizens of Providence were unhappy when some of the vessels serving the city were transferred to Stonington. In the 1840s and 1850s both forms of competition intensified. For example, in 1845 five different companies operated steamers between Providence and New York, and a new steamboat line began operating between Fall River and New York.[8]

Fall River entered the port rivalry in 1847, when a new steamer service to New York was established in conjunction with the recently completed rail route to Boston. As the "Fall River Line," this was to become the most famous of all the steamboat services on the Boston–New York route. The reasons for its success are many; most significant were its ability to command adequate financial resources and the shrewdness of its managers.

The first company to operate the Fall River service was the Bay State Steamboat Company, organized in 1846 by Colonel

Thomas Borden and his brother, with a capital of $300,000. Borden had operated a small steamboat between Fall River and New York in 1845 and 1846, but there was no connecting boat train until 1847. In May of that year the Bordens joined with the managements of the Old Colony Railroad and the Fall River Railroad to operate a passenger train to the wharf in Fall River connecting on a close schedule with the boat to New York. Two vessels were used in the service: the *Massachusetts* and the *Bay State*.[9]

The Fall River company rapidly increased its passenger and freight business. In 1850 the revenues were sufficient to permit the payment of a 6 per cent dividend. By 1853 travel was heavy even in the winter months: during December, 1,409 passengers traveled from Fall River and 903 from New York; freight revenue for the month was $5,621.34, and total income was $12, 469.78. Revenue continued to increase during the 1860s,[10] and this growth enabled the company to charter and build new and superior vessels that added to the prestige of the line. Because of the competition of the established lines at Stonington and New London, this success is quite impressive.

Steamship Service in Northern New England

North of Cape Cod regular steamboat service started somewhat later than on Long Island Sound. By the early 1830s there were lines running between the smaller coastal towns and cities in Maine. Their history is beyond the scope of this work, but they were stimulants to the local economies and aided in the establishment of the resort business along the Maine coast. It was the companies serving the larger cities like Bangor and Portland that figured most prominently in the economic growth of Maine.

Portland had service to Boston by 1830, but the ownership of the vessels changed frequently. The Eastern Railroad operated a steamboat line between Portsmouth and Portland until the railroad was completed to Portland, whereupon the steamers were transferred to service between Kennebec and Penobscot river ports and Portland. There was additional service to Eastport, Maine; St. John, New Brunswick; and Halifax, Nova Scotia. For many years the Eastern Railroad had a large investment in steamers and wharf property in Maine. Along with the Boston & Maine Railroad, the Eastern owned a substantial interest in the Penobscot Steam Navigation Company, which was organized to operate steamers between Portland and Bangor.[11]

In 1833 the city of Bangor had an organized steamboat company known as the Boston & Bangor Steamship Company. Then in 1843 the Sanford family entered the business. Captain Menemon Sanford had run in competition with Commodore Vanderbilt on Long Island Sound, and when forced from that area he entered the Boston and Bangor trade. In 1845 the Sanford family established Sanford's Independent Line. The Sanford name was retained until 1882, although the family lost control of the company in 1875.[12]

At Portland the Porter family was prominent in the steamboat business. They had formed the Cumberland Steam Navigation Company, which in 1844 was succeeded by the Portland Steam Packet Company. The latter was capitalized at $100,000. Most of the stock was purchased by Portland interests including Captain J. B. Coyle, who had been an engineer on the steamers of the Navigation Company, and whose name was to be conspicuous for many years in the Portland coastal trade. This consolidation of interests enabled the steamers to meet the competition of the recently completed railroad to Boston. The Portland Steam Packet Company was to become dominant in the Portland-Boston service because it served as the Boston outlet of the Grand Trunk Railway, which opened in 1853.[13]

Two other lines of importance to Maine had their beginnings in the 1840s and 1850s. One operated between Boston and the Maritime Provinces of Canada. Limited service to the Maritimes had begun in 1836, but no permanent companies were formed until the International Steamship Company was organized in 1860, with J. B. Coyle a director. Although its terminus was in Boston, considerable Portland capital was invested in the company. The steamers called at Portland and intermediate points on their runs between Boston and St. John. In 1856 service commenced between Portland and New York, inaugurated by H. B. Cromwell & Company. The company was succeeded by the New England Screw Steamship Company in 1860, with J. B. Coyle as president. Although the new company had superior passenger accommodations and faster vessels, it was supplanted in a few years by the Portland & New York Steam Packet Company.[14]

The Maine coast was quite adequately served by steamers, and many of the companies prospered. The Portland Steam Packet Company reported in 1863 that after twenty years of operation it had carried 1,400,000 passengers and 2,500,000 tons of freight.[15] The state had reasonably good service to the Maritimes, Boston, and New York, as well as intrastate routes serving its many islands, rivers, and port towns. The Civil War did not materially injure the Maine routes, and after 1865 traffic and frequency of service increased.

Although Boston had good connections with Maine and the Maritime Provinces, it did not have an all-water service to New York. This situation was in part the result of the inherent danger of rounding Cape Cod, but a more significant factor was probably the commercial rivalry between the two cities. Some intermittent service was started in 1852, but no regular line was organized until after the Civil War.

Where there had been only slight interest in establishing a Boston–New York line, suddenly in 1864 and 1865 two groups entered the field. The Neptune Steamship Company, operating between New York and Providence, decided to send three of its six vessels to Boston to run on the outside route (around Cape Cod) to New York. Central Wharf in Boston was leased for this purpose. Unfortunately the steamers were under charter to the federal government, and it refused to release them. At the same time General James S. Whitney, former collector of the port of Boston, along with Oakes Ames, Peter Butler, John B. Taft, and others, had three or

four steamers that had just returned from government charter. Whitney, anticipating the move of the Neptune Line,
made arrangements to load the steamers with freight for New
York. Before long, business had increased to such proportions
that it was deemed advisable to form a stock company. Some
Boston merchants and several railroad companies subscribed
to the stock, which totaled $100,000, and the Metropolitan
Steamship Company was a reality. Confronted with this formidable opposition and unable to get its vessels from the government, the management of the Neptune Line decided to
sell its steamers to the Metropolitan Steamship Company for
$300,000.[16]

By 1869 the Metropolitan Steamship Company had eight
freight steamers and a capitalization of $500,000. It owned
its vessels free and clear, and the business was reported profitable. Most of the profit was employed to improve facilities,
for no dividends had yet been declared. The company had
good credit and the management was judged to be "shrewd."[17]

Changes among the Sound Lines

As the the steamboat business began to settle into more organized patterns north of Cape Cod, similar developments
occurred among the lines plying Long Island Sound. A line
from New Bedford to New York had opened in 1853, but it
suspended operations at the outbreak of the Civil War. At
Fall River the Bay State Steamboat Company was prospering,
its monthly income in 1862 and 1863 averaging around
$20,000.[18] At Providence, Stonington, Norwich–New Lon-
don, Bridgeport, and New Haven, stability was also beginning to be achieved.

Financial embarrassment, however, was not yet a thing of
the past. Despite the prosperity of the Bay State Steamboat
Company, the directors were considering sale of the company. In 1862 the Old Colony & Fall River Railway (formed
by consolidation in 1854 of the Fall River Railroad and the

Old Colony Railroad) completed an extension from Fall River to Newport. The extension had been opposed by Fall River interests. Officials of the railroad claimed that the opposition was led by the Bordens, who controlled the Bay State Steamboat Company as well as large Fall River textile interests. They also claimed that several thousand more people traveled to Boston via the Fall River route than to New York because steamers were unable to arrive in New York in time to make connections for the south and west; if Newport were the terminus for passenger operations, these connections in New York could be made. Understandably Fall River interests were reluctant to see their city become a way station. Nevertheless, on 5 June 1863, at the office of the American Print Works, President Richard Borden was authorized to sell the Bay State Steamboat Company, including its charter rights, steamers, and real estate in Newport and elsewhere, to the Boston, Newport & New York Steamboat Company. After the sale, passenger operations were transferred to Newport; the freight terminal remained at Fall River.[19]

At Providence the company known as the Neptune Steamship Company was founded in 1863, originally to operate between there and New York. The management had plans for expansion, but as noted in the previous section, the company failed to establish itself at Boston. Early in 1866, however, a consolidation was effected between the Neptune Line and the Stonington Line under the name of Merchants' Steamship Company. The terminus of the Stonington route was moved to Groton, Connecticut, where the New York, Providence & Boston Railroad had extended its tracks. The capital stock in the new venture totaled $2,750,000 and sold at $175 a share. The company had "splendid boats" and was considered a "tip top line." It ordered two large and luxurious vessels that were to be named *Providence* and *Bristol,* and they were to be the finest in the trade. The company was reported as "undoubtedly safe to all appearances."[20]

Then disaster struck. One of its best steamers, the *Commonwealth,* burned at her berth in Groton, and the wharves were destroyed also. Neither loss was insured. The company rebuilt

the *Commonwealth,* but soon afterward she was wrecked off
Orient Point. Groton never again served as a terminal; Stonington regained its former status. These difficulties the company probably could have survived; those that followed in
rapid succession overwhelmed it. The *Commodore* went
ashore near Stamford and was a total loss. The *Plymouth
Rock* suffered a similar fate at Saybrook. Bankruptcy followed in the autumn of 1866, and service from Stonington
was suspended. The *Bristol* and the *Providence,* on which the
company had spent $1,350,000, were sold for $350,000. In
the failure the stockholders of the Merchants' Steamship
Company received three cents on every dollar invested.[21]

Out of the wreckage three new companies emerged. The
Providence & New York Steamship Company was formed by
Providence interests, including the Sprague family. The Merchants' Steamship Company sold six steamers and its Providence real estate to the new company for $690,000. The
Spragues apparently used the new line to haul their own
freight, often filling the steamers with it. The line was so
prosperous that the next year a 5 per cent cash dividend and
a 5 per cent stock dividend were declared. It remained prosperous until the 1870s, when it was hit by a series of financial crises.[22]

The second company to emerge from the disaster of the
Merchants' Steamship Company was the Narragansett
Steamship Company, which purchased the unfinished *Bristol*
and *Providence.* Soon it had them running between New
York and Bristol, Rhode Island, where passengers took a train
to Boston. The route almost at once became known popularly
as the Bristol Line. The capital stock of the company totaled
$1,100,000. Observers reported that it was doing a "splendid"
business and was "well and economically managed."[23] The
Bristol Line came into strong competition with the Norwich
Line, the new Stonington Line, and the Boston, Newport &
New York Steamboat Company.

The third company was the Stonington Steamship Company. It was organized in 1867 under Connecticut statutes.

The authorized capital stock was $500,000—20,000 shares at $25 par. Of these, 13,080 shares were subscribed, with the New York, Providence & Boston Railroad taking 10,200 shares. D. S. Babcock, former New York agent of the Neptune Line, was made president. His cousin, Samuel D. Babcock, was president of the railroad. Operations commenced the following year when the balance of the capital stock was fully subscribed. The railroad took an additional 6,696 shares, giving it a total of 16,896 shares.[24]

Changes had occurred earlier in the decade at Norwich. In the late 1850s the Norwich & Worcester Railroad had suddenly found the New York boat withdrawn when the Norwich & New London Steamboat Company discontinued operations and sold its equipment. This experience made its impression. On 11 July 1860 the officials of the railroad took a leading role in the organization of the Norwich & New York Transportation Company. The company was organized under Connecticut laws, and its charter gave it the right to transport mail, freight, and passengers between New York, New London, and Norwich or other places. At the first stockholders' meeting, held in the offices of the Norwich & Worcester, the railroad subscribed to 8,000 shares (par $25) out of a total of 12,000 shares. Wharves were secured in New York and elsewhere, and the stock of the Norwich & New London Steamboat Company was purchased by issuing Norwich & New York Transportation Company stock. In 1861 a contract was signed between the new steamboat company and the Norwich & Worcester Railroad, which established train connections with the boats at wharves owned or leased by the railroad. The Norwich & New York Transportation Company used these wharves free of charge and, in return, agreed to furnish and maintain regularly two first-class steamers for passengers and two substantial freight boats to operate between Thames River points and New York. In April 1861 the regular terminal was moved from Allyn's Point, below Norwich, to New London. This was the result of a trackage agreement between the Norwich & Worcester Railroad and the

New London Northern Railroad, which gave Norwich & Worcester trains the right to operate over New London Northern tracks and to use its wharf and terminal facilities in New London.[25]

It should be evident that the New England railroads very early decided that independent steamship companies could be a threat to their earnings. Any sudden termination of service was a severe blow to the railroads. At Stonington and Norwich actual control was secured over the connecting lines. Similar moves were made at Bridgeport; the Housatonic Railroad and the Naugatuck Railroad owned securities of the Bridgeport Steamboat Company, which had been formed in December, 1865, with an authorized capital stock of $250,000.[26] The Old Colony & Newport Railway had an arrangement with the Boston, Newport & New York Steamboat Company that in its early years worked well, but within a few years problems began to arise.

The Rate War of 1867–69

The period immediately following the Civil War was a time of increasing passenger travel and freight business. All the new companies sought to gain a share of this business, and the competition resulted in a general rate war among the lines operating between Boston and New York. The problem was compounded by the fact that the Bristol Line was controlled by a group headed by James Fisk, Jr., who also had a large interest in the Erie Railroad. The line was said to be run for the benefit of the managers and not the stockholders.[27] Thus it could operate more recklessly than the other lines.

The traffic during 1867 and 1868 was heavy, but competition forced rates so low that none of the companies earned an adequate return. The fare between New York and Boston dropped to one dollar. Finally, early in 1869, representatives of the Old Colony & Newport Railway interests, the Stonington Line, the Boston & Providence Railroad, the Providence,

Warren & Bristol Railroad, the New York, Providence & Boston Railroad, and the Narragansett Steamship Company met to discuss an agreement ending the rate war.

The agreement, which was signed on 14 April 1869, provided for the withdrawal of the Boston, Newport & New York Steamboat Company from the Newport Line and the freight line to Fall River, and the discontinuance of the Bristol Line.[28] A new route was to be established over the Old Colony & Newport Railway in conjunction with the Narragansett Steamship Company. The contract of the Narragansett Steamship Company (Bristol Line) with the Providence, Warren & Bristol Railroad and the Boston & Providence Railroad was "annulled and cancelled." Fall River again became the terminal of the route through Newport, and Newport again became a way station. Hereafter Fall River remained the terminus of the steamers, and the Narragansett Steamship Company adopted the trade name "Fall River Line."[29]

The agreement also fixed passenger and freight rates. Through fares between New York and Boston were set at $5.00, of which $1.25 was paid into a common fund. This fund was apportioned between the Old Colony & Newport Railway and the Boston & Providence Railroad. Fare reductions could be made only by mutual consent unless the all-rail fare between Boston and New York was reduced. In that case reductions could be made so that the rail-boat fare was a dollar less than the all-rail fare. Freight rates were to be maintained according to the tariffs existing before the rate war, and all special contracts were to be canceled. Thirty-seven per cent of the freight revenue went to the rail lines and 63 per cent to the boats. The Boston & Providence officials agreed that in any arrangements they might make with any steamboat company for transportation of through freight between Boston and New York, the steamboat company would be required to become a party to the agreement of 14 April 1869. If the steamboat company refused, the Boston & Providence was to decline to run its freight trains in connection with said company and refuse to make through rates with it.[30]

This agreement virtually ended rate competition between the Sound lines; it worked well in its early years. Officials noted with satisfaction that the "ruinous competition" that had plagued the Boston–New York lines during the previous two years "will . . . hereafter be avoided," and anticipated that the business would be carried at remunerative rates.[31] The agreement typified a new attitude in the transportation business that in time would be accepted by most transportation men: competition in rates injured the strong as well as the weak.

Settlement of the rate war brought needed stability to the business and showed a certain amount of maturity among the managers and owners. The business now required relatively large amounts of capital. Equipment had to be modern, accommodations reasonably comfortable, and service more frequent. For anyone with an old surplus steamboat to enter the business successfully had become more difficult. At the larger ports an agreement with a connecting railroad was almost mandatory in order to assure more than just port-to-port traffic. Although steamboating had not yet reached maturity, it had come a long way. By 1870 the managers had, if nothing else, recognized that there was enough business for all.

2. Trends and Troubles, 1870–81

THE NEW decade held great promise for the New England coastal steamship companies. The economic disruption caused by the Civil War was nearly past, the rate war in southern New England had subsided, and prosperity seemed assured. Yet concomitant changes were taking place that would limit the expansion and prosperity of the companies.

Developments during the 1870s

At a congressional hearing in 1870 some of the owners and managers of coastal steamship lines expressed concern or outright pessimism regarding the future of coastal trade. Taxes, construction costs, and the growth of railroads were among the factors cited as injuring its prosperity.[1] Certainly there were valid reasons for concern, but the pessimism was overstated. The recently constructed railroads were taking some business from the coastal lines, but there was enough new business for all, and the earnings of the steamship companies in the 1870s refuted the pessimism expressed at the hearing. The only consequential threat to the steamship companies was to be that of railroad competition or railroad control. Already several railroads had invested in these companies in order to insure their connections. This trend most of the coastal steamship companies would find impossible to check.

The railroad network in New England was expanding and consolidating. After the Connecticut River bridge near Old Saybrook was finished in 1870, only the Thames River still had to be crossed by ferry on the all-rail shore line route between Boston and New York. While physical connections were being made, certain railroad companies were expanding. The New York & New Haven Railroad leased the Hartford & New Haven Railroad, and in 1872 they consolidated as the New York, New Haven & Hartford Railroad. In 1869 the Boston, Hartford & Erie Railroad had leased the Norwich & Worcester Railroad. The former went into receivership in 1870, but when it was reorganized as the New York & New England Railroad, it retained the Norwich & Worcester lease as well as control of the Norwich & New York Transportation Company.[2] As the rail systems expanded, they often had access to far greater financial resources than independent steamship companies.

It is worth noting that as these railroads achieved all-rail connections to New York City, they also retained their interests in the steamship lines. The first New England railroads had been built along the river valleys running approximately north and south, and the steamship routes provided through connections to New York. The construction of east-west rail links had no major impact on the prosperity of established coastal routes, for other, compensatory forces were at work. What did change was the type of operation. The decade of the 1870s proved to be the last when companies with slow, small steamers and uncomfortable accommodations could prosper.[3] Passengers patronized the lines that provided comfort, and shippers were demanding fast and dependable freight service. Spurred by improved railroad schedules, night trains with sleeping cars, and more comfortable coaches and parlor cars, the steamboat companies built new and superior vessels. The sleeping car and the operation of night trains meant direct competition between all-rail and rail-water routes where it had never before existed.

Developments during the 1870s

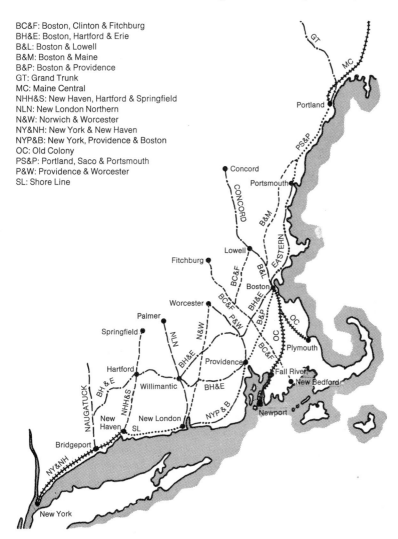

BC&F: Boston, Clinton & Fitchburg
BH&E: Boston, Hartford & Erie
B&L: Boston & Lowell
B&M: Boston & Maine
B&P: Boston & Providence
GT: Grand Trunk
MC: Maine Central
NHH&S: New Haven, Hartford & Springfield
NLN: New London Northern
N&W: Norwich & Worcester
NY&NH: New York & New Haven
NYP&B: New York, Providence & Boston
OC: Old Colony
PS&P: Portland, Saco & Portsmouth
P&W: Providence & Worcester
SL: Shore Line

MAP 1. *Principal New England Railroads Having Connections with Coastal Steamship Lines, about 1870 (Adapted from Baker,* Formation of the New England Railroad Systems)

There were two factors that enabled the coastal steamship companies to remain prosperous despite these challenges. The first was the rapid increase in New England manufacturing, especially cotton textiles, woolen goods, boots and shoes, and paper products. These items were ideally suited to the service supplied by the coastal steamship lines and the connecting railroads. Because the finished products—especially the textiles, woolens, and footwear—were of high value, transportation costs were less significant than the quality of the service needed for delivery. After the Civil War New York became the principal market for such goods, even though Boston was much closer to many of the factories. Businessmen in Boston recognized the problem but were unable to find a solution.[4] Dependable and rapid service to the New York market meant business for the steamship lines and influenced entrepreneurs choosing a location for their facilities. Such service, in conjunction with the cheaper cost of raw materials and fuel shipped by sea, brought about a concentration of industry in the regions under study and the development of a unique transportation system. In time each would rely on the other for survival.

The second factor was the rise of the summer resort business. This was particularly true in northern New England, where after about 1885 the coastal lines increasingly depended upon this business. Many resorts could be reached much more easily as well as more cheaply by steamer than by railroad. Inland resorts were accessible by a rail-water journey that avoided most of the heat and dirt of a long rail journey. In 1870 there were many established resorts such as Saratoga, Newport, and Martha's Vineyard. Compared to those that existed a mere decade later, however, these resorts were insignificant. Early in the decade resorts in northern New England were underdeveloped. To reach many areas in Maine and New Hampshire that later became popular resorts required a fairly lengthy stage ride. That travel to these areas was still something of an adventure can be seen by advice given in a travelers' guide published in 1868: the traveler should not drink water "in unaccustomed places," nor rely on timetables published in railway guides. The descriptions given of some "resorts" reinforce the author's warnings.[5] Comfortable and dependable transportation, which both railroads and steamboats supplied, made development of these resorts possible.

Changes among the Sound Lines

For a few years after the settlement of the rate war of 1868–69 relations among the companies south of Cape Cod were satisfactory. Earnings were quite good, ranging between 3 per cent and 15 per cent per annum, but two of the companies were soon in financial difficulty. These were the Narragansett Steamship Company and the Providence & New York Steamship Company. Their failures were related to the depression that struck in 1873.

Because of the character of its management, the Narragansett Steamship Company has a unique place in the history of the Fall River Line. It was headed by James Fisk, Jr., and he provided more color in the short time he controlled the line than anyone before or after him. In 1868 the Fall River Line, then operated by the Boston, Newport & New York Steamboat Company, was considered second in quality to the Bristol Line, operated by the Narragansett Steamship Company.[6] When Narragansett Steamship took over the Fall River Line as a result of the agreement of 1869, the prestige and quality of the *Bristol* and *Providence* became identified with that service. Fisk loved to dress in ornate uniforms and promenade around Pier 28, Hudson River, in New York before the departure of the steamer to Fall River. It was he who began the practice of having bands on the steamers, an innovation soon adopted by the other Sound lines. The furnishings of the steamers were also in keeping with Fisk's love of opulence and display.[7] Once such standards were established, the Fall River Line maintained them in all future vessels.

Another noted personality having an interest in the Narragansett Steamship Company was Jay Gould. His relations with the Erie Railroad and his fights with Cornelius Vanderbilt were well known. Gould was never as active as Fisk in the management of the Fall River Line. Nevertheless, his connection with the company aroused misgivings regarding its management because of the way he had destroyed the credit of the Erie. It was said in financial circles that Narragansett Steamship was heavily mortgaged and badly in debt to creditors in Newport and Fall River; cash-only transactions with the company were recommended.[8]

When Fisk was murdered in 1872, Gould became president of the steamship company. The flamboyance declined after Fisk's death, but the financial situation did not improve. Under the agreement of 1869 the Old Colony & Newport Railway had paid $100,000 to the Narragansett Steamship Company, successor to the Boston, Newport & New York Steamboat Company, but the railroad was not entirely satisfied with the new relationship. In 1873, three years before the contract expired, the management of the railroad was already speculating that it might be advantageous to control its own steamers.[9]

While the financial condition of the Narragansett Steamship Company was under a cloud, its reputation for dependability increased. The *Nautical Gazette*, the only marine periodical of the period, praised the company lavishly. Clean linen, not always common at that time, was said to be a feature of the Fall River Line. The *Bristol* and the *Providence* were recommended as comfortable and safe.[10] Upon such items a reputation was built, one which later managements very carefully nurtured.

The Fall River Line, at best only a minor subsidiary among Gould's investments, declined in importance after Fisk died. The dissatisfaction of the Old Colony Railroad (in 1872 the Old Colony & Newport Railway changed its name to Old Colony Railroad) made the position of the Narragansett Steamship Company insecure, for the railroad had the financial resources to establish its own line to New York.[11] The decision of Gould to get out of the steamboat business was probably influenced by these factors.

On 1 April 1874 the General Court of Massachusetts granted a charter to the Old Colony Steamboat Company. It could operate in the waters of Narragansett and Mount Hope bays, New York, and intervening waters, using as many vessels as needed. The directors of the Old Colony Railroad had made their decision: only a company controlled by the railroad would be satisfactory.[12]

The Old Colony Steamboat Company was organized on 29 May 1874; at the stockholders' meeting of 11 June the capital stock was fixed at $900,000. The Old Colony Railroad owned $741,000 of the total, thereby insuring absolute control of policy and operations. Most of the directors and principal officers were the same for both companies, and Onslow Stearns was president of both. Authorization was given to a committee of three to negotiate for the purchase of the assets of the Narragansett Steamship Company. The negotiations were successful. By 11 June the Narragansett Steamship Company had sold its properties to the new corporation for $1,800,000 and settled its affairs.[13] To the general public the outward changes on the Fall River Line were few; to the financial community the situation was a marked improvement. One observer considered the credit of the new company "abundantly good."[14]

Although the Old Colony Steamboat Company was controlled by the Old Colony Railroad, the two companies were separate entities. Each maintained its own accounts, and through rates were proportioned between them. This arrangement was advantageous to the railroad because it was not liable for any contracts or losses incurred by the steamboat company. Its only loss would be its investment in steamboat stock. Of the through passenger fares the steamboat company received 65 per cent and the railroad 35 per cent. The former retained all meal, stateroom, and bar receipts. On freight the steamboat company received between 60 per cent and 80 per cent of the rate.[15]

In his report to the stockholders in 1875, the president of the Old Colony Railroad noted that business had been poor on the New York route. In spite of this the Old Colony Steamboat Company declared an 8 per cent dividend. Clearly the railroad had made a propitious investment. In 1876 business increased, primarily because of the Centennial Exposition in Philadelphia. The management observed: "The results thus far have satisfied the directors of the wisdom of the stockholders in authorizing the purchase of this [steamboat] property."[16]

In 1874 the directors authorized the purchase of stock in another steamboat property. Seeing the growing potential of the summer tourist business on Nantucket, the Old Colony invested $30,681 in the Nantucket & Cape Cod Steamboat Company.[17] The investment in this stock grew until, by the mid-1880s, the railroad had a considerable interest in the lines to Martha's Vineyard as well as Nantucket.

Still another steamboat route that was to come under the control of the Old Colony Railroad was the one based in New Bedford. Service from that port to New York had begun in 1853, as textile manufacturing began to replace whaling in the New Bedford economy. The Civil War brought a suspension of operations, since the steamers were in government service, but after the war the company resumed operations and prospered on the passenger and freight business generated by the new industry. A considerable area of the waterfront formerly devoted to whaling was cleared, and new facilities were built to handle coal and general cargo. In 1874 the company was reorganized as the New Bedford & New York Steamship Company, adding two new steamers and increasing its capital stock from $75,000 to $400,000.[18] The Boston, Clinton & Fitchburg Railroad, which had leased the New Bedford Railroad in 1873, used the New Bedford Line as its outlet to New York, running boat trains that furnished considerable freight. The management of the railroad had plans to make New Bedford a major Atlantic port for through traffic from the West.[19]

These plans never materialized because of the financial difficulty encountered by the Boston, Clinton, Fitchburg & New Bedford Railroad after 1876. Only with the aid of its creditors did it avoid receivership.[20] The steamship company also had financial problems beginning about 1876. Around

New Bedford rumors were heard that the railroad planned to gain control of the line, but the railroad was in no condition to pursue this goal. In 1877 the steamers were making three trips a week and were said to be "doing a losing business." No doubt the rate war that had begun between the Boston–New York lines was responsible for some of these losses. Within a short time the debts of the New Bedford & New York Steamship Company were almost equal to its assets. In 1878 Otis Seabury, president of the company, and two other individuals gave a personal loan to the company, with two of the steamers as collateral. By early the following summer three vessels had been attached, debts were increasing at an alarming rate, and the directors were seeking a purchaser for the steamers.[21]

At this time the Old Colony Railroad leased the Boston, Clinton, Fitchburg & New Bedford Railroad. The lease to the stronger road promised a larger return to New Bedford Railroad stockholders than would be possible if the railroad remained independent, but it placed the steamship company in a worse position; sale of the steamers to the Old Colony seemed the best answer. On 27 June 1879 the directors of the Old Colony Steamboat Company appointed a committee to consider whether to purchase the steamers *City of Fitchburg* and *City of New Bedford,* which had been built by the New Bedford Line in 1874, or whether to construct one or two new freight boats. In August the Old Colony purchased the vessels, which were converted for freight service and operated on the New Bedford–New York route. Passenger service was discontinued. The New Bedford & New York Steamship Company continued in existence until at least 1886, but it ended all service in 1880.[22]

Its control of traffic at New Bedford and Fall River made the Old Colony system dominant in southeastern Massachusetts. The two cities were growing rapidly and would supply valuable high-grade freight ideally suited to the rail-water service to New York. The Old Colony was already the largest railroad in the state, and its boat lines were becoming the most prosperous on the Sound.

While several of the ports in southern New England were

prospering because of co-ordinated rail-water service between Boston and New York, Providence was less fortunate. First-class through service from Boston to New York had ended more than a decade before the Civil War. The local passenger service provided by the Providence & New York Steamship Company was acceptable, but it was in no way comparable to that of the Fall River, Stonington, or Norwich lines. The company's freight boats did have connecting rail service, but Sprague freight often occupied much of the capacity of the steamers.[23] In 1872 the Providence Line steamer *Metis* was rammed and sunk off Watch Hill, Rhode Island, with considerable loss of life. Since the *Metis* was not insured, the loss cost the company between $125,000 and $150,000. Despite the disaster, the business continued to be moderately prosperous, and the stock, which had been selling at about half its par value, did not decline noticeably.[24]

The following year, however, the collapse of the A. & W. Sprague Manufacturing Company, which controlled the steamship company, brought hard times to the Providence Line. The breakup of the Sprague empire involved substantial litigation, but efforts to free the Providence & New York Steamship Company from Sprague control proceeded more rapidly.[25]

In March 1874 the directors of the Providence & New York Steamship Company agreed to merge with the Stonington Steamship Company. Until the terms could be agreed upon, the former would lease its property to the Stonington company. The profits were divided, and the operations were directed by the management of the Stonington Steamship Company. By April 1875 the two lines had merged under the new title Providence & Stonington Steamship Company. The former Providence Line properties were valued at about $1,400,000, and the holders of its stock accepted as payment stock in the new corporation. The Stonington management was retained, with D. S. Babcock as president. Authorized capital stock totaled $1,500,000, of which $1,260,000 was issued. Observers regarded the new company as "one of the best managed" in New England. The New York, Providence

& Boston Railroad retained a controlling interest in the new company, owning $804,900 of the stock.[26]

Steps were taken immediately to improve the quality of service. In 1877 the *Massachusetts* was completed, setting new standards for Sound travel. The arc lights in her main saloon were said to be the first installation of electric lights on board ship. The dining hall was on the main deck, a feature probably copied from the Stonington Line steamer *Rhode Island*. Moving the dining hall from the lower deck to the main deck made the facilities far more pleasant for the passengers.[27]

The following year the company restored through Boston–New York service on the Providence Line. On 9 December 1876 Henry A. Whitney, president of the Boston & Providence Railroad, signed a five-year contract with D. S. Babcock establishing the conditions for the service. The railroad agreed to furnish first-class train service to connect with the boats at Fox Point, in Providence, where baggage, freight, and passengers between New York and Boston were to be transferred. All loading and unloading expenses were to be borne by the steamship company. The newest steamers, *Massachusetts* and *Rhode Island*, were to run daily except Sunday from May to November; the rest of the year the line was to carry freight only. The steamship company was to receive 75 per cent of the rates and fares unless the passenger fare dropped below $2.50, whereupon the railroad was to receive not less than 62.5 cents as its portion. Meal, stateroom, and bar receipts were to be retained by the steamship company. The agreement did not apply to the participation of the railroad in rail-water service via the Stonington route nor participation in the all-rail route between Boston and New York.[28] This new contract resulted in monthly passenger revenue during 1877 more than triple the amount when service was local. The president of the New York, Providence & Boston Railroad was pleased with the contract, even though he realized that the new route would "undoubtedly" reduce the amount of traffic carried on his railroad between Stonington and Providence. Increased dividends from the steamboat company would make up some of the loss, and future possibilities were considered good.[29]

In 1876 the principal rail-water routes between New York and Boston—via New London–Norwich, Stonington, Providence, and Fall River—were controlled by railroad companies. Their motives were clear, for independent connections were uncertain in the best of times, and at other times perhaps nonexistent. The Old Colony Railroad had tried several kinds of agreement, but its directors finally recognized that the company had to control its steamboat connection to New York.

The companies west of Stonington were prospering in the 1870s. The Norwich Line did well despite the financial collapse of the Boston, Hartford & Erie Railroad. Only for the years 1874–76 and 1879 did the company fail to declare any dividend, and before and after those years dividends were between 8 per cent and 20 per cent annually.[30] Except for a few months in 1873 and 1874 New London continued to be the principal terminus of the Norwich Line. The boat trains met the steamers at the wharf of the New London Northern Railroad, and in the summer special through trains operated between New London and the White Mountains. The New London Northern also co-ordinated its train schedules with the steamers. Freight business on the Norwich Line was often heavy enough to require an extra freight boat. Some freight service still operated to Allyn's Point, where special trains for Boston met the steamers. This service speeded the delivery of fresh fruit to the Boston market.[31]

When the Vermont Central Railroad, predecessor of the Central Vermont Railway, leased the New London Northern in 1871, it made a temporary agreement to have railroad freight travel to New York via the steamers of the Norwich & New York Transportation Company. However, the railroad "immediately saw the necessity of controlling its own traffic, to control delivery and to secure the business in New York." It soon purchased two old steamers to serve this route, and the freight agreement with the Norwich Line was terminated, although the Norwich Line boat trains continued to use Vermont Central tracks. The Vermont Central steamboat service did not actively compete with the Norwich & New York Transportation Company because it served primarily Vermont Central territory and carried no passengers.[32] In later years it became an important differential route to the West.

The condition of the New Haven and Bridgeport lines was truly one of affluence. The Bridgeport Steamboat Company paid dividends ranging from 9 per cent to 120 per cent annually; the New Haven Steamboat Company paid between 5 per cent and 70 per cent.[33] At the New Haven wharves there were connecting boat trains for Springfield run by the New York, New Haven & Hartford Railroad, a special service instituted because the principal railroad station in New Haven was a considerable distance from Belle Dock, the New Haven Line terminus. Freight service was also well co-ordinated with the New Haven Railroad, and the company operated a day boat to New York as well as a night boat. The New Haven Steamboat Company was considered a "gilt-edged concern" with as much traffic as it could handle. In the mid-1860s and later in 1875 it had competitors, but it outlasted them.[34] Despite the agreements that the Bridgeport and New Haven companies had with the local railroads, they managed to retain their independence throughout the remainder of the century.

The Lines North of Cape Cod

The decade was a satisfactory one for the coastal steamship companies based north of Cape Cod. In Boston the Metropolitan Steamship Company was doing quite well. Because its stock was owned by a relatively small number of people, it published no annual reports, which makes difficult any detailed assessment of its business affairs. However, its history to 1905 indicates that it was a well-managed company with continually increasing traffic. It had connections in New York for Philadelphia and Baltimore, and rail connections in Boston with all the railroads west and north of the city.[35]

During the early 1870s the Metropolitan Line had a close relationship with the Clyde Line, but this seems to have terminated by 1875. The capital stock of the company was said to have been $500,000, and in 1872 it had $75,000 cash on hand.[36] Such a financial condition would have warmed the heart of any entrepreneur.

The traffic between New York and Boston was sufficient for the Metropolitan Steamship Company to order a new steamer. She was named *General Whitney* in honor of Henry A. Whitney, president of the company. Financial conservatism in no way impaired the design of the *General Whitney*—which cost $285,000—and she incorporated significant features new or rare in New England coastal steamers. She was an iron propeller vessel with a high freeboard, making her more suitable for the rough weather often encountered on the outside route around Cape Cod. The vessel can be classed as a steamship, as opposed to the low-freeboard side-wheelers often referred to as steamboats. The freight handling facilities on the *General Whitney* were much improved over those on existing steamers. She had special cribs to keep baled cotton from shifting, four independent hoisting engines to operate her seven freight cranes, and easily handled port shutters.[37] The Metropolitan Line handled considerable baled cotton and manufactured cotton goods from textile cities like Lowell, Lawrence, and Haverhill. The *General Whitney* enabled the company to offer superior service in competition with the lines from Fall River, Providence, and other ports south of Cape Cod. Because of such progressive ideas, the Metropolitan Line was soon considered the most prosperous coastal steamship route operating out of Boston.[38]

The down-East lines shared in the increasing business, largely because of growth in manufacturing and in summer resort business. The coastal lines to Maine and Canada had an advantage over those south of Cape Cod: a railroad system along the coast was practically nonexistent. The coast of Maine has many deep indentations and innumerable harbors, small rivers, and islands. Railroad construction in this area was very expensive, and except for Portland and Rockland there were no cities of significant size to provide traffic. The return on such an investment made railroad construction unattractive. This gave the coastal steamship lines a freer field, which they did not neglect. The interstate routes also prospered because they provided better service than the railroads.

As we have seen, the Portland–New York route was served by several companies before the Maine Steamship Company was established in the spring of 1868. It succeeded the Portland & New York Steam Packet Company, which had been sold at auction.[39] Until 1875 the new corporation fared well, declaring annual dividends as high as 80 per cent, and seeing its stock sold above par. Then it met competition from the Cromwell firm that had formerly been active in the Portland–New York trade. However, the Cromwells failed shortly, and their failure left the field to the Maine Steamship Company. The company underwent some refinancing in the late 1870s after which its prosperity was unbroken. The rate war that began in 1877 between the companies in southern New England cut revenues, but this setback was temporary. Business between New York and Portland increased for several reasons. Portland was the winter port for Montreal and thus provided considerable freight tonnage. It was also the principal city of Maine and a leading rail center. As a result, freight was sent there to be shipped to New York. New York was a major market for Maine manufactures and agricultural products as well as a source of supply for raw materials like baled cotton. Although the trip from Portland took thirty to thirty-five hours, it was faster than freight could be moved by rail. With two trips a week the normal schedule, the steamers of the Maine Steamship Company had all the cargo they could handle.[40] In fact, by 1880 cargoes were taxing the capacity of the company's two steamers. Poor rail service between New York and Portland provided the Maine Steamship Company with increasing numbers of passengers. The necessity of changing trains and railroad stations in Boston made an unbroken sea voyage seem very attractive, especially during the warm months.

During these years the railroad officials often appeared oblivious to the inconvenience to passengers of changing trains. In 1870 the president of the Maine Central Railroad observed that "the change of cars at Portland is rather agreeable . . . after riding an hundred or more miles in a car" from Boston. Transferring freight from one car to another was quite another matter; it cost the railroad money, and the lack of through service upset the president.[41] This contrast in attitudes illustrates that the era of catering to passengers had not yet arrived.

Service to the Maritime Provinces continued under the International Steamship Company. Now it had connections with the Maine Steamship Company so that passengers could purchase through tickets and check baggage to their destination. The shortsightedness of Maine railroads is seen again in 1875, when the officials of the Maine Central and the European & North American Railroad were unable to renew their arrangement for the operation of a night train between Boston and St. John, New Brunswick. The management of the Maine Central believed that operating such a train between Boston and Bangor would not be remunerative and that the attempt to divert "a large and growing business from the water to the [rail]road" did not then look promising. The through rail service was not considered again for several years.[42] Considerable traffic that otherwise would have gone by rail stayed with the steamships. All of these factors made the International Steamship Company a healthy corporation, and its stock often sold above par whenever it could be found on the market. Ownership of the company remained concentrated among Portland investors.[43]

At the end of the Civil War a new steamship service began along the Maine coast. The new company received its charter in January 1864, by a special act of the Maine legislature, as the Portland & Machias Steamboat Company. The company was organized late in 1865, with Captain Charles Deering the guiding spirit. Then in 1867 the name was altered to Portland, Bangor & Machias Steamboat Company because Bangor was the terminus for one of its steamers.[44] The company operated two steamers from Portland: one stopped at Rockland, Camden, Belfast, Searsport, Bucksport, and Bangor; the other served Rockland, Castine, Deer Isle, Southwest Harbor, Bar Harbor, Mount Desert Island, and Machias.[45] Many of these points were becoming summer resort centers, and few had direct rail service. As a result, the company did a fair, though never very prosperous business. J. B. Coyle, manager of the Portland Steam Packet Company, was a director, but apparently he was not active in the management of the company. After 1874 the company began to feel the effects of railroad competition, as new rail lines were completed to places like Rockland, Bucksport, and Belfast. The company, as a result, dropped service to Bangor and concentrated on the coastal route to Machias and Mount Desert Island.[46] At times barely meeting expenses, the company struggled on, with its future in doubt.

The Portland Steam Packet Company suffered somewhat from railroad competition but not enough to endanger its financial position. The Boston & Maine and the Eastern Railroad were fighting each other, as well as the steamboats. No co-operative agreement between the ship companies was reached until the next decade, when, under the leadership of J. B. Coyle, the Packet Company joined with the International Steamship Company in purchasing the steamer *Falmouth*. This was one of a series of moves that brought the lines serving Portland into a close relationship.[47] Coyle seems to have had a major role in getting the Maine companies to co-operate with one another. Such arrangements made it easier to meet the threat posed by the railroads.

At the end of the decade certain patterns were evident. Topographical features created quite marked contrasts between the principal steamship lines based north of Cape Cod and those south of the cape. The northern lines were all independent of railroad control, whereas the majority in southern New England were under railroad control. This pattern began to develop well before the Civil War. In that period the southern coastal lines provided the only satisfactory route to

New York. The coastal lines to the north and east of Boston remained independent because the railroads expanded outward from Boston rather than building from inland to points on the coast and thus had no need for steamer connections to Boston. The steamship companies, like the Portland Steam Packet Company, that paralleled railroads, continued to provide alternative services, usually at lower cost. They retained sufficient traffic to provide good earnings while the northern railroads looked primarily to interior New England for new sources of traffic. In addition, many of the northern steamboat companies did not duplicate railroad routes, as did many of the lines in southern New England. Finally, the marketing conditions at Boston were quite unlike those at New York. At Boston rapid delivery from northern New England was not normally required; when it was, the rail facilities were adequate to handle the business.

The Rate War of 1877–81

During the 1870s one of the most common forms of competition among transportation companies was the rate war. It had the disadvantage of injuring the strong companies as well as the weak ones. Numerous attempts had been made by New England transportation companies to end these wars, but most proved unworkable. What spurred them to settle their differences was the most widespread rate war the region had ever experienced.

The agreement signed in 1869 between the Fall River Line group and the Stonington Line group worked satisfactorily until 1874. The reasons for the subsequent conflict are not clear, but the formation of the Old Colony Steamboat Company may have been partly responsible. Whatever the cause, the New York, Providence & Boston Railroad and the Stonington Steamship Company brought suit against the Old Colony Railroad and the Narragansett Steamship Company to recover money alleged to be due under the agreement. The attorney for the Old Colony group entered a demurrer stating that the agreement permitted the "right to combine to destroy competition" in freight and passenger traffic; such contracts, he continued, promoted monopolies and were "against public policy."[48] There is no record of a decision by the Rhode Island Supreme Court, thus indicating that the Old Colony demurrer was sustained. Additional supporting evidence is the signing of a new agreement between the Sound lines in the spring of 1875. It terminated the war in freight rates that had been in progress for several months. Freight tariffs were raised from 25 per cent to 40 per cent. Passenger rates had remained stable throughout the period. Signatories were representatives of the Stonington, Providence, Fall River, Norwich, and Metropolitan lines.[49]

Harmony reigned for almost two years, but then the conflict was renewed. This time it was far more severe and encompassed a wider area. Two events were largely responsible for this rate war. One was the re-establishment in May 1877 of the through Boston–New York service via the Providence Line. The Old Colony interests were understandably concerned about this new service, which was certain to reduce passenger travel on the Fall River Line. The new Providence Line passenger service operated from May to November, during the only months that passenger service was profitable. Also, the Providence Line had through connections to the White Mountains, which were somewhat closer by rail to Providence than to Fall River.

The establishment of an all-rail freight line between New York and Boston was the second reason for the renewed conflict. The new route was a co-operative venture of the New York, New Haven & Hartford Railroad and the New York & New England Railroad. This new competition was the reason given by officials of the Old Colony for withdrawing from the freight compact signed in 1875. Within a very short time freight rates had dropped to two-fifths of those prevailing under the compact.[50]

Before long, recriminations were being made by officials of all the companies involved. In annual reports to the stockholders, the managements either placed responsibility for breaking the compact on another company or pleaded that such a step was taken to protect the company's own well-being. The president of the New York, Providence & Boston Railroad charged the Old Colony group with unfair tactics in trying to prevent the establishment of a first-class Providence line. Onslow Stearns, president of the Old Colony Railroad, maintained that the Norwich Line had caused the cut in passenger fares by establishing a $6.00 round-trip fare between New York and Boston. The old fare had been $10.00. The Fall River Line was forced to cut its round-trip fare to $7.00. In the matter of freight rates, Stearns stated that the Old Colony had never inaugurated any reductions; the reductions were made solely to match the cuts by other companies.[51]

Attempts were made during 1877 to restore the former tariffs, but the companies could not reach an agreement. The management of the New Haven Railroad offered to withdraw the all-rail freight line if the Providence & Stonington Steamship Company and the Old Colony Steamboat Company would agree to restore the through passenger fare to the $10.00 rate. The Old Colony refused. The New York, Providence & Boston management charged that the refusal was due to the re-establishment of through service on the Providence Line. If this service was not withdrawn, an Old Colony official was alleged to have said, his company would inaugurate and continue the fight until the "weakest went to the wall."[52]

The Old Colony maintained a rather pious attitude during 1877 and 1878. Onslow Stearns claimed that the Old Colony Railroad was less dependent upon the New York traffic than were the other companies involved in the rate war. He also refused to cut passenger fares because doing so might attract enough additional business to interfere with the established quality of the Fall River Line service.[53] After 1878 the company could hold out no longer.

No company achieved any real benefit from these reductions. Despite the increased traffic on some routes, earnings were lower, and a few companies lost money. Officers of the companies involved did their best to assure stockholders that everything possible had been done to keep earnings high. All hoped for an early termination of the conflict.[54]

To compound the difficulties, two new, low-fare steamboat lines were put into operation. Such lines, known as fighting lines, were not a novelty, but they had not been used for several years. In 1878 a low-fare line started between Allyn's Point and New York. The boat connected with the Norwich & Worcester Railroad, and the one-way fare was $1.00. This forced the Fall River Line to reduce its fare to $1.50, the same as that of the Stonington Line. During the following summer the Fall River Line restored the $3.00 fare, as did the Providence Line when it opened in May 1879. Then in June, using the two oldest vessels in its fleet, the Old Colony inaugurated the so-called Newport Line, with the through fare set at $1.00. Freight and passenger trains met the boat at the Newport wharf. The ostensible purpose of this service was "to relieve the stress upon the regular boats." The Newport Line steamers *Old Colony* and *Newport* also carried the Fall River freight, enabling the withdrawal of the regular Old Colony freight boats during the summer season of 1879. With the addition of these two routes, six steamboat lines operated in the New York to Boston rail-water service during the summer of 1879. Three of these charged a fare of $1.00. As one wag observed: "It is cheaper and safer to go to Boston on a steamboat than to stay ashore."[55]

The rate war was a boon to travelers. Occurring at a time when resort and excursion traffic was already rising, the low fares attracted considerable extra patronage, which increased the revenue on most lines. The Stonington Line, with its dollar fare, carried in 1878 and 1879 more than twice the number of passengers it had carried annually during the years 1869 to 1872. The Fall River Line carried about 400,000 passengers during the summer season of 1879—a record. Despite this heavy business neither the Old Colony Railroad Company nor the Old Colony Steamboat Company declared a dividend that year. The next year, when dividends were restored, the steamboat company decided to construct a new steamer in the same class as the *Bristol* and the *Providence*, an indication that the company was not suffering too heavily.[56]

A peripheral outgrowth of these years was a sharp increase in passenger travel during the late fall and winter months. December to March was normally a poor time for passengers on the steamers; harsh cold and snowstorms sometimes reduced passenger lists to a dozen or two on vessels able to carry several hundred people. In the autumn of 1879 the Fall River Line continued Sunday service an extra month because of this increased business.

The impact of the rate war on the railroads was severe. Trains between New York and Boston that had averaged three hundred passengers now averaged less than fifty.[57] Clearly these conditions could not continue very long without destroying the financial stability of southern New England's transportation network.

Although exact figures are difficult to locate, it is clear that freight rates underwent a similar decline. They were at least 25 per cent to 60 per cent lower during the rate war than in 1876. No doubt officials of these companies concurred with the statement that freight rates were "next to nothing."[58] As was true in passenger operations, the low rates attracted additional freight business.

For a while in the summer of 1879 the Stonington Line reduced its through fare to fifty cents one way, and the Norwich Line announced that its fares were subject to "daily reductions." During the following spring even the Fall River Line reduced its through fare to one dollar. Such fares created a problem in public relations. It was now much less expensive to buy a ticket between New York and Boston than to many intermediate points. Although the cheaper tickets were good only for "continuous passage," passengers used them for intermediate stations whenever possible.[59] These conditions of uncertainty and instability became more and more intolerable.

During 1879 and 1880 several attempts were made to end the rate cutting, but despite every effort no understanding could be reached. The management of the Old Colony still demanded as the price of settlement the termination of through service on the Providence Line. With fares sometimes fifty cents and freight rates at an equally unprofitable level, economic logic sooner or later had to prevail over all other considerations.[60] The greatest obstacle was getting agreement among so many companies. In 1869 only two groups had been involved; in 1880 there were four groups totaling eight companies.

Finally, on 18 January 1881, satisfactory terms were agreed upon and a contract was signed.[61] The provisions were explicit, touching on all the major issues that had precipitated the original difficulties. First-class all-rail passenger fares between New York and Boston were set at a minimum of five dollars; the first-class rail-steamer fare was to be four dollars from June 1 to October 1 and three dollars the remainder of the year. Freight rates were fixed at approximately two-thirds the level in 1876. The contract allowed the Metropolitan Steamship Company a 15 per cent to 20 per cent differential on some goods because of its second-day delivery to New York; rail-water routes south of Cape Cod offered next-morning delivery from many points. All rebates and the issuance of free passes were forbidden. In addition to this contract, officials of the Stonington Line and the Fall River Line signed a separate agreement dividing revenues of the "through passenger business" accruing to both.[62]

The immediate effect of the agreement was a decline in traffic, but the higher rates increased revenue considerably. The prevailing sentiment was that business was "more satisfactory" under the new conditions.[63] After this agreement no significant rate wars occurred during the nineteenth century. The New England transportation companies had finally learned that no one gained from them. Indeed, this impression was so strong that George Henry Watrous of the New Haven Railroad believed that rate cutting was one of the "greatest curses" affecting the industry.[64]

The 1881 contract in no sense ended competition, though it did change it. Henceforth competition would be confined to service—the dependability of freight delivery, the elegance of a company's steamers, and such intangible items as courtesy and the type of passengers traveling on each line. This type of competition brought stability to the business, and memories of recent events quickly discouraged any thoughts of renouncing the contract. Events after 1877 made clear to all that the transportation business had undergone a major change during the decade. The railroads were now dominant throughout southern New England, and their presence was very noticeable as far north as Maine. Steamship company officials could no longer make decisions without assessing the impact of these decisions on the railroads.

The Repercussions of a Collision

While still engaged in the rate war, the Providence & Stonington Steamship Company was involved in a series of accidents that reflected on the reputations of the other lines as well as on its own. The gravest of its misfortunes occurred on the foggy night of 11 June 1880, when the company's steamers *Narragansett* and *Stonington* collided in Long Island Sound. It was the most serious disaster in these waters in several years. The *Stonington* sustained only damage to her bow, but the *Narragansett* caught fire and sank with a loss of thirty lives. Over two hundred of her passengers were rescued by the *Stonington* and two other steamers.[65]

There was bitter censure of the captain and crew of the *Narragansett* as well as the management of the company. The *Nautical Gazette* was particularly vitriolic. The editor charged that the life preservers on the *Narragansett* were bad or rotten, that the lifeboats were improperly launched, and that panic seized the crew.[66] The magazine had previously been critical of the management of the Providence & Stonington Steamship Company, apparently because its president, D. S. Babcock, before assuming that position had been involved in the Pacific Mail Steamship Company scandal. The hostility of the *Nautical Gazette* had continued during the rate war, when it blamed the intransigence of the company for prolonging the conflict. Also, on a night in 1879 when neither the Norwich Line nor the Fall River Line steamers left their berths because of poor weather, the Providence & Stonington Steamship Company had allowed the *Massachusetts* to sail. She became involved in a minor accident for which the management had to share some of the responsibility.[67]

The collision between the *Stonington* and the *Narragansett* brought to a culmination the hostility of the *Nautical Gazette*.[68] Babcock wrote an open letter to the press defending the crew and the company. Fortunately for the company, the formal investigation by the United States Steamboat-Inspection Service exonerated the management of any interference with the officers of its steamers, although the management was charged with assigning too few licensed engineers and watchmen. The captains of both vessels were blamed for the collision, and the captain of the *Narragansett* was censured for failing to fight the fire.[69]

Later the same year (1880) the *Rhode Island* went ashore at the entrance of Narragansett Bay. Only her engines were salvaged, to be used in the construction of a new steamer of the same name. Despite these two misfortunes the company did not suffer too severely financially; its earning power was "never seriously affected." Insurance covered most of the losses on the *Narragansett* and the *Stonington,* and the *Narragansett* was salvaged and rebuilt by the company. The company paid no dividends from 1881 to 1884, but did have a surplus after charging off all losses resulting from the accidents. Despite its difficulties the steamship company retained its normal share of the New York–New England business.[70]

These disasters inevitably tarnished the reputations of all the Sound lines. Prompted by a collision between a tug and the *City of Worcester* of the Norwich Line, the *New York Times* published an editorial that objected to the high speed of the Sound steamers when running through the East River, where the collision had taken place. The callous manner of the officers on these steamers was also criticized. They would "rather run down a small boat than turn out of their course." The *Nautical Gazette* defended the officers of the Sound steamers and accused the *Times* of being "brutal, malicious and vindictive in the extreme." The formal investigation cleared the officers of the *City of Worcester*, thus vindicating the position taken by the *Gazette*.[71]

Incidents like these illustrate the difficulties encountered along the hazardous route between New York and New England. Certainly many of the disasters were avoidable and inexcusable. Fortunately, the officers of the coastal lines recognized that the public would not tolerate continued disregard for the safety of passengers. The result was that steamers built after 1880 began to incorporate features that provided a much improved margin of safety. That the coastal steamship companies were successful in retaining the confidence of the public can be seen in the record of dividends paid by the companies during this and the following decades.

3. Growth and Consolidation, 1881-99

BETWEEN 1881 and 1899 the coastal steamship lines underwent considerable change. Passenger and freight traffic increased on almost all lines, and to accommodate this traffic all the major companies constructed new and larger steamers. Even the depressions that occurred did not affect earnings to any significant extent. Perhaps the most important development was the consolidation of the individual companies into larger corporations.

The Steamship Lines in the 1880s

Although some aspects of the business were transformed in this period, on the whole the 1880s were more peaceful than the 1870s as far as competition went. The relative calm was broken in southern New England only once: the People's Steamboat Company began operations in 1886, thus challenging the Bridgeport Steamboat Company. Formed by leading businessmen of Bridgeport, People's entered into a heated fight with the older company, involving extra boats, low fares and freight rates, and racing. During the next few years the Bridgeport Steamboat Company suspended dividends, but its general financial condition remained good. In 1889 it began

buying stock in the People's Steamboat Company, and by
1890 the Bridgeport Steamboat Company was managing
both lines. The following year dividends were again declared.
The incident was closed on 1 July 1892, when the Bridgeport
Steamboat Company leased all the property of the People's
Steamboat Company for fifty years.[1] No similar incidents occurred in southern New England.

The other Sound lines and railroads remained quite content with the new conditions. New, fast, six-hour trains between Boston and New York no doubt injured passenger business on the steamship lines, especially during the depression
years of 1885 and 1886, but the more prosperous companies
continued to declare dividends. So satisfactory were relations
that in February 1886 the Old Colony lines and the New
York, Providence & Boston lines renewed their agreement on
the division of the through passenger receipts.[2]

Two significant changes took place in the ownership of the
steamship companies to the north, where, otherwise, conditions were stable, with increasing freight and passenger business. The Bangor-Boston route of Sanford's Independent Line
had come under new owners in 1875, when control of the
company passed from the Sanford family to a group of Boston bankers. They changed the name to Sanford Steamboat
Company; in 1882 the title became Boston & Bangor Steamship Company. The freight agent was Calvin Austin, a man
who was to become a very prominent figure in coastal shipping.[3]

The second change was the entry of the Maine Central
Railroad into the steamboat business. When the decade began, the Portland, Bangor & Machias Steamboat Company
had already encountered financial difficulty, and its future
was in doubt. The season of 1880 was profitable, and the
stock of the company rose to about ten dollars a share. Increasing summer travel to Mount Desert Island was becoming a major source of revenue. Then in the summer of 1881
the *City of Richmond* was lost, a blow from which the company was unable to recover. Early in 1882 stockholders voted
to sell the real estate and steamer to a new corporation to be
called the Portland, Bangor, Mt. Desert & Machias Steamboat

Company. The new company was organized on 20 January 1882, with a capital stock of $125,000. The shares of the old company were reckoned at five dollars each; the stockholders received about 10 per cent of their original investment.[4]

The new company acquired all the property of the old one, including the *City of Richmond,* which was rebuilt. The prospects for the new corporation seemed good, for the management was composed of men of ability. The first year of operation brought a 10 per cent dividend. Earnings continued satisfactory, enabling improvements to the steamers as well as the payment of dividends.[5]

In 1884 a radical change occurred in service to Mount Desert Island. The Maine Central Railroad opened a rail line to a place on Hancock Point called Mount Desert Ferry, where a steamer met the trains for the transfer of passengers to Bar Harbor. This meant considerable competition for the steamboat company and resulted in poor earnings in 1884. During the summer of that year the railroad acquired 1,064 shares of steamboat company stock. This gave the railroad a controlling interest, and it had an option to purchase the remainder of the stock. The price paid was fifty-five dollars a share—five dollars above par. The next year it purchased an additional 1,132 shares. The Maine Central now owned about 2,200 shares out of the 2,500 outstanding, with the remaining 300 owned by the Boston & Maine Railroad. The Maine Central ended boat service to Bangor, and the name of the company was changed in 1886 to Portland, Mt. Desert & Machias Steamboat Company.[6] Following the practice of other railroads, the Maine Central operated the company as a separate corporation, but many of the officers and directors served both companies.

Other changes were inaugurated almost immediately. In place of the Portland and Bangor service a thrice-weekly service was established during the summer months between Portland, Rockland, and Bar Harbor. This accommodated the growing summer business to the area. The same boat also served Machiasport. Service during the winter months was suspended in 1886 because of a lack of patronage. The new schedule permitted the sale of the *Lewiston* to the Boston &

Bangor Steamship Company; the rail line to Mount Desert Ferry had eliminated the need for the two-boat service.[7]

Except for the International Steamship Company, the decade was prosperous for all the Maine companies, and they were able to construct new steamers and pay dividends. The International Steamship Company suffered a succession of misfortunes not unlike those suffered by the Providence & Stonington Steamship Company. The *Falmouth* burned at her berth in Portland, and two other steamers were wrecked, one being a total loss. The company survived, but changes in the management were made. J. B. Coyle became president, thus bringing this company into an even closer relationship with the Portland Steam Packet Company and the Maine Steamship Company. Coyle, Portland agent of the Maine Steamship Company, was held in the highest esteem by the local business and financial community.[8]

The Boston & Maine Railroad, after gaining control of the Eastern Railroad, its rival on the Portland-Boston route, made no serious attempts to acquire any steamboat lines. Keen competition did continue between the steamboats and the Boston & Maine. Certainly the close relationship among the steamboat lines out of Portland and the ability of J. B. Coyle gave the companies added strength in competing with the Boston & Maine for traffic. Finally, in the late 1880s the Portland Steam Packet Company and the railroad reached an agreement. A scale of rates was established designed to give the steamers the heavier classes of freight. Without the competition of the coastal lines rail tariffs would no doubt have been higher.[9]

The Establishment of the Interstate Commerce Commission

During these years a continual problem for many transportation companies and shippers was the instability of rates. Until 1881 few of the formal agreements between New England transportation companies had worked to anyone's satisfaction, and they were usually abrogated within a few years. Agitation for federal control of rail rates increased during the early 1880s, and it did not go unnoticed in Washington.[10] New England was far from unanimous in its support for a federal railroad commission to regulate rates. The Maine Railroad Commission noted that there was not the ill feeling toward the local railroads that existed in the South and West. The steamboat interests were opposed to any regulation of port-to-port water rates, but were in favor of the regulation of rail rates. The Interstate Commerce Act of 1887 gave the Interstate Commerce Commission authority over rail-water rates, but port-to-port rates were excluded from the original act. In 1889 there was an unsuccessful attempt by railroad interests to have coastwise rates placed under the authority of the commission. As might be imagined, those favorable to the coastwise companies responded with a harsh dissent.[11]

The Interstate Commerce Act did benefit, temporarily at least, some of the steamboat companies in Maine not under railroad control or influence. Railroads having water competition at certain points attempted to adjust rates to comply with the act while remaining competitive with the water lines. This brought protests from noncompetitive points; eventually these inequities were resolved to the satisfaction of all interested groups. The Maine Central, however, did not at once attempt to meet competitive water rates. The International Steamship Company was delighted and picked up considerable extra business. Finally, after a ruling by the Interstate Commerce Commission, the railroads were allowed to meet the water rates without violating the short-haul clause of the Interstate Commerce Act.[12]

The immediate impact of the commission on the steamship companies was slight. These companies had generally resolved satisfactorily their differences and after 1887 had few conflicts. Not until after 1900, when it was endowed with additional authority, did the Interstate Commerce Commission become a valuable asset in checking the abuses of monopoly then threatening the New England transportation system.

The Impact of the Summer Resort Business

As noted earlier, there were substantial increases in passenger travel. Several reasons may be found. A crucial one was the population growth in New England and the Middle Atlantic states. Although New England lagged behind the rest of the nation in the percentage of growth, all six states added population in every decade between 1870 and 1900.[13] The number and size of the industries of the region also increased, which meant that business-related travel became significant during the months when vacation travel was light. Salesmen and businessmen often favored the coastal steamers because of their comfort and their early arrival at their destination.

The greatest stimulus to passenger travel was the annual summer migration from the cities to the mountains, lakes, and seashore. New England was ideally suited to capture a large portion of this business because of its pleasant summer weather. Southern New England had long been a favorite of people seeking to avoid the oppressive summer heat of New York City, while Cape Cod held the same attraction for the affluent residents of Boston. Newport had, in fact, been a summer resort in the colonial period. Northern sections of New England, because of poor transportation, lagged in attracting summer visitors. Travel in Maine around 1870 was quite difficult, if not primitive. Guide books noted that there were many attractive sights in Maine, but physical comforts in the state were few. "In many places, he [the traveler] will not find road or inn at all, but must trudge along painfully on foot, or by rude skiff over the lakes, and trust to his rifle and his rod to supply his larder." Mount Desert Island was described as an "out-of-the-way nook of beauty" having poor connections with the rest of the state. The nearest railhead was Bangor, a forty-mile stage ride. The infrequent steamer service to Mount Desert Island was hardly designed to encourage extensive tourist travel.[14] Conditions were not dissimilar in the mountains of New Hampshire. Some rail lines penetrated the mountains, but many hotels still could be reached only by a lengthy stage ride.

By 1880 several developments had begun to change this. Perhaps most influential was the growing number of people who could afford the luxury of a summer vacation. These people demanded facilities equal to those to which they were accustomed at home. The transportation companies began to promote resort areas by publishing pamphlets extolling their virtues. Simultaneously schedules were improved and additional summer trains and boats were added to accommodate the trade. New rail lines were sometimes constructed solely to reach resort areas. This stimulated the construction of new hotels and the enlargement and modernization of existing ones to handle the anticipated patrons. Alone, none of these developments would have been sufficient; together they created a booming business where in some instances nothing had heretofore existed.

An example of the effort by the railroads to increase their share of the tourist business is the construction of the branch line serving Bar Harbor by the Maine Central Railroad. In 1882 the president of the railroad pointed out that there had been a large increase in the road's passenger traffic due to the "increased travel to Maine by tourists and pleasure seekers." The potential of this business seemed limitless. Recognizing the profits to be made, the railroad constructed the branch from Bangor to Mount Desert Ferry, built a terminal, and purchased a steamer to carry passengers the eight miles to Bar Harbor. The sole purpose of this branch was to serve the summer passenger business, for freight business on Mount Desert Island was negligible. As noted, at the same time the Maine Central purchased a controlling interest in the Portland, Bangor, Mt. Desert & Machias Steamboat Company, which was one of the two all-water routes to the island. The Maine legislature passed a special act permitting the Maine Central to operate steamers as an extension of its rail line. Because it was considered an extension, the ferry service operated as an integral part of the railroad, and its accounts were included in the railroad accounts.[15]

Service on the branch began in 1884. In the first year or two a limited train, consisting entirely of parlor cars, operated from Boston to Mount Desert Ferry. Later, additional trains were added, including night trains with sleeping cars. New and finely furnished steamers were also constructed or purchased. This service attracted people to the Frenchman's Bay area, and among them were some of the country's most wealthy families.[16]

Not until 1886 did the state of Maine make a survey of the value of the tourist business in the state; in that report Bar Harbor merited special notice. During the previous twenty years millions of dollars had been spent there on "cottages," and the score of large hotels was insufficient to meet the demand. In 1887 an agent reported that the number of guests at hotels and cottages during the summer was 23,263 and that they spent an estimated $1,213,810. Real estate prices in the Bar Harbor area were very high. Some of the so-called cottages constructed in the 1880s and 1890s cost between $250,000 and $500,000; John D. Rockefeller, Jr., was said to have spent $1,000,000 on his.[17] There is little doubt that easier accessibility brought this prosperity to Mount Desert Island, with the Maine Central line from Mount Desert Ferry being a major factor and improved steamer service also attracting additional tourists.

The inland resorts were far from neglected. In Maine, Poland Springs was considered "one of the most famous in the state." The Maine Steamship Company as well as the railroads carried large numbers of passengers for Poland Springs. There were "hundreds" of other resorts in the state and the business increased practically every year. New Hampshire, with its famous White Mountains, was another favorite.[18] The Sound lines provided through rail-water service to the mountains and advertised widely these connections.

In southern New England the coastal lines also nurtured the local resorts. The Old Colony Railroad had acquired a large interest in the steamboat companies connecting Martha's Vineyard and Nantucket with the mainland. In March 1886 the two separate corporations serving the islands were merged as the New Bedford, Martha's Vineyard & Nantucket Steamboat Company, with the Old Colony owning over $15,000 of its stock. The connections with the Fall River Line were good. A train met the boat at the Fall River wharf and traveled express to the New Bedford wharf that was the terminus of the island steamers.[19]

In June of 1886 the Fall River Line inaugurated a daily double-service each way between New York and Fall River. The passenger business had increased to such an extent that this was the only means of accommodating it. One steamer each way made a stop at Newport; the other ran nonstop to Fall River. This proved a success and was continued for several years until corporate mergers permitted other arrangements.[20]

Co-ordination of rail and steamer service was usually excellent; advertisements in newspapers, magazines, and guide books illustrate this fact. Almost all the steamship lines had through connections to the major resort areas of New England, and there were special tours lasting a week or more, plus one- or two-day excursions. Most boat trains carried the finest equipment available. Cape Cod, coastal Rhode Island and Connecticut, the mountains of New Hampshire, coastal and inland Maine, and virtually all other resort areas in the region were accessible by public transportation. Some were easier to reach then than they are today because the water distance was shorter than the overland route.

More indicative of the prosperity of the coastal lines was the construction of new passenger steamers, some of which were significant contributions to marine architecture. The Norwich Line fixed the pattern for new steamers. Its *City of Worcester* was in 1881 the largest iron vessel in her class. She was lighted by electricity and gas, and had a large freight capacity. She received considerable praise for her design and handsome lines.[21] Most famous of all the steamers built during the decade was the Fall River Line side-wheeler *Pilgrim*, which was completed in 1883. Numerous articles about her appeared in the marine and technical journals, all of which were lavish in their praise. Although she was not the first iron-hulled vessel in Sound service, she was quickly nicknamed "The Iron Monarch of Long Island Sound." The *Pilgrim* had numerous technical innovations marking a considerable advance over earlier vessels, including a double bottom, electric lighting throughout, and a huge single-cylinder walking-beam engine with a cylinder diameter of 110 inches. Her furnishings were equally striking. At the time she was the largest steamboat ever built.[22]

Other New England companies constructed steamers, but none matched the *Pilgrim*. The Providence & Stonington Steamship Company rebuilt the *Rhode Island* and the *Stonington;* in 1889 it received from the builders the *Connecticut*. Though the *Connecticut* was a finely furnished steamer, it turned out to have been a costly mistake to equip her with oscillating engines. The companies serving Maine also added to their fleets, but these companies were more frugal in providing luxuries for their patrons.[23]

In 1889 the Old Colony Steamboat Company added another steamer to its fleet, the *Puritan*. Measuring 419 feet in length, she was 39 feet longer than the *Pilgrim* and cost $1,200,000.[24] The economics of operating such vessels demanded large numbers of passengers, and it is evident that the patronage was there, because in the 1890s still larger and more opulent steamers were ordered.

The Growth of the Freight Business

While passenger business was booming, a similar expansion occurred in the freight business. New England had long been a major center of manufacturing, and after the Civil War there was extensive growth in industries using the coastal steamship lines. Some steamer manifests from this period are available for the eastbound voyages, and they show extensive commerce. The Fall River Line in particular did a lucrative business hauling baled cotton for the New England mills.[25] Other lines shared in this prosperity, although none approached the tonnage carried by the Old Colony Steamboat Company.

A manifestation of this boom in freight traffic is found in the construction of several steamers designed especially for freight service and in the increased freight capacity of the passenger boats. The Old Colony Steamboat Company built two freighters, the *City of Fall River* (1883) and the *City of Brockton* (1886); the Metropolitan Steamship Company constructed the *H. F. Dimock* (1884), the *Herman Winter* (1887), and the *H. M. Whitney* (1890); and the Providence & Stonington Steamship Company built the *Nashua* (1885). Some of these freighters were quite speedy, making their runs almost as fast as the passenger boats. The *City of Fall River* could make the trip between Fall River and New York in about ten hours, giving her an average speed of about eighteen miles per hour. She could carry one hundred carloads of freight.[26] This capacity was an addition to the already considerable freight capacity of the regular passenger boats. In the late 1880s freight was heavy on all the southern New England routes. During the spring of 1887, to handle the tonnage between New England and New York City, the Norwich Line needed four steamers, the Stonington and Providence lines three each, the Old Colony Steamboat Company four, and the Central Vermont line three.[27] It would seem that the Metropolitan Steamship Company was also doing well, since it constructed two vessels between 1887 and 1890.

J. B. Coyle said in 1880 that the freight business in Maine was profitable only three months out of the year. There are many indications, however, that by the end of the decade the business was profitable most of the year. The freight manifests for the down-East lines were quite different from those in southern New England. Agricultural products like potatoes, vegetables, dairy products, molasses, and flour, plus wool and leather, comprised the largest proportion of goods shipped by steamer out of Portland. The lines serving the Maritimes carried similar items as well as a large amount of dried and fresh fish and shellfish.[28]

South of Cape Cod the manifests on eastbound trips were comprised primarily of raw materials dominated by baled cotton. Other eastbound commodities were flour, sugar, and leather. The westbound cargoes reflected the industries of the area served by each line. Bridgeport and New Haven sent brass goods, firearms, and other manufactured items. From New London eastward, finished textiles were important, along with confectionaries, boots and shoes, and other manufactured goods.[29]

The events of this decade proved that there was enough business for all the companies and that they could share it without resorting to rate wars. Their self-imposed stability had been maintained, and few complaints were heard about existing conditions.

With the advent of fast and reasonably safe railroad passenger service, the coastal lines had to rely on freight to provide the largest portion of their earnings. This was true of all the companies in New England except the Old Colony Steamboat Company, which during the 1880s earned more from passengers than from freight. Among the companies in southern New England all earned between one and a half and three times as much revenue from freight as from passengers.[30] Certainly the condition of the Metropolitan Steamship Company proves that the profits from freight were ample. Freight was the mainstay of the coastal lines in Maine because the summer season was too short for the passenger business alone to sustain the service.

The Situation in the 1890s

The most conspicuous development during the 1890s was the consolidation of transportation companies in southern New England. The New York, New Haven & Hartford Railroad accomplished this through a variety of methods; by the end of the decade the New Haven controlled not only the principal railroads of the area, but also many of the steamship lines operating in Long Island Sound.

Operation of the coastal steamship lines in New England varied little from practices that had evolved in the preceding decades. Passenger and freight business continued to increase, except for a temporary decline during the depression that began in 1893. Fortunately, none of the steamship companies experienced the disastrous decline in earnings during the depression that forced many American railroads into receivership.[31]

Toward the end of the 1890s Charles W. Morse, a Maine businessman who had made a fortune in the ice trade, took the initial steps to join four Maine steamship companies in a consolidation that in 1901 was incorporated as the Eastern Steamship Company. This new company would become a major rival of the New Haven Railroad, for both would be competing for control of the coastal steamship service in New England.

The Rise of the New Haven Railroad

The New York, New Haven & Hartford Railroad had been formed in 1872 by the merging of the New York & New Haven Railroad, the Hartford & New Haven Railroad, and the Shore Line Railroad connecting New Haven and New London. In 1881 the New Haven acquired stock control of the New Haven & Northampton Railroad and the following year leased the Air Line Railroad.[32] The New Haven now controlled important segments of the three principal rail routes between New York and Boston. The old Hartford & New Haven reached Springfield, Massachusetts, there connecting with the Boston & Albany Railroad to Boston, and the New Haven & Northampton was a parallel line to the west of the Hartford & New Haven that also connected with the Boston & Albany. The Air Line Railroad from Middletown to Willimantic, Connecticut, formed a second route using New York & New England tracks between Willimantic and Boston. The Shore Line route gave the New Haven whatever traffic moved over the third route between New London, Providence, and Boston, but this line did not become important until the Thames River was bridged in 1889. Equally significant, the

New Haven had the finest route into New York City from New England. Many threats were made by rivals to construct a parallel line, but the New Haven management was always able to thwart these attempts.[33] Nevertheless, during the 1880s the power of the New Haven Railroad in southern New England was never absolute; the company did not control or effectively influence any of the Sound steamship lines from ports east of New Haven and so had no dictatorial power over certain classes of through traffic.

Only one railroad in southern New England compared in size with the New Haven: the New York & New England Railroad. During the late 1870s and the first half of the 1880s, when the two enjoyed generally harmonious relations, they co-operated in establishing a through night passenger train between Boston and Washington. Charles P. Clark, general manager, and William F. Hart, president of the New York & New England, personally organized the New England Transfer Company to ferry the Boston-Washington trains and fast freight trains between Harlem and Jersey City, where the yards of the Pennsylvania Railroad were located. In 1880 the Transfer Company was bought by the New Haven and the New York & New England Railroad, each purchasing half of the stock.[34]

During 1882 and 1883 the co-operation between the two railroads suffered considerable strain when the New England management, finding itself in financial difficulties, attempted to lease its road to the Erie Railroad. In Boston there was a large and powerful group opposed to this move. In spite of valiant efforts, the New York & New England was unable to meet its obligations and was forced to apply for receivership. On 31 December 1883 a federal judge in Connecticut appointed Charles P. Clark, who had just been elected president, as the sole receiver. Clark resigned as president and operated the New York & New England for the next two years as receiver. His appointment assured renewed harmony between the New Haven and the New York & New England, for Clark was also a director of the New Haven.[35]

Clark economized wherever possible and worked toward

improving passenger and freight service. He was successful, and in 1886 the New York & New England emerged from receivership with Clark as president. At this point he urged the New Haven to lease his railroad, but the proposition was not received favorably by the New Haven management.[36] In 1887 Clark was ousted by a dissident group of New York stockholders. For him it was not at all a misfortune; he was elected president of the New Haven. For the New York & New England the next few years were to be ones of disaster.

*The Struggle for Dominance in
Southern New England*

The new management of the New York & New England proposed to construct its own line into New York City parallel to the main line of the New Haven. Clark at once took defensive action. He improved the New Haven main line to accommodate the increasing traffic, enlarged the terminal facilities, reduced rates, and hired capable subordinates.[37] This response helped to check the New York & New England scheme.

Although possessing considerable financial strength, in battling the New York & New England the New Haven had a major weakness: it lacked its own entrance into Boston. After 1889 the most suitable route was over the New York, Providence & Boston Railroad and the Old Colony Railroad. To buy or lease these roads was no simple matter, and before attempting it the officials of the New Haven had to make careful preparations. Most important was getting permission from the Connecticut General Assembly to increase the authorized capital of the New Haven by $35 million and to exchange its stock for that of any Connecticut railroads it might lease. After an epic battle in 1889 between the lobbyists of the New Haven and the New York & New England, the General Assembly approved the New Haven request. Four years later the Assembly permitted the New Haven a further increase in its capital to $100 million and allowed the railroad to use these securities to lease roads wholly in adjoining states.[38] This new authority was a powerful weapon, which the management of the New Haven employed skillfully.

Another and more useful weapon of the New Haven was its ability to divert traffic away from the New York & New England. The first step to isolate the latter was made in 1887 when the New Haven purchased the one-half interest the New York & New England owned in the New England Transfer Company. The following year the New Haven withdrew from the through freight line with the New York & New England and the Pennsylvania Railroad. At the same time the New York Central Railroad refused to route any traffic from New York City via the New York & New England.[39] All attempts of the New York & New England to bypass the New Haven and the New York Central failed.

With its flanks reasonably secure the New Haven could now concentrate on securing its own entrance into Boston. In the fight with the New York & New England the officers of the New Haven were aided considerably by the construction of the bridge across the Thames River by the New York, Providence & Boston Railroad. The bridge connected with the Shore Line and so made that road part of a continuous rail route to Boston. With its charter rights amended in 1889 by the Connecticut General Assembly, the New Haven took positive steps toward controlling this route east of New London. At the same time it did everything possible to harass the New York & New England. The New Haven canceled the operation of some jointly operated trains, while others met with unexplained delays. Freight formerly sent over the New York & New England was routed via the Shore Line, and local rates were instituted on traffic that had been carried on lower through rates. These tactics had the desired effect. In Boston, however, many merchants complained bitterly about the changes in service and deliveries.[40] The Massachusetts General Court conducted an investigation of the matter, but it could not save the New York & New England. Every effort the railroad made the New Haven checkmated; the end was only a matter of time.

On 1 April 1892 the New Haven leased the New York, Providence & Boston Railroad. Since at the time there was no compelling reason for granting this lease, the terms offered by the New Haven had to be very favorable. Within a year the road was absorbed by the New Haven. This left only one gap to close in controlling the line into Boston.[41]

The following year the New Haven completed its New York–Boston line when it leased the Old Colony Railroad. In 1887 the directors of the Old Colony had approved the lease of the Boston & Providence Railroad, which was the most satisfactory route between Providence and Boston. In order to secure this forty-four-mile line the New Haven had to lease the whole six-hundred-mile Old Colony system. The Old Colony management had used good judgment in securing the Boston & Providence because of the latter's strategic position. Once the New Haven controlled the New York, Providence & Boston Railroad, the Boston & Providence was the inevitable choice for an entrance to Boston. The New Haven had purchased enough Old Colony stock by February 1893 to insure favorable action on its offer. The lease took effect 1 March 1893.[42]

These two leases brought a radical change in the control of transportation in southern New England. Not only had the New Haven achieved its goal of a through line to Boston, but it had also entered the steamboat business. By leasing these railroads it gained control of the majority of stock in the Old Colony Steamboat Company and the Providence & Stonington Steamship Company. Its position in southern New England was almost impregnable. Nevertheless, the New York & New England was not yet willing to concede victory to the New Haven.

During 1892 the New York & New England Railroad had come under the control of Archibald A. McLeod, president of the Philadelphia & Reading Railroad, which served the anthracite coal region of Pennsylvania. McLeod wanted to control his own distribution routes for anthracite in New England. To handle the anticipated traffic he secured control of the recently completed Poughkeepsie Bridge across the Hudson River. This bridge eliminated costly and inefficient ferries formerly used by the New York & New England. In 1892 he created the Philadelphia, Reading & New England Railroad to operate the combined roads. Next McLeod secured the Boston & Maine Railroad, and in October 1892 he was elected its president. This combination posed a real threat to the New Haven.[43]

J. Pierpont Morgan, the investment banker who since 1891 had been a director of the New Haven, was not at all favorably disposed toward McLeod's invasion of New England. In addition, McLeod had alienated Morgan by transferring the financing of his railroads from Drexel, Morgan & Company to Speyer & Company. Morgan was determined to eliminate the McLeod threat. A raid was made on the securities of the Philadelphia & Reading, driving them down to a price that forced the railroad to apply for receivership in February 1893.[44] McLeod still retained his New England railroads, but without the Philadelphia & Reading his position had become precarious.

Throughout 1892 and into 1893 the harassment of the New York & New England had continued. Not only had the New Haven deprived the New York & New England of most of the profitable through freight traffic, it also was operating two additional express passenger trains between New York and Boston. These express trains deprived the New York & New England of any profits it might have made on its train. Starting in 1892 the New Haven refused to furnish any boat train to Boston to connect with the Norwich Line except one at three o'clock in the morning.[45] Needless to say, the Norwich Line lost considerable through business to the Stonington, Providence, and Fall River lines.

McLeod and the management of the New Haven, in the midst of all this hostility, did take one positive step when they decided to end competition for freight traffic. They divided New England along the tracks of the Boston & Albany. North of that railroad was to be the preserve of the Boston & Maine; south of it was New Haven territory. Neither company was to solicit traffic or seek control of railroads in the territory of the

other.[46] The immediate reaction of the public was not particularly harsh, and no serious challenge was made. The
agreement worked very well for fifteen years.

Meanwhile, Morgan interests had been purchasing large
amounts of securities of the New York & New England, and
by the end of 1893 it was again in receivership. Whether the
securities had been purchased solely to bring this about is not
certain, but circumstantial evidence lends support for such a
conclusion.[47] Whatever the reasons, McLeod retired in 1894,
and the New Haven, because of its controlling interest in
New York & New England securities, could now dictate the
fate of the company.

By the end of 1894 the New Haven was clearly master in
southern New England, and the agreement between it and
the Boston & Maine meant that there was no threat to its position by New England railroads or steamship companies. The
one potential threat had been removed by the state of Massachusetts after considerable investigation of the situation.

The state of Massachusetts prohibited railroads entering
Boston from leasing or combining without legislative consent. No difficulties had been experienced in gaining consent
to the lease of the New York, Providence & Boston. The Old
Colony Railroad, however, was almost completely within the
state and had two lines running into Boston. In addition, the
businessmen of the city were not entirely happy with traffic
and terminal conditions in Boston after the New Haven began routing through freight over the Old Colony. The investigation conducted in 1893 by the Massachusetts General
Court heard testimony that brought to light the ruthless nature of the competition between the two railroads. The testimony illustrated that only a few gained real benefits from the
type of competition that had disrupted relations between the
New Haven and the New York & New England.[48]

Despite the charges and countercharges the legislature decided to confirm the lease of the Old Colony by the New Haven. The lease guaranteed a 7 per cent return on Old Colony
stock and provided for the exchange of ten Old Colony shares
for nine of the New Haven—a favorable exchange for the

Old Colony stockholders.[49] A question still unweighed was whether a corporation chartered in two states should be allowed to increase its capital in the first state to purchase securities of corporations located in the second state. It is unfortunate that such practice was not forbidden at this time, for the directors of the New Haven employed this technique after 1903 to purchase control of other transportation companies in New England, and it contributed much to the troubles of the company.

The Consolidation of the New Haven's Position

After gaining control of the roads to Boston the management of the New Haven proceeded to take steps to bring its recent acquisitions into a closer relationship with the railroad.[50] The New York, Providence & Boston was absorbed into the New Haven system just two weeks before the Old Colony lease took effect. A similar policy of consolidation was instituted regarding the steamship companies.

When the New Haven leased the New York, Providence & Boston, the latter owned 12,776 of the 20,000 shares of Providence & Stonington Steamship Company stock. On 13 February 1893, when the railroad ceased to exist, the New Haven acquired full title to the steamship stock.[51] At a meeting of the directors of the Providence & Stonington Steamship Company, held on 23 May 1893, they recommended that the company sell the remaining stock to the New Haven for $150 a share. To carry this out it was necessary to secure permission from the Rhode Island General Assembly. On 21 February 1895 the assembly passed the required enabling act. There is some question whether the legislators realized that the ultimate purpose of the New Haven was to liquidate the company.[52] In fact, the purchase made little difference, because policy decisions for the steamship company were already being made by the New Haven. In September 1896 liquidation of the steamship company was attempted at a stockholders' meeting, but strong dissent from a vocal minority forced a postponement until the New Haven management could eliminate these stockholders. Finally, on 10 July 1898, the New Haven took over actual operation of the steamship company, the corporate existence of which was retained as a sort of legal fiction in the Providence office of Edward G. Buckland, then an attorney for the New Haven. He had one share in his name and was authorized to represent the other 19,991 shares by proxy.[53]

The absorption of the Old Colony Steamboat Company followed a somewhat different pattern. When the Old Colony lease was consummated, the Old Colony Railroad turned over 9,673 (out of 12,000) shares of the steamboat company to the New Haven.[54] On 9 June 1893 the Old Colony Railroad was authorized to acquire the remaining stock, which was subsequently to be turned over to the New Haven. The New Haven, however, did not have the required permission of the Massachusetts Railroad Commission to buy the stock from the Old Colony Railroad. The legality of New Haven ownership was questioned by the commission. The New Haven arranged to transfer the steamboat company stock to William E. Barnett (trustee), and to have him transfer it to Drexel, Morgan & Company. This allowed Charles F. Choate, Old Colony Railroad president, to write the Railroad Commission that the Old Colony had not purchased said minority stock. Satisfied with this answer, the commission granted permission for the New Haven to acquire the remaining stock which it in fact already owned.[55]

Thus, the two most prosperous Sound lines in the Boston–New York service were firmly under New Haven domination. With the New York & New England Railroad in receivership and the New Haven having its own rail entrance into Boston, the New Haven control over traffic was now unchallenged. The Norwich Line was still independent, but its fate awaited the reorganization of the New York & New England.

The New York & New England emerged from its second receivership in 1895 as the New England Railroad with, again, Charles P. Clark, now president of the New Haven Railroad, as its president.[56] There was little doubt that the road would soon become a part of the New Haven system. On 1 July 1898, the New Haven leased the railroad, ending the notorious career of this unfortunate corporation. With the lease came the Norwich & New York Transportation Company, which was then wholly owned by the Norwich & Worcester Railroad. In 1899 the New Haven transferred the terminus of the Norwich Line from the Central Vermont Railway dock to its own wharf opposite the New Haven passenger station in New London.[57]

Within a few weeks after the Norwich Line came under New Haven control, operation of the steamship lines was taken over by the marine district of the New Haven Railroad, and the accounts of the individual lines were consolidated. It now became easier to shift the steamers from one line to another. These changes simplified operations and facilitated bookkeeping.[58] The legal existence of each company continued, however, thereby protecting the railroad from excessive liability arising from any marine disaster. This arrangement remained in effect until 1904.

The Reaction to the New Haven Monopoly

Considering the magnitude of the developments between 1892 and 1898, the reaction to the New Haven monopoly was strikingly muted. No doubt part of the reason for the lack of widespread opposition was that the New Haven was a New England owned corporation. The New York & New England Railroad had been manipulated by outsiders, a fact that struck fear into the entrepreneurs of New England. The New Haven could claim that it always placed the welfare of New England first because it was owned by its citizens. Many businessmen and bankers were convinced that only a powerful company like the New Haven could check outside encroachments and improve service between New England and the rest of the country.[59]

Another factor supporting the New Haven was that consolidation was in vogue throughout the transportation business, and mergers were defended by many influential men. Charles A. Prouty, a prominent member of the Interstate Commerce Commission, stated before the Industrial Commission in 1899 that "railroad consolidation tends to do away with discrimination." There was evidence in New England to support Prouty's position. Since New England had been divided between the New Haven Railroad and the Boston & Maine Railroad, rates had been reduced and service improved. Prouty added that the number of complaints received in his office from New England shippers was small compared to the number received from other regions.[60] The chairman of the Interstate Commerce Commission, Martin A. Knapp, concurred in these views.[61] In 1899 the Interstate Commerce Commission made quite emphatic its position: "A railroad is essentially a monopoly." While competition existed at points served by two or more railroads, elsewhere monopoly ruled. The natural result of railroad competition was "to create preferences between localities."[62] Furthermore, New England had seen what competition among railroads and steamship companies did to the stability and efficiency of transportation. Many in New England were quite ready to test the stability that was said to accompany monopoly; instability and the accompanying uncertainty of competition were an anathema to businessmen.

Monopoly had its pitfalls, however, and the management of the New Haven was sometimes clumsy in avoiding them. This was especially evident in Providence. There a certain jealousy had long existed because Fall River had the prestige and service of the Fall River Line; the leading businessmen of Providence believed that their city was the proper terminus for such a line. Business and commercial groups agitated for the transfer of two Fall River Line steamers to the Providence Line so that their city could enjoy during the summer the double-service which had for several years been a feature of the Fall River Line. Their efforts were in vain. At the same time there was increasing dissatisfaction with the service provided by the Providence Line. Businessmen accused the New Haven of "using every effort to divert trade from our steamship lines." Especial reference was made to the Merchants & Miners Transportation Company, which operated a line between Providence and Baltimore. The *Providence Journal of Commerce* urged local businessmen to patronize this company because it was free of railroad control and because steamship lines were "the natural highway of commerce."[63]

By 1896 rumors were prevalent in Providence and New Bedford that independent steamship lines were about to be established to compete with the lines of the New Haven operating from those cities. The depressed business conditions seem to have prevented the immediate creation of this competition. In Providence continued complaints were heard that the New Haven was "bottling up" the city.[64] Clearly the executives of the railroad would have to exercise the utmost prudence in operating their transportation system if they were to allay the suspicions of those New Englanders who were suspicious of monopoly whatever its benefits might be.

The end of the decade marked a plateau in the history of the relationship between railroads and steamship companies in New England. The New Haven had done much to rationalize transportation in southern New England while leaving northern New England to the Boston & Maine. The New Haven had achieved a rail monopoly by a policy of buying, leasing, and bankrupting the necessary railroad companies. Some of the steamship companies owned by these railroads were consciously sought; others were acquired incidentally. Little doubt can be entertained that the Fall River Line was an alluring prize in leasing the Old Colony Railroad. Its independence would have made it a potential threat to New Haven domination and could have been used as an effective form of blackmail in unfriendly hands. Some might argue that with control of the all-rail routes to New York City, the New York, New Haven & Hartford had no need for the steamboat lines; no greater misconception may be imagined.

There is a certain ironic twist to the achievements of the New Haven. At the very moment that it secured its monopoly a new challenge appeared to threaten all that had been accomplished. Within ten years electric street railroads had grown from a small installation in Richmond, Virginia, to high-speed interurban lines that were threatening railroads in areas of concentrated population. As early as 1893 the New Haven had recognized their danger.[65] These electric railroads as well as new steamboat lines forced alterations in the course of New Haven strategy; unfortunately, at about the same time the management embarked on an expansionist policy that would ultimately bring financial disaster to the New Haven system.

4. Technical and Operational Developments, 1870–1916

AT THIS point it is necessary to evaluate and describe the operational aspects of the rail-water service. Without such a discussion it would be impossible to judge fairly the charges made against the New Haven during the years after 1908. Railroad ownership of the coastal lines could easily have resulted in a gradual decay of the quality of service and inattention to advances in marine architecture and technology. Comparisons between the independent companies and those operated by the railroads will indicate the treatment accorded the latter.

Technical Developments

Fundamental to all else was the design and construction of the steamers. The record here is uneven depending upon the section of New England under discussion. In 1870 the standards of marine architecture were similar among all the coastal steamship lines. The typical vessel had a wooden hull and was powered by a single-cylinder beam engine. The size of the steamers varied according to their service. Those employed on the Sound lines were larger and more luxurious; those north of Cape Cod were smaller and more Spartan.[1] Despite their wooden construction, steamers lasting twenty years were not uncommon, and some lasted thirty or more.

Steamship Design and Construction, 1870–1910

The first significant signs of change in the design of New England coastal steamers appeared in the 1870s. These changes were not widespread, but they were noticed by those perceptive in marine affairs. Because the steamers incorporating new ideas were not always products of the larger companies, their significance was sometimes overlooked.

Construction of iron-hulled vessels was by no means novel, but few of the New England companies had built any. The Norwich & New York Transportation Company was the first New England company after the Civil War to favor this material. In 1867 the Norwich Line received from Harlan & Hollingsworth the iron side-wheeler *City of Lawrence.* In 1873 the Metropolitan Steamship Company chose iron when it ordered the *General Whitney,* a screw steamer designed especially for the outside route between Boston and New York. The *General Whitney* was precursory in other ways too. She had twin screws and a high freeboard like an ocean steamer rather than the low freeboard so familiar on steamers operating along the New England coast.[2] No other company operating between New York City and New England points adopted these features for several years.

During the remainder of the decade, designs varied little from the conventional. The details were sometimes improved upon, but the basic design of passenger steamers remained unchanged. The coastal steamboats were distinguished by their fine lines and high-quality finish. They had relatively shallow hulls and depended on their sponsons and paddle wheels for additional stability. The hulls were generally narrower in proportion to their length than were those of later, propeller vessels. On most of the Sound passenger side-wheelers the length of the hull was between seven and eight times the width; the screw steamers built after 1890 usually were six to seven times longer than they were wide. The largest steamers like the *Puritan, Priscilla,* and *Pilgrim* drew less than fifteen feet.

To strengthen the long wooden hulls, it was necessary to construct elaborate hogframes—actually trusses—on each side of the vessels to prevent the hulls from sagging at the bow and stern. Considering that many of these side-wheelers were over three hundred feet long, it is a credit to the architects and builders that they were such sturdy and reliable vessels. Because of rapid technical advances, the early steamboats had not been finished as well as the later ones. After the Civil War major technical advances were less frequent and designs were changed more slowly. The stabilization of design meant that vessels would be serviceable longer, which made it possible to improve the quality of joiner work and furnishings.[3]

Despite the innovations in the *General Whitney* and the *City of Lawrence,* the other New England steamship companies followed older practices and ordered wooden side-wheelers. The Stonington Steamship Company received the *Rhode Island* in 1873, and in 1877 the newly formed Providence & Stonington Steamship Company completed the *Massachusetts.* These vessels were over 320 feet in length and, for the period, quite modern.[4] Most of the Sound steamers constructed after the Civil War had their boilers in the hold instead of on the guards. For many years placing the boilers on the guards had been considered a safety feature, but by 1870 marine architects recognized the practice as a hazard, since it exposed the boilers to damage in a collision or in rough seas.

The 1880s marked the real turning point for the adoption of iron and steel construction. The success of two steamers built in 1881 and 1883 assured that within a short time practically all large steamers would have iron or steel hulls. The first of these steamers was the *City of Worcester,* built for the

Norwich & New York Transportation Company. Costing about $408,000, she was an expensive vessel, but her owners were well pleased with her. Her iron hull eliminated the need for hogframes and at the same time made her stronger and lighter.[5] The largest steamer of her class when completed, the *City of Worcester* soon lost this honor to a new leviathan of the Old Colony Steamboat Company.

Confronted with a rapidly increasing passenger business, the management of the Old Colony Steamboat Company had their supervisor, George Pierce, design a new steamer that was nearly 50 feet longer than the *City of Worcester*. The *Pilgrim* measured 390 feet on deck and 375 feet on the water line. Her beam was 50 feet, and the width of the main deck was 88 feet, 6 inches. At 3,500 registered tons she was the largest coastal steamboat in the world. Quickly dubbed the "Iron Monarch of Long Island Sound," she captured the imagination of those interested in marine affairs. Despite her striking size and appearance, the *Pilgrim* did not depart radically from conventional steamboat design. Her single-cylinder beam engine and side-wheel propulsion were not unlike those of her sisters. Her 110-inch cylinder was one of the largest ever cast, but it differed in no significant way from earlier engines installed on the *Providence*, the *Bristol*, and the *City of Worcester*. Nevertheless, the Old Colony Steamboat Company and George Pierce deserve credit for several improvements. The *Pilgrim* had a double-bottom hull of iron divided into 103 watertight compartments. The engine and boiler spaces and the kitchen were enclosed in iron bulkheads to reduce the danger of fire. In addition, she was lighted throughout by electricity, eliminating the highly combustible illuminating gas. For the $853,000 paid for her, the company received a fine and reliable vessel. During her first season the *Pilgrim* made 190 consecutive trips totaling 34,200 miles.[6]

The previous year the Old Colony Steamboat Company had completed a new freight boat, the *City of Fall River*, the first of several freighters ordered specifically to handle the ever increasing tonnage between New York City and southern

New England. This freighter was a wooden vessel of standard design, but she did incorporate two mechanical innovations. Her two-cylinder compound beam engine of two thousand horsepower was a novelty for side-wheel steamers used in the New England coastal trade. In addition, she had feathering paddle wheels. Although common in Europe, these had not been widely adopted in the United States. They had moveable buckets that hit the water at a more nearly perpendicular angle than did the paddles of a rigid wheel. The *City of Fall River* proved so successful that an almost identical freighter, the *City of Brockton*, was added in 1886.[7]

Two other steamers constructed during the decade were also in the nature of experiments. The 2,554-ton side-wheeler *Nashua*, built in 1835 for the Providence & Stonington Steamship Company, had a compound oscillating engine. Company officials hoped that this type of engine would give the *Nashua* more speed and a lower fuel consumption than their older freighters. The oscillating engine was an advantage on a freight boat, because it connected directly to the shaft, thereby eliminating the working beam, which took considerable space in the center of the vessel.[8] In Boston the Metropolitan Steamship Company received the iron screw steamer *H. F. Dimock*, which was powered by a compound engine. A water ballast tank was installed to permit the trimming of the ship when lightly loaded. The machinery spaces were sheathed in iron, and steam jets were located in every compartment to smother any fire. The *H. F. Dimock* was, like the *General Whitney*, an ocean-type vessel, but capable of higher speed. She could make the New York–Boston run in approximately twenty hours.[9]

The other New England lines continued to reproduce the standard model of coastal steamer. The new *Rhode Island* (1882) of the Providence & Stonington Steamship Company was only a slightly larger version of her predecessor. In 1882 the Portland Steam Packet Company ordered the *Tremont*, a wooden side-wheeler similar to those built during the previous decade. The same year the Boston & Bangor Steamship Company added the *Penobscot*. An indication of the more utilitarian furnishings on the steamers of the northern lines is the fact that the *Penobscot* cost about $200,000, or $34,000 less than the freighter *City of Fall River*.[10]

Between 1889 and 1894 a remarkable variety of steamers were constructed, and their specifications indicated future trends. The most notable of the older-style steamers was the large wooden side-wheeler *Connecticut*. Of the wooden Sound liners only the *Bristol* and the *Providence* were larger. Influenced by the success of the oscillating engine on the *Nashua*, the officers of the Providence & Stonington Steamship Company ordered a compound engine of this type for the *Connecticut*. The *Connecticut*, however, proved to be a costly mistake. At a time when the principal competitors of the Providence & Stonington Steamship Company had large iron steamers and were ordering steel ones, constructing a wooden steamer was shortsighted. In addition, the *Connecticut*'s large engine was difficult to keep in proper working order; during the 1890s there were many times when the *Connecticut* was out of service because of machinery failures. Never again was this type of engine installed in a Sound steamer. In effect, the *Connecticut* was obsolete before she was launched.[11]

The *Connecticut* had her brief moment of glory, but the Old Colony Steamboat Company quickly recaptured the attention of the public. Designed by George Pierce, the 403-foot *Puritan* was ordered in 1887 and entered service early in 1889. Again the Fall River Line had the honor of owning the largest steamer of her class. Like the *Pilgrim*, she had a steel hull of the conventional steamboat type: flat on the floor and wall sided with long, sharp, wedgelike ends. The *Puritan* had considerably more buoyancy than the *Pilgrim*, permitting a greater beam. Because of the success of the compound engines on the *City of Fall River* and the *City of Brockton*, the *Puritan* was equipped with a massive compound beam engine. The technical journals of the period were in awe of the various parts of the engine. The working beam was the largest ever cast. The *Puritan* was the first of the Old Colony passenger boats to be equipped with feathering paddle wheels; all later vessels were so equipped. The publicity accompanying the building and launching of the *Puritan* added to the already high prestige of the Fall River Line. Few companies could afford to spend $1,200,000 on one steamer.[12]

After the burning of the *Bristol* at her Newport berth in December 1888 the management of the Old Colony Steamboat Company ordered a new steel steamer to replace her. The *Plymouth* continued the refinement of the steamboat type and was one of the finest efforts of George Pierce. She was not as large as the *Pilgrim* or the *Puritan* because she was designed for winter service, when there was less demand for accommodations, and she could carry more freight in relation to her size than the other passenger steamers. The most distinguishing feature of the *Plymouth* was her four-cylinder, double inclined, triple expansion engine, which lowered the center of gravity and freed a large area above the main deck not needed for the working beam. The *Plymouth* more than met all expectations, and many considered her the finest of the later steamers on the Fall River Line.[13]

Still the Old Colony fleet could not cope with the increasing demand for service. Thus, in 1891 the company announced that a team headed by George Pierce was preparing specifications for a new steamer equal in power and capacity to the *Puritan*. The same year the company also ordered another freight boat, the *City of Taunton*, which was similar to the *City of Fall River* and the *City of Brockton*.[14]

The side-wheel steamer *Priscilla* broke all existing records for coastal steamers and was the largest of the vessels designed by George Pierce. Measuring 424 feet on her water line, she was 21 feet longer than the *Puritan*. The greatest difference between the two was the engines. Satisfied with the results of the inclined engine of the *Plymouth*, the company installed an 8,500-horsepower, double inclined, compound engine in the *Priscilla*. To supply steam she needed ten boilers. When completed and furnished the *Priscilla* cost $1,378,000. Again the Old Colony Steamboat Company had demonstrated that only the finest steamers operated on the Fall River Line.[15]

Meanwhile, the Providence & Stonington Steamship Company made a sharp break with tradition when it ordered the *Maine* and the *New Hampshire*. Since the *Connecticut* had been a source of continual difficulty, the company abandoned the old steamboat type. The *Maine* and the *New Hampshire* were steel vessels, and each was powered by one triple expansion engine turning a single propeller. They were fine vessels in every respect, but their cost reflects the smaller resources of the company. Each cost $449,000, which added together was less than the price the Old Colony Steamboat Company paid for the *Puritan*.[16] Yet the *Maine* and the *New Hampshire* were just the sort of steamer needed. Their operating costs were low, and they were seldom out of service for any reason except periodic maintenance.

At the same time significant developments were occurring at New Haven. In 1889 Chester W. Chapin, president of the New Haven Steamboat Company, realized that the company needed a new steamer. He wanted a steamer completely different from the company's wooden side-wheeler, *C. H. Northam*. Being an enthusiastic yachtsman, he discussed the matter with the well-known yacht designer A. Carey Smith. Smith had designed several yachts for Chapin, and the two men were on close terms. Smith had never attempted anything as large as a steamboat and was hesitant about such an undertaking, but Chapin was insistent. He gave Smith carte blanche and ordered the engineering department to give its complete co-operation. Smith drew five sets of plans before he had a design that he believed was suitable. When the plans arrived at the Harlan & Hollingsworth yard in Wilmington, Delaware, the marine architects there were "astonished" by the lines. A beam of 48 feet in relation to a length of 300 feet on the load water line was thought too broad a cross section to be driven through the water at the desired speed. Smith replied that the cross section "had nothing to do with it, that the general form gave speed to a boat." Other aspects of the design were similarly criticized, but with Chapin's resolute backing Carey Smith prevailed.[17]

Another controversy arose over the number of boilers to be

placed in the steamer. Smith was told that four was the maximum number that could be fitted into the hull. After a meeting with the chief engineer of the New Haven Steamboat Company, Smith said that six were necessary. Despite the bewildered protests in Wilmington, six boilers were installed. The trial trip vindicated the ideas of Smith and Chapin's faith in him. The new steamer, christened *Richard Peck*, proved to be one of the fastest on the Sound. She cruised easily at twenty miles per hour, her coal consumption was half that of the *C. H. Northam*, and she could carry ten more carloads of freight.[18]

The *Richard Peck* was the first of several steamers designed by Smith. So impressed were the executives of the Norwich & New York Transportation Company with the design and performance of the *Richard Peck* that they selected Smith to design a new passenger steamer for the Norwich Line. The results were equally satisfactory. The *City of Lowell* was somewhat speedier than the *Richard Peck* despite an additional eighteen feet on the water line. On her trials the *City of Lowell* attained a speed of 22.25 miles per hour. It was generally agreed that the *Peck* and the *Lowell* were among the finest vessels on the Atlantic coast. Chapin had Smith design another steamer for the New Haven Steamboat Company. The *Chester W. Chapin*, named in honor of the president's father, was built to run in competition with the steamers of the New Haven's Providence Line. Like the others she was a fine piece of work, and her yachtlike lines were quite pleasing to the eye.[19] The work of A. Carey Smith illustrated the rule that form follows function.

The officers of companies in northern New England were hesitant to adopt the designs proving so successful in Sound steamers. Wooden construction continued in Maine. In 1890 the *Portland* joined the fleet of the Portland Steam Packet Company; a few years later the almost identical *Bay State* joined her. Not until the *Portland* was lost with all her passengers and crew in November 1898 was the management shaken out of its traditional ways.[20] The *Governor Dingley*, completed in 1900, replaced the *Portland*. She was a steel steamer propelled by a three-cylinder triple expansion engine turning a single propeller. With a broad beam to aid stability and a high freeboard, the *Governor Dingley* was typical of all later steamers built for the outside routes.[21]

The management of the Maine Steamship Company showed greater awareness of the need for change than did officials of other lines down East. In 1890 and 1891 the *Cottage City* and the *Manhattan* entered the New York–Portland service. These wooden propellers were much better suited to the exposed outside route than the old side-wheelers. By later standards their speed of 13 miles per hour was slow, but it was with these steamers that the company earned the reputation of operating one of the best-paying coastal runs out of New York.[22] In 1896 the Maine Steamship Company received the steel propeller *John Englis*. She was more than fifty feet longer than the *Cottage City* and cost twice as much. Capable of cruising at 19.5 miles per hour, she cut the schedule to approximately 20 hours, which made the route more competitive in securing the trade between Maine and points south. During the summer of 1897 many passengers found staterooms unobtainable. This demand for space resulted in an order for another steamer almost identical to the *John Englis*.[23] Upon completion of the *Horatio Hall* daily service was to commence, but the federal government ended that plan when it requisitioned the *John Englis* for use as a hospital ship during the Spanish-American War. The *Englis* was replaced in 1901 by the *North Star*. It was the *John Englis* and the *Horatio Hall* that the Portland Steam Packet Company used as models in designing the *Governor Dingley*.[24] Considering that J. B. Coyle was influential in both the Maine Steamship Company and the Portland Steam Packet Company, it is somewhat surprising that the latter did not follow sooner the lead of the Maine Steamship Company.

It was evident by 1900 that considerable emphasis was being placed on speed and capacity. Technical advances permitted increases in both these factors while at the same time reducing operating costs. Practically all new construction employed steel hulls, triple expansion engines, and screw propulsion. Only the Fall River Line resisted the trend.

Not only the passenger boats but also the freighters were emphasizing these factors. For example, most of the new freighters were equipped with cargo booms to facilitate the handling of bulky items. The Central Vermont Railway leased two large freighters to replace its slow, obsolete vessels.[25] The Old Colony Steamboat Company and later the New England Navigation Company built several freighters with speeds approaching those of the passenger steamers.

The pinnacle of construction activity and innovation was reached between 1904 and 1908. During that period the New England Navigation Company—successor to the marine district of the New Haven Railroad—built two new side-wheelers, the *Providence* (1905) and the *Commonwealth* (1908), and the express freighter *Boston* (1904). The *Commonwealth* was the largest and most expensive side-wheeler ever employed in coastal service. She and the *Providence* continued the high standards of the Fall River Line. They had double-bottom hulls buttressed with many watertight compartments and bulkheads. Each had a four-cylinder inclined compound engine similar to the one on the *Priscilla*.[26]

During this time there appeared a new and formidable competitor of the New Haven. The companies north of Cape Cod, including the Metropolitan Steamship but not the Maine Steamship Company, were now controlled by Charles W. Morse. He merged the Maine companies into a new corporation known as the Eastern Steamship Company, which started to build steamers at a startling rate. The Eastern Steamship Company began a new trend by ordering the first turbine-powered ship constructed in the United States. The *Governor Cobb* fulfilled the expectations of her builders and owners, and was followed by four more turbine steamers.[27] The most famous were the sister ships *Harvard* and *Yale*. They were Morse's pride, and he spared no expense in their construction. Since they were intended for the outside route between Boston and New York, the *Harvard* and the *Yale* had to be fast enough to equal the train-boat schedule of the Fall

River and Providence lines. Morse had them designed in Scotland, built in Chester, Delaware, and equipped in New York City. Propelled by triple screws, they could sustain a speed of at least 24.7 miles per hour, and their top speed on one trip was reported to have been 28 miles per hour. The steamers cost $1,225,000 apiece, but Morse got what he wanted. Simultaneously he gave the officials of the New Haven Railroad some sleepless nights.[28]

Spurred by Morse, the New Haven ordered three freighters built for a new freight line to be established between New York and Boston, but capable of service on any of the company's lines. The *Massachusetts* and the *Bunker Hill* were powered by two four-cylinder triple expansion engines and the *Old Colony* by triple screws actuated by three Parsons turbines. They too were capable of speeds in excess of twenty miles per hour. On a record trip the *Massachusetts* averaged twenty-three miles per hour between Fall River and Pier 18, Hudson River, New York. These three freighters together cost over $2 million, a clear illustration of the threat posed by the steamship combination headed by Charles W. Morse.[29]

By 1908 the great days of construction were almost over for the New England coastal lines. New vessels, to be sure, were ordered, but never again was the region to witness the spectacle of two or three new steamers a year. Changing economic patterns, increased operating costs, and the arrival of the automobile and motor truck ended the need for new leviathans to serve on the Fall River Line and the Metropolitan Line.

Propellers and Paddle Wheels

Most New England companies were slow to adopt the propeller; they preferred the paddle wheel, with which they were familiar. Many of the coastal lines connecting New England with the southern states had built screw steamers before the Civil War, and companies engaged in coastal service in other sections of the United States also had adopted this form of propulsion for new steamers. New England, however, lagged

far behind.[30] Of the more prominent New England companies, only the Metropolitan Steamship Company had completely abandoned paddle-wheel propulsion in new construction. Many claimed that propeller vessels suffered far less
damage from ice than did side-wheelers. Conversely, others
argued that the side-wheelers provided far more usable space
above the main deck because of their sponsons and that side-
wheelers could be stopped more quickly in emergencies.

The perfection of the high-speed triple expansion engine in
the 1870s and 1880s provided an economical alternative to
the beam engine. Capable of utilizing much higher boiler
pressures, this type of engine furnished more power with less
weight than the beam engine. An example is the *City of Lowell*, with two 2,500-horsepower triple expansion engines having cylinders of 26, 40, and 64 inches. The *Pilgrim* needed a
huge 110-inch cylinder to provide 5,300 horsepower, and her
engine was a simple engine using steam only once. The mas-
siveness of the *Pilgrim*'s engine necessitated extremely heavy
parts, whereas those on the *City of Lowell* were much lighter.
The working pressure of the *Lowell* was 165 pounds, that of
the *Pilgrim* 50 pounds. The *City of Lowell* had a reputation
for economical operation; the *Pilgrim* was notoriously expensive to operate because of her high coal consumption.[31]

Norwich Line officials gave careful consideration to the
merits of paddle wheels and propellers when designing the
City of Lowell. Their decision certainly was correct. A paper
read before the Society of Naval Architects and Marine Engineers in 1906 noted that the efficiency of the propellers of the
City of Lowell reached "the unusually high value of 78.3 per-
cent," and that "The two factors in the performance of the
Lowell [*sic*] which are primarily responsible for her economical amount of power per ton of displacement, are the high-
screw efficiency and an exceptionally low hull resistance."[32]
A. Carey Smith's ideas were vindicated. The *City of Lowell*
was not an isolated example, but typical of the advances being made by the combination of scientific methods and practical experience.

Nevertheless, later side-wheelers were much improved

1. Poster used sometime between 1865 and 1872.

2. *Massachusetts*, built in 1876–77 for the Providence &
Stonington Steamship Company. The trusses, or hogframes,
prevented the narrow wooden hull from sagging fore and aft.

3. *City of Brockton*, freight steamer built in 1886 for the
Old Colony Steamboat Company. She was one of the first side-
wheelers to have feathering paddle wheels and a compound-beam
engine. Her freight capacity was 800 tons.

4. *Commonwealth*, built in 1908 for the New England Navigation Company. She was the largest and most expensive side-wheeler ever employed in coastal service.

5. *Bunker Hill*, express freighter built in 1907 for the Boston Merchants Line. She was capable of speeds in excess of 20 miles per hour and was one of the vessels that put the Metropolitan Steamship Company out of business.

6. Views of the steamship *Pilgrim*, flagship of the Fall River Line, from *Frank Leslie's Illustrated Weekly* of 30 June 1883.

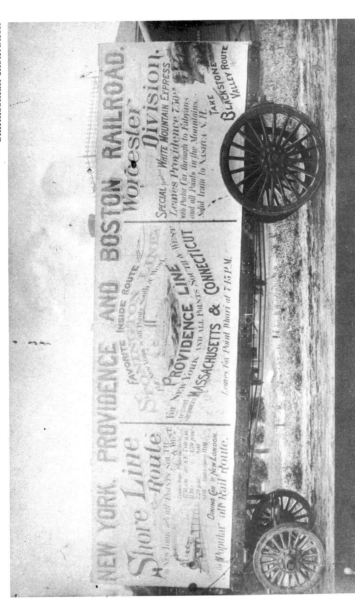

7. New York, Providence & Boston Railroad advertisement of its services and those of the Providence & Stonington Steamship Company, sometime between 1889 and 1892.

8. Freight yard off India Street, Providence, of a Merchants and Miners Transportation Company line. This drawing is from the Providence Board of Trade Journal of August 1890.

9. Hudson River Piers 18 and 19 in 1905 or 1906. The *City of Brockton* is in midstream, heading for the Sound, and the *Pilgrim* is heading in. The *Rhode Island* lies alongside Pier 18 and the *Puritan* at Pier 19.

10. Electric freight trucks transferring freight from receiving platform to steamer, Fall River Line, Pier 14, Hudson River.

11. Stowing freight on board the steamer. Use of electric trucks made Pier 14 one of the most efficient freight stations in Manhattan.

over the early models, as the evolution of the type on the Fall River Line indicates. The feathering wheel was of utmost importance in permitting the high speeds of the 400-foot steamers. This type of wheel could be smaller and still furnish the necessary power. The *Pilgrim* had rigid paddles on a 41-foot wheel; the feathering wheels on the larger *Priscilla* were 35 feet, on the *Providence* 30 feet, and on the *Commonwealth* 35 feet. The later steamers also utilized higher boiler pressures and a different type of engine. The inclined engine lowered the center of gravity, which was important as engines became heavier. The steam pressures used on steamers built after 1890 ranged from 135 pounds on the *Priscilla* to 174 pounds on the *Plymouth*. Engine speeds on the side-wheelers remained around 25 revolutions per minute compared with 125 revolutions on the *Richard Peck, City of Lowell,* and *Maine*.[33]

The Steam Turbine

In spite of all the improvements in the reciprocating steam engine, the most important technical advance in propulsion was the perfection of the steam turbine. The success of the *Governor Cobb* proved that this form of power was suitable for commercial steamships. The turbine had the advantages of simplicity and low vibration. Turbine steamers could operate at sustained high rates of speed without causing excessive wear on the turbine; a reciprocating engine could not sustain high rates of speed without excessive wear. The *Harvard* and the *Yale* were able to maintain their schedules because of their turbine propulsion. Even the smaller *Belfast* and *Camden* of the Eastern Steamship Company, designed for the run between Boston and the Penobscot River ports, were powered by turbines. After receiving the *Governor Cobb*, the Eastern Steamship Company and its successor corporations never ordered another large steamer powered by reciprocating engines.

The horsepower of the turbines was about the same as that of reciprocating engines in similar vessels. The *Governor*

Cobb had 5,000-horsepower turbines, and the *Belfast* and the *Camden* turbines developed about 4,000 horsepower. They used steam at a pressure of 150 pounds, very low compared to later turbines. At a steam pressure of 155 pounds the turbines on the *Harvard* and the *Yale* were rated at 10,000 horsepower. The turbine steamers built by the Morse companies used three Parsons turbines: one high-pressure and two low-pressure turbines. Each low-pressure turbine was equipped with a reversing turbine.[34] Considering that W. & A. Fletcher Company had never before constructed a turbine, the company and Consolidated Steamship Lines, which controlled the Metropolitan Steamship Company, deserve credit for pioneering successfully this mode of propulsion in the United States.

For a company that was a leader in building modern turbine steamers, the executives of the Eastern Steamship Company made a startling decision in 1905 when they ordered a wooden stern-wheel steamboat for the Kennebec River line between Bath and Augusta. The *City of Augusta* did not quite meet the standards of other steamers built by the company. On her maiden trip up the Kennebec she struck a ledge because of steering difficulties. She was then returned to her builders, who corrected this deficiency and raised her deck, which was too low to allow the handling of the normal freight carried on the line. Even progressive officials could make small mistakes.[35]

Corporations that resisted the new trends made some very costly mistakes. Probably the Providence & Stonington's *Connecticut* is the extreme example. No doubt her unsatisfactory performance had much to do with influencing the Norwich Line to abandon side-wheel propulsion. At times the public was the victim, as in the breaking up of the *Portland* in a severe storm north of Cape Ann, with the loss of three hundred lives. The combination of wooden construction and exposed paddle wheels could not withstand the force of wind and water. The fault lay not in the workmanship but in the design. The *Portland* was not the best that existing technology offered for the area she served.

Improvements in Efficiency

Had not the increases in size and speed of coastal steamers been accompanied by large savings in fuel consumption, operating costs would have become prohibitive. The surface condenser and the compound and triple expansion engines were major factors in conserving fuel. The older steamers used jet condensers that discharged the condensed steam overboard, whereas the surface condenser permitted the continuous re-use of water. This made possible the utilization of purified water, which prolonged the life of the boilers. More efficient boilers and fireboxes also were of considerable help. It is not difficult to comprehend the advantages of the compound and triple expansion engines over the simple ones.

The *Pilgrim*, for example, was noted for her enormous coal consumption. When new she burned an average of eighty-five tons a trip. When the size of the furnaces in her boilers was reduced, the consumption of coal decreased to between seventy-five and eighty tons a trip. Nevertheless, her operating costs were said to be the highest of any steamer on Long Island Sound.[36] Similar complaints were not heard regarding later steamers. Progress in hull design, propulsion machinery, and boiler efficiency brought remarkable reductions in coal consumption per indicated horsepower. The *Priscilla* burned approximately fifty tons of coal on the ten-hour run between New York and Fall River.[37] The *Maine* and the *New Hampshire*, on the shorter run between Stonington and New York, burned about twenty-four tons, compared to an average of thirty-eight tons consumed by the *Connecticut*.[38] The Hartford & New York Transportation Company effected similar savings when it built its first propeller, *Hartford*, in 1892. The side-wheelers had consumed about fifty tons a trip between New York and Hartford; the *Hartford* burned about thirty tons.[39] In July 1893 the cost of coal for the *Maine* was $1,903.22; for the *New Hampshire* it was $1,799.16. During the same month the *Connecticut* burned $4,084.80 worth of coal and the *Massachusetts* $3,537.97. During September 1897 the cost of coal for the *Pilgrim* while operating on the

Providence Line was $6,249.64, compared to $3,608.18 for the *Plymouth*.[40] The above figures provide convincing evidence of the effectiveness of the technological improvements. Operating costs were high, however, even on the later steamers. For example, in 1899 the fuel for the *Priscilla* cost $41,249.44 and for the *Puritan* $41,388.60.[41] A large amount of business was required to operate these steamers profitably.

It is interesting to note that many steamers burned anthracite coal. The smoke ordinances in New York City were probably partly responsible, but even without them, the cleanliness of this type of coal was important. The Maine Central steamers in Frenchman's Bay used anthracite, although no smoke ordinances existed there.[42]

The use of oil was a later development. The only steamers equipped to burn oil before World War I were the *Harvard* and the *Yale* and later the *Massachusetts* and the *Bunker Hill*. The reason for conversion was primarily the convenience of using oil in the New York–Boston service. It provided more uniform heat than coal, did not clog the flues, and left no ashes. The limited layover time in New York made it extremely difficult to get 235 to 240 tons of coal on board and at the same time handle the freight. Although it cost $60,000 more a year to burn oil in the *Harvard* and the *Yale* than to burn coal, the convenience of oil was worth the cost. After World War I, when labor costs increased significantly, oil became more competitive with coal because it eliminated the need for stokers and the excessive dust that accompanied taking on coal.[43]

The Demand for Speed

The effect of technological changes on the speed of the coastal steamers was less remarkable than on other characteristics. The Fall River Line steamer *Metropolis* had, before the Civil War, averaged more than 20 miles per hour on the 181-mile run. Until the *Puritan* entered service, her record of 8 hours and 50 minutes, made on 19 June 1865, was unmatched. On 8 June 1899 the *Puritan* completed the run in 8 hours and 27 minutes. The *Massachusetts* shattered this record on 4 June 1907 with a time of 7 hours and 48 minutes, giving her an average speed of 23 miles per hour.[44] The average had risen only about 3 miles per hour, but considering the increased size of the later steamers, it was a significant improvement.

On the longer runs the increases in speed were more noticeable. During the 1870s and 1880s the trip between New York and Portland required 35 hours. After the Maine Steamship Company received the *John Englis*, the running time was on occasion reduced to less than 20 hours, and on one trip to 17.5 hours. The *Horatio Hall* and the *North Star* could also maintain these schedules. Sometimes the speedier steamers did not have the good sailing qualities of the older ships. The *John Englis*, for example, was a bad roller, and the owners were not unhappy when the government purchased her.[45]

The famous "flyers," *Richard Peck, City of Lowell, Priscilla, Massachusetts, Old Colony, Bunker Hill, Harvard,* and *Yale,* could travel between 22 and 28 miles per hour.[46] Then as now the American public was enthralled by speed and attracted to the companies providing the fastest schedules.

The increase in speed was not confined to passenger steamers. The express freighter *Boston* (1904) had twin screws enabling her nearly to match the fastest steamers in the fleet of the New England Navigation Company.[47] The freight boats required this speed to make their scheduled arrival times, especially if they had been delayed by late arrival of the boat trains.

Improvements in Safety, 1870–1916

Assuring the safety of a steamer in the days of wooden construction and gas lighting was a formidable task. A collision often ruptured gas lines, and the escaping gas could easily be ignited by sparks from the boilers or from the lights themselves. A fire with any headway was virtually impossible to contain. During the period under study remarkable advances in safety were made. All steamboat companies tried to keep abreast of the latest technology, but the Old Colony Steamboat Company and later the New England Navigation Company were the leaders in this field.

The acceptance of iron and steel construction and electric lighting were among the most important safety advances made between 1870 and 1916. The success of the *Pilgrim* was especially significant. The new type of double hull construction was put to the test when the *Pilgrim* was barely a year old. While sailing through the East River in May 1884 the *Pilgrim* struck an uncharted ledge, which ripped a hole nearly one hundred feet long in her outer hull. After the accident she proceeded to her berth as if nothing had happened, discharged her passengers and freight, and then waited until the dry dock was prepared to receive her. As the *Nautical Gazette* commented: "The Fall River Line may well feel proud of owning such a mammoth life-boat as the *Pilgrim* has proven to be."[48] All the later Fall River Line steamers had this type of hull. In succeeding years similar accidents to the passenger steamers proved the value of double hull construction in conjunction with watertight bulkheads. This type of hull became standard on most large passenger steamers built after 1900.

The fine performance of the incandescent lighting system on the *Pilgrim* quickly convinced the management of the Old Colony Steamboat Company of its value. In 1884 the *Bristol* and the *Providence* were rebuilt and their lighting systems converted to electricity. During the same year the Norwich & New York Transportation Company removed all the gas lights from the *City of Worcester*, which had been equipped with both gas and electric lights.[49] The Providence & Stonington Steamship Company was reluctant to abandon gas. As late as 1886 one of its officers declared that the Pintsch lighting system was "preferred for many good reasons."[50] Obviously these "good reasons" were not enough, for electric lighting was being installed in practically all new passenger steamers.

Of all the safety precautions none was more important than those taken for fire protection. All the iron- and steel-hulled steamers had wooden joiner work above the main deck, and their carpeting and furnishings were highly combustible. On the Fall River Line the precautions taken were always far above legal requirements. The *Pilgrim* when new had one steam and two hand fire pumps, plus many hydrants and extra hose.[51] The Old Colony Steamboat Company trained special fire-fighting brigades on its passenger steamers to respond quickly to emergencies. By 1890 all Fall River Line steamers had electric thermostats in strategic locations to warn of fire long before it had gained much headway.[52] As improved safety devices were developed, they were included on each new steamer and added whenever possible during the rebuilding of the older ones. On the *Providence* (1905) and the *Commonwealth* every stateroom had a thermostat that activated alarms in the pilot house, engine room, and crew's quarters. The first installation of automatic sprinklers on a passenger steamer occurred in 1907, when the *Plymouth* was rebuilt. A sprinkler system had been successfully installed on one of the freight boats, and it was decided to include similar systems on the *Plymouth* and the *Commonwealth*. The only other coastal steamers so equipped during these years were the *Harvard* and the *Yale*. Freight decks, machinery spaces, and kitchens on the *Commonwealth* were lined with sheet steel. What is impressive is that these installations were made before they were required by law.[53]

Other companies took adequate safety precautions and met all government requirements, but the railroad-owned Fall River Line deserves much credit for its foresight and leadership. Only the Eastern Steamship Company and the Metropolitan Steamship Company, among New England companies, approached the standards of the Fall River Line. In the 1880s the Fall River Line already had acquired a reputation for safe operation. While the editor of the *Nautical Ga-*

zette was so hostile toward the management of the Providence & Stonington Steamship Company, he had only praise for the Fall River Line and its personnel. The reputation of the Fall River Line spread to Europe as well.[54]

Wireless equipment was adopted almost as soon as it was perfected, all the coastal lines adopting it at about the same time. Life-saving equipment also improved over the years. A glance at the logbooks of the steamers shows the precautions taken by the officers.[55]

The generally excellent safety record of the New England lines accounts for their continued prosperity despite improved railroad service. The size of the new steamers built in the twentieth century must have given a secure feeling to the traveler and, until the *Titanic* disaster, provided an aura of indestructibility.

Operational Developments

The Effect of Consolidation

The consolidation of the steamship companies in New England permitted large savings through the greater utilization of steamers and the centralization of shop facilities. The advantages of increased size are particularly evident in the better utilization of the steamers by the larger companies and the ability of these companies to provide spare boats in cases of emergency.

The New England Navigation Company and the New England Steamship Company, which after 1905 alternated as operating companies for the lines owned by the New Haven Railroad, had a regular schedule of maintenance for all the steamers. During the winter one passenger and one freight steamer were kept ready for each line. These could be in service on twelve hours' notice. Because of its large fleet of different types of steamers, the New England Steamship Company could operate the steamers best suited to the season of the year and the demands of the service. Examples may be found in the utilization of the large side-wheelers used on the Fall River and Providence lines. The *Commonwealth* was in service only about five months of any one year and the *Priscilla* about six months of the year. Because of their size it would have been uneconomical to operate them during the coldest months. However, the *Plymouth* operated for about eight months and the *Providence* for almost ten months a year. These two steamers were smaller and less expensive to operate, but quite adequate to handle the business. Of the whole fleet of twenty-one steamers owned by the New England Steamship Company in 1916, seven were normally out of service at any one time. Only a large corporation could afford to use a steamer as large as the *Commonwealth* only five months a year and to have one-third of its fleet idle at any one time.[56] The Eastern Steamship Company was able to follow the same practices in its operations.

Another benefit of consolidation was the ability to operate elaborate shop facilities for maintaining and overhauling steamers. The New Haven lines had exceptionally fine shops. At Newport was located a very elaborate complex of shops capable of doing every type of repair and construction except drydocking. The Newport shops dated from at least 1870, when the Narragansett Steamship Company also maintained shops in Fall River. By 1873 two hundred skilled workers had been added to the force already in Newport. It took a large gang to maintain the seven steamers then owned by the company.[57] The Providence & Stonington Steamship Company had its repair facilities adjacent to its terminal in Stonington. Located there were a boiler shop, general repair shops, and a Pintsch gas plant to supply the steamers.[58] As these companies came under New Haven control, the officials of the marine district realized that one large shop complex for all the lines would be more suitable and economical.

Thus in 1900 the officials of the marine district of the New Haven decided to enlarge the facilities at Newport. The company spent $250,000 on new brick buildings and new machinery. Four berths were available, two of which were more than five hundred feet long and the others about four hundred feet in length. Employing between three hundred and five hundred workers, the shops were the principal employer in the city of Newport. The facilities contained a power house, machine shop, carpenter shop, paint shop, blacksmith shop, a derrick capable of handling the largest machinery or boilers on the steamers, and a large open area on the wharf for outside work.[59] An indication of the capacity of the facilities is the fact that several steamers were partially constructed at Newport. Many of the interior furnishings on the *Providence* (1905) and the *Priscilla* were installed there.[60] Because the company could provide a continuous work schedule, the Newport shops "materially reduced the cost of repairs and eliminated the profits of outside contractors."[61] Here again size was definitely an asset.

Interior Furnishings and Facilities

At least since the completion of the *Providence* and the *Bristol* in the 1860s the emphasis on display and the use of elaborate furnishings had not waned. All the Sound lines were forced to conform or suffer losses in the through business to competitors. In decorating the interiors a general style or color combination was often selected and followed throughout the public cabins and saloons. The *Puritan, Plymouth,* and *Priscilla* were decorated in a nineteenth-century version of Italian Renaissance style. The *Chester W. Chapin* had all her carpets especially designed in Persian style. The "French Renaissance strongly influenced by Louis XVI period" was the theme on the *Providence* (1905).[62] The *Commonwealth* had a potpourri of styles in her principal public areas including Louis XVI, Italian Renaissance, modern English, Venetian Gothic, Louis XV, and French Empire.[63] Many considered her furnishings less successful than those of her predecessors. The *Harvard* and the *Yale*, of course, featured the crimson and the blue of their namesakes.[64]

No matter what the theme or colors, lavish use was made of Wilton carpeting, mahogany and other costly woods for paneling and carvings, gilding, opulent furniture, murals, mirrors, and other trappings of Victorian and late Victorian decor. These furnishings achieved their purpose: they made a setting that added to the pleasures of travel and provided, for many passengers, a taste of unaccustomed luxury. Having electricity in the 1880s, before most cities, the steamers were often a source of wonder as well as pleasure.

The regular staterooms were plainly furnished and usually had two bunks. On steamers constructed before 1900 there were inside staterooms without windows and outside rooms with windows. The later steamers often were constructed with only the more popular outside rooms. The larger steamers usually had a few bridal suites with brass beds, plus a few staterooms at higher prices for wealthier travelers desiring privacy.[65] The *Harvard* and the *Yale* had no less than thirty staterooms with complete baths and brass bedsteads. This was luxury equal to that of the trans-Atlantic liners.[66] For those unable or unwilling to pay for a stateroom, free bunks were available in the men's cabin and ladies' cabin.

Another primary attraction of the coastal lines was the cuisine. All the lines provided good food and varied menus; some had excellent reputations for their cuisine. A good meal afloat was often the highlight of the trip, and "There [was] no better way to popularize a line than through the medium of a good table fare."[67] Not only were the meals an epicure's delight, but also they were served in an attractive setting. Steamers built before 1870 had their kitchens and dining cabins on the lower deck. The *Rhode Island* (1873) and the *Massachusetts* began the trend of placing the dining cabin on the main deck.[68] This permitted better ventilation and gave the diners a better view from their tables. When the Providence & Stonington Steamship Company designed the *Maine* and the *New Hampshire,* the dining cabins were placed on the gallery deck, from which an excellent view was had of the coastline and harbors.[69] Other companies gradually adopted the practice of placing the kitchen and dining facilities on the main or gallery deck. The dining cabins of necessity were quite large. The *Pilgrim* could seat 170 persons in hers; the *Commonwealth* could seat 216. Dining in the latter must have been especially pleasant. Her dining saloon was located on the hurricane deck, which was forty feet above the water. There the traveler could enjoy his meal while admiring the scenery through the five-foot windows that encircled the saloon.[70]

The logistics of supplying the steamers involved considerable planning, particularly in the days before mechanical refrigeration. To supply the *Pilgrim* for each trip during the summer season required such items as 2,200 pounds of meat, 300 pounds of fish, 40 pairs of fowl, 5 dozen assorted game, 6 to 8 barrels of potatoes, 2 barrels of turnips, 1 barrel of onions, 6 bags of peas, 3,000 oysters, 1,500 clams, 50 quarts of berries, 6 baskets of peaches, 300 pounds of butter, 300 loaves of bread, 500 quarts of milk, 1 barrel of flour, 60 pounds of coffee, 20 pounds of tea, 10 pounds of chocolate, 200 pounds of sugar, and 270 dozen eggs.[71] A few years after the New Haven Railroad took over the Sound lines, it established a central commissary department at Pier 14, Hudson River, New York, to supply all the lines under its control. As in the case of the Newport shops, centralization resulted in savings for the company.[72] Adding together the commissary supplies, linen, silverware, liquor, and other necessary items, the enormity of the preparations for each trip can be appreciated.

Among the other amenities to attract patronage were the nightly band and orchestra concerts. Begun on the Fall River Line when Jim Fisk was in his heyday, the practice was adopted by the Norwich, Stonington, and Providence lines. Only the Fall River Line, however, carried a band throughout the year.[73] In 1879 the Fall River Line began publishing its own paper, the *Fall River Line Journal*, distributed free to the passengers. Containing verses and poems, schedule information, and articles of interest, it became a regular feature of the line. Again the competition imitated this practice.[74]

Operating Expenses, 1880–1916

The cost of operating these services was not small. Although complete figures are difficult to find, enough are available to indicate that operating expenses increased in every decade. Since separate accounts for each line were not always kept, it is impossible to determine the operating costs for some lines. Officials of the New England Steamship Company claimed that they were unable to determine precisely which lines were making or losing money.[75] Comparisons between different companies are meaningless because of the lack of uniform accounting procedures.[76] There was no Interstate Commerce Commission to supervise steamship accounting. The packet lines on the Atlantic coast reporting to the Bureau of Corporations had an operating ratio of 81 per cent, but because of the variety of service and traffic these averages provide only a superficial view.[77]

Operating costs definitely rose during the years under consideration. During July 1884 the operating expenses on the Providence Line were $39,077.01; in July 1891 they were $61,075.56. By July 1897, because the consolidation of the lines under New Haven management had altered traffic patterns, the expenses had dropped to $48,712.57. On the Stonington Line similar increases are evident: from $26,513.64 for the month of July 1884 to $36,557.54 in July 1891. For the Old Colony Steamboat Company monthly expenses rose from $227,467.39 in July 1889 to $291,545.99 in July 1892.[78] Taking operational costs for individual steamers one finds an identical trend. During August 1910 it cost an average of $1,995.02 to operate the *Harvard* and the *Yale* for a single trip. In August 1915 the *Massachusetts* and the *Bunker Hill*, which were considerably less expensive to operate, had expenses of $1,895.75 per trip. Clearly, costs had risen significantly between 1910 and 1915. Laying-up expenses were another costly item. For the *Harvard* and the *Yale* the total was $52,594 in 1908 and $65,923 in 1909, and they were then new vessels.[79]

As Calvin Austin, president of Eastern Steamship Company, said, an independent company could not operate profitably the seasonal service provided by steamers like the *Harvard* and the *Yale*. The management of the Hartford & New York Transportation Company had recognized this several years before. When the New Haven purchased the company in 1906, Charles C. Goodrich, the general manager, said that an independent company could not afford to operate the service of the Hartford Line. The passenger business between Hartford and New York City did not earn enough profit to permit the company to purchase the new steamers necessary to remain competitive with the railroads. An example of the problem is the increased size of the crew required during the summer. Sometimes the payroll for a steamer in passenger service was as much as one-third higher in the summer than it was in the winter.[80] As wages and other costs increased, these conditions affected all the companies. Despite the monopolistic tendencies of these large corporations, only they could afford to continue steamship service on the scale to which the public had become accustomed.

Labor on the Coastal Lines

Working conditions in the coastal merchant marine were generally superior to those in the foreign merchant marine. The principal reason for this was that after 1874, unlike seamen in a foreign port, the seamen in the coastal service could "quit" without being charged with desertion and perhaps imprisoned. According to Andrew Furuseth, secretary of the Seamen's Union, "Being free to quit work, he [the sailor] was free to organize." Because landings were more frequent and cargo had to be handled more often, the work in the coastal service was more demanding than in the deep-sea service.[81] To attract good workers it was necessary to pay somewhat higher wages than were paid to seamen in foreign service. This did not apply, however, to the lower ranks in the coastal service. Menial jobs and physically demanding work like stoking were done for meager pay and often by foreigners or immigrants.[82]

Wages varied considerably from one company to another. One of the best-paying companies was the Old Colony Steamboat Company. Its senior captains on steamers like the *Pilgrim* and the *Providence* received at least $2,500 in 1887, which was more than $1,000 higher than the average salary in 1889 for captains working out of Boston. The Old Colony officers in the deck and engineering departments also received salaries much higher than the Boston average. Of course the officers in charge of the large passenger steamers on the Sound lines had tremendous responsibility, especially in the days before wireless and adequate navigational aids. For the deck hands, firemen, oilers, and other lower ranks the pay scale was about the same as the Boston average. But the higher wages paid by the Old Colony to officers attracted able, ambitious men to the company, and many who entered in the lower grades eventually became officers.[83] Pride in their company was common among the employees of the first-class lines as can be seen by the long service of many employees.

The employees had additional benefits such as uniforms and subsistence while in service. The wearing of uniforms by the officers was a rather late innovation. The introduction of uniforms sometimes produced humorous results. During 1875 the band members on the Fall River Line, pretending to be ship's officers, often showed excessive interest in the female passengers. Their uniforms were soon altered to preserve the dignity of the regular ship's company.[84]

Wages do not appear to have risen significantly before 1900. This contributed to the labor unrest that occurred toward the end of the century. In 1899 a wildcat strike was called on the steamer *New Hampshire* shortly before her scheduled departure from New York. The New York press was outraged, not only by the strike, but also by the failure of the New Haven management to provide transportation for the stranded passengers from the wharf to Grand Central Station. In 1903 the ocean and harbor tugboat crews called a strike in New York Harbor, but the failure of nonunion men to honor it considerably lessened its effectiveness.[85] In February 1907 the New England Navigation Company had to grant a pay raise to its captains, pilots, and mates.[86] Calvin Austin, president of the Eastern Steamship Company, later the same year claimed during the preceding ten years wages had risen an average of one-third, and over-all operating expenses were 40 per cent higher than in 1897. Between 1908 and 1914 wages in the engineering and stewards' department rose another 15 per cent. The unions also were able to force an increase in the size of the engineering force on freight vessels.[87]

The increasing wages and the difficulties of dealing with certain groups employed by the coastal lines forced the steamship companies to change procedures and adopt labor-saving devices. This occurred at the terminals when electric trucks began to replace hand trucks. The management of the Metropolitan Line decided to convert its steamers to oil as much to avoid the difficulties with the stokers as to avoid the time-consuming job of coaling in New York. It took about forty men to keep steam on the express liners *Massachusetts* and *Bunker Hill*. According to Calvin Austin, the stokers were the "meanest things that God put on the face of the earth that we have to deal with, and when we put oil aboard, we washed that class out."[88]

On balance, however, the years before World War I were reasonably good for the operating personnel. The companies provided pensions for employees with long service, and working on the Fall River Line or another important line gave one a certain prestige.[89] Labor difficulties did not become critical until after World War I. Ultimately the high cost of labor was a major factor in the demise of the New England coastal lines.

After 1908 the New Haven Railroad was criticized harshly for neglecting its steamship lines. This was hardly a fair evaluation. The New Haven and its predecessors were quite conscious of advances in technology and safety. Whenever possible they incorporated these advances in the new steamers. On several occasions the Fall River Line had the finest equipment that existing technology offered. Compared with the steamers built by several independent steamship companies in New England, steamers built by the Sound lines controlled by railroads were generally more advanced in design and more elaborately furnished.

By 1900 it was evident that large financial resources were required to operate first-class steamship service. Railroad ownership could provide this capital. Consolidation permitted economies at all levels of operation and provided a pool of managerial talent that was unavailable to smaller companies. These were only some of the benefits of railroad control, but without them the rail-water service would have been inadequate to the needs of New England.

5. Rates, Schedules, and Service, 1881–1916

REGARDLESS OF technological improvements, without favorable rates and dependable service the rail-water lines would have withered. The changes and refinements made by the New Haven Railroad resulted in a highly sophisticated transportation system that was well suited to the requirements of the region.

Passenger Service

The Growth of Tourism

The basic pattern of passenger operations was well established by 1870. The rate wars, which ended in 1881, showed that competition had to be confined to service and convenience. After 1880 a few railroads acquired steamboat lines as extensions of their rail routes, but the steamboats no longer were the principal passenger carriers between major New England coastal cities. Even so, they shared in the growth of the passenger business, which was linked inseparably with the growth of tourism.

To accommodate better the increasing numbers of passengers, the Sound lines augmented their service. There had long been resistance in New England to the operation of transportation on Sunday. At one time only interstate trains had been permitted to operate on that day. Nevertheless, by late in the 1870s Sunday night steamers were scheduled during the warmer months on all the principal New England lines. In 1879 the Fall River Line continued its Sunday trips until after Christmas to serve touring theatrical companies. The Norwich Line encountered some opposition in Connecticut to a similar move, but the petitions opposing these trips had no apparent effect.[1] The Fall River Line provided a daily-except-Saturday double-service (two boats in each direction) during the summer to meet the demand for staterooms. It continued until the middle of the 1890s, when the facilities on the Providence Line were improved and so ended the necessity of the double-service.

The lines in northern New England likewise increased service during the summer. The Maine Central Railroad operated its service to Mount Desert Island primarily to accommodate the tourists. The Portland, Mt. Desert & Machias Steamboat Company provided three weekly trips during the summer as opposed to one a week in the early spring and late autumn. The Maine Steamship Company during the 1890s added a third trip to its summer schedule; by 1897 it was operating five trips a week. At the same time the Portland Steamship Company (formerly Portland Steam Packet Company) ran a double-service during the summer.[2]

In 1904 the management of the New Haven Railroad, as part of a reorganization of its freight service, reopened the New Bedford Line to passengers during the summer months. This was especially appreciated by the summer residents of Martha's Vineyard and Nantucket, because the island steamers used the same wharf in New Bedford.

The establishment of summer passenger service on the Metropolitan Line with the *Harvard* and the *Yale* attracted more attention than any other change during the years under study. Begun in September 1907, this service was comparable in luxury to that of the Fall River Line. Although heavily patronized, it never proved a very profitable venture because of the high operating costs of the ships in conjunction with the short, four-month season.

Additional evidence of the expansion of passenger travel can be found among the railroads. The New Haven had three daily five-hour trains between New York and Boston by 1910. In 1913 fifteen through trains were operating in each direction on the Shore Line. In 1902, after considerable agitation from Maine businessmen, the Boston & Maine Railroad and the New Haven Railroad opened a through service between New York and Portland, Maine. The train went via Worcester and carried through cars to Mount Desert Ferry and Rockland. Officials of the New Haven had maintained that such service would be unprofitable, but the number of passengers who desired to avoid the inconvenience of crossing downtown Boston soon proved them incorrect. By the summer of 1913 three trains each way were required to handle the business.[3]

Despite rail competition, the steamship lines had little difficulty retaining a profitable share of the passenger business in the warmer months. Modern steamers and faster schedules were great assets to the coastal lines, and they were always ready to advertise these advantages.

Aspects of the passenger business that developed relatively late were the tour and the excursion. In the 1880s these had become well established, and they continued to increase in popularity. Many variations could be found in the excursions, which included two- or three-day trips to a city or resort; one- or two-day shopping trips to cities like Boston and New York; special trips to the America's Cup races or the Harvard-Yale crew race on the Thames River; and Sunday trips from New York City up the Hudson River to the Poughkeepsie Bridge, or to New Haven. The run to the Poughkeepsie Bridge was for many years a popular Sunday outing, and when the weather was fair the *City of Lowell* was usually loaded to capacity. Excursions gave employment to steamers otherwise idle and brought in revenue from people who might never have been able to ride the Sound steamers. The excursion fares were quite inexpensive; the New York–New Haven fare was only seventy-five cents.[4]

The tour, which required more time, utilized a variety of routes and means of transportation, and it generated a large amount of business. The Old Colony Steamboat Company summer folder for 1893 listed over five hundred different tours to resorts and cities in the northeastern United States and Canada.[5]

The resort business depending on summer hotels, cottages, or the palatial summer homes of the rich became of considerable value in the 1880s; in the next two and a half decades it provided the primary source of cash income for some sections of New England. The state of Maine is an especially good example of its importance. In 1887 an estimated 100,000 tourists visited Maine. The Maine Central Railroad claimed that 75,000 of these arrived by rail and the majority of the rest by water. During their visit they spent between $6 million and $10 million.[6] The impact of tourism was reflected not only in the number of visitors and the money they left in the state, but also in the investment in real estate. To cater to the desires of the guests required an almost continuous expansion and modernization of the facilities. In 1908 the real estate directly connected with the summer resorts and private cottages was valued at $113 million. Throughout the state of Maine were scattered 1,200 summer hotels.[7] Then as now, intense competition existed among those seeking to attract the tourist and his money.

Only during depression years did the growth of tourism lag. In 1908 the out-of-state tourists left $20 million in Maine. To a relatively poor state, this was an important source of income. Not all the visitors were arriving in the summer. Hunting and fishing were gaining in popularity, and the conditions in northern New England attracted many to that area—especially to Maine. Publicity journals contained numerous articles and photographs on the wonders of the outdoor life in Maine. It was the only state in New England where large game existed in any abundance, and the numerous lakes and the long coastline provided excellent angling.[8]

Without the transportation provided by the railroads and steamship lines Maine could never have achieved such a rapid growth in tourism.[9] The services were continually expanded. In 1901 the Maine Central inaugurated a steamer service between Rockland and points in Penobscot Bay. Because many of the better resort sites were located beyond the rail lines of the company, the management found it "expedient and profitable" to construct and operate steamers from its Rockland terminus. Without the steamers the business would have vanished. During fiscal year 1914, the services of the Maine Central in Penobscot Bay and Frenchman's Bay had a deficit of $52,530, which resulted in an operating ratio of about 167 per cent. Nevertheless, the patronage given the rail lines of the company justified the cost.[10]

The steamship lines throughout New England shared in the prosperity. One of the favored routes from New York to northern New England was by the Fall River Line to Boston and thence either by rail or steamship. The Maine Steamship Company and the Portland Steamship Company also brought large numbers of visitors, and each constructed new steamers to handle the passengers. The tariff files list many routes for which through tickets were sold; they often included a steamship journey. New England resorts felt the pressures and enjoyed the profits of the business made possible by the expanding network of rail lines, electric interurban lines, and steamship lines.

The steamers built after 1880 did not necessarily bring any significant increase in capacity, but nearly all had a much larger number of staterooms. No longer would the traveling public tolerate sleeping in a common cabin. For their 1,200 passengers the *Providence* and the *Bristol* had only 250 staterooms. Out of 1,000 berths on the *Puritan* over 700 were in staterooms. The trend accelerated on the later boats. The *Plymouth* had 770 berths in first-class accommodations out of a total of 861 berths; the *Providence* (1905) had 881 out of 992.[11] Among the Maine companies the tradition of the common men's cabin and ladies' cabin lingered, but the trend to staterooms was inexorable. In 1884 the *Tremont* had 100 staterooms and a passenger capacity of 700, whereas the *Portland*, completed in 1890, with about the same capacity had 156 staterooms. The *Governor Dingley*, built in 1900, had 220 staterooms for her 700 passengers. On vessels of the Maine Steamship Company and the Boston & Bangor Steamship Company similar improvements occurred.[12] The express trains carrying parlor and sleeping cars forced the most conservative managements to provide facilities equal to or surpassing those of the railroads.

The increase in passenger travel between 1875 and 1914 is startling. In the summer of 1875 the Fall River Line carried an average of 21,000 passengers a month during July and August; in 1912 the average was about 40,000 a month.[13] On the Stonington Line the yearly average between 1881 and 1884 was 100,000. During the middle of that same decade the Norwich Line was carrying about 50,000 a year. In 1912, when only the Norwich Line was in operation, it carried 109,400 passengers.[14] The 1912 total is an impressive one considering the competition the Norwich Line had from the two new year-round lines operating between Providence and New York. The Providence Line in the years between 1881 and 1884 carried an average of 29,800 passengers during its five-month season. In the 1912 season, 70,243 rode the line. During 1913 and 1914 the number carried dropped to 58,581 and 50,452 respectively, but these totals do not include the passengers traveling on the Bay State Line and the Colonial Line, which provided a twelve-month service to the city. The New Bedford Line in the seasons of 1912 and 1913 carried an average of over 20,000 passengers.[15]

In Maine the trend was the same. In 1895 the Maine Central steamers out of Mount Desert Ferry carried just over 45,000 passengers from June to September; in 1915 over 54,000 rode the steamers during those months. The total for 1915 did not include any passengers carried by the Eastern Steamship Corporation. In 1880 the number of passengers traveling by steamer between Boston and Portland totaled 113,500; in 1912 about 700,000 were handled at Franklin Wharf by the lines of the Eastern Steamship Corporation to Boston and New York.[16]

The importance of the summer business cannot be over-emphasized. On the lines of the New England Steamship Company, which had more winter patronage than most of the companies north of Cape Cod, 59.6 per cent of the passenger revenue was earned from June through September.[17] This emphasizes the tremendous cost of operating large steamers that could be utilized profitably only during a brief, four- or five-month season.

Steamship and Railroad Fares

After 1881 passenger fares remained quite stable although some fighting lines entered the field during the first decade of the twentieth century. With one exception the New Haven refused to cut the fares on its first-class lines; instead, it started low-fare lines using older surplus steamers to fight the new companies. As had occurred in the rate war ending in 1881, the passenger fares dropped to as low as one dollar and on occasion to fifty cents, but these reductions never spread beyond local port-to-port rates as had happened in 1877. Rate cutting on the New Haven's first-class lines occurred only when Charles W. Morse was operating the *Harvard* and the *Yale*. Then the New England Navigation Company reduced its through New York to Boston fare from $4.00 to $3.65. The company restored the $4.00 fare after the Morse threat subsided.[18]

Fares on the coastal lines were far cheaper than those by rail. On the first-class steamer lines between Boston and New York the regular $4.00 fare averaged 1.73 cents a mile. The local fare between Fall River and New York was 1.67 cents and from Providence 1.65 cents a mile. From New London the average per mile rate for the $1.50 fare was 1.25 cents.

Passenger Service

By contrast the New York–Boston rail fare averaged 2.3 cents a mile in 1894; in 1914 it was 2.06 cents a mile. North of Boston the steamship fares averaged about the same as those on the Sound lines. Between Boston and Bangor the fare remained at $3.50 until 1914. Using rail mileage, this fare averaged 1.46 cents a mile. The all-rail fare of $6.50 cost 2.6 cents a mile and the $8.00 fare from Boston to Bar Harbor via Bangor came to 2.75 cents a mile.[19]

The steamship lines had a decided advantage in the setting of fares because after 1900 the railroads could not operate passenger trains profitably if the fares were below two cents a mile.[20] Between 1880 and 1910 some rail fares did decline, but the trend was short-lived. The Boston–New York fare via the Shore Line dropped from $5.53 unlimited in 1884 to $5.30 unlimited and $5.00 limited in 1894. By 1913 it had been reduced to $4.75. In 1887 the New York to Bar Harbor rail fare was $13.45 unlimited and $11.95 limited; in 1911 the fare all-rail via Worcester was $12.55 limited or unlimited.[21] The 1911 route eliminated the necessity of changing trains at Boston as had been required before 1900. Shortly before World War I, however, rail and steamship fares began to increase.

Often fares were quoted at two prices. The more expensive, unlimited tickets were usually good until used, and permitted stopovers at any place en route. Limited tickets sometimes were restricted to continuous passage or to no more than a one- to four-day stopover en route at one place.

As was the case with rail fares, the steamer fares included only the cost of passage; staterooms, meals, and other special services were extra. On the steamers free berths were available, but most passengers preferred staterooms. An inside stateroom was usually $1.00, and a cooler and better ventilated outside stateroom, $2.00 or $3.00. On the longer runs the prices were higher, because of the greater period of occupancy. In 1913 the Maine Steamship Company charged $3.00 for an inside room and $4.00 for an outside room. For those desiring more luxurious accommodations, most steamers had a limited number of rooms with regular beds. A few of the express steamers built after 1900 had rooms with full baths. A stateroom with a bedstead cost $5.00 or $6.00, while one with a bath was around $8.00. Comparable prices on the New Haven Railroad for Pullman accommodations were $1.50 for an upper berth, $2.00 for a lower berth, and $4.00 or $5.00 for a compartment.[22]

As the steamship lines came under railroad control or themselves merged into larger companies, the practice of through ticketing became general. By the 1880s the tariffs quoted several routes to the leading resorts. Between Bar Harbor and New York the traveler had the choice of as many as eight combinations by rail, water, or rail and water. A through ticket eliminated the formerly bothersome chore of purchasing one or more tickets en route. If the instructions given to the ticket agents of the Maine Central Railroad are indicative of those given by other railroads, the traveler who did not have his itinerary selected in advance might be ticketed for a less desirable route. The company instructed its agents to "endeavor to obtain the *longest haul for this company,* unless such route would be to the passenger's decided disadvantage as to train connections, or otherwise."[23]

In the through service on the Sound lines the division of revenue was fixed by agreement between the railroad and the steamship company. The latter retained all revenue from staterooms, meals, and the bar. The division of the New York–Boston fares on the Fall River Line was 65 per cent to the steamboat company and 35 per cent to the railroad. On the Stonington Line the division was set in 1869 as 37 per cent to the rail lines and 63 per cent to the steamers. In 1878 this changed to 45 per cent to the railroad and 55 per cent to the steamers. The Norwich Line and the Norwich & Worcester Railroad established these same divisions to all points north and west of Worcester. South of Worcester the steamship company retained a larger share. The passenger divisions remained fairly constant until 1910, whereas the freight divisions underwent changes favoring the railroads. The Maine Central boats received the local fare between

Rockland or Mount Desert Ferry and point of destination; in through ticketing the local rate was added to the through rate.[24]

The Boat Trains

Because of excellent co-ordination between trains and steamers, those steamship routes controlled by railroads had a decided advantage over the independent lines. On the first-class lines like the Fall River Line and the Providence Line the trains operated on express schedules and carried the finest equipment. These luxuries and the brief time between train arrival and boat departure were vital in the competition with the ever improving all-rail service. At stations like Fox Point in Providence special arrangements had to be made to run the boat train to the wharf, because of the lack of any satisfactory connection between Union Station and the wharf. At Fall River, Stonington, and New London the wharf stations were located either close to the regular passenger station or on branches that connected conveniently with the main line and the regular stations. At Rockland the Maine Central Railroad constructed a spur track to the waterfront to serve the Portland, Mt. Desert & Machias Steamboat Company steamers. The Mount Desert Ferry terminal likewise handled primarily passengers and baggage.[25]

The boat train on the Fall River Line, operated by the Old Colony Railroad, always carried the finest equipment. It was assigned vestibuled cars when they were rare in New England and had special engines and parlor cars for use only on the boat train. At its demise in July 1937 it was the oldest American passenger train in continuous operation. In addition to the express train, the Fall River Line had a second train making several stops, and during the summer there were trains directly to and from the White Mountains and Cape Cod.[26]

When the New York, Providence & Boston Railroad operated the Stonington Line, its boat trains had fine equipment and operated on a fast schedule. The Providence Line had first-class service to Boston and the White Mountains. The Norwich Line could never compete successfully for a large share of the eastbound, New York to Boston passenger traffic because of the distance from Norwich to Boston. The Boston passengers had either to take a train before 4:30 A.M. or take a train around 6:30 A.M., which arrived in Boston after 10:00 A.M. On the Providence and Fall River lines the trains could leave as late as 6:30 A.M. and still reach Boston by 8:00, a more convenient hour for businessmen. The New Haven Line once had through service to Springfield, but when the New Haven Railroad consolidated the rail lines around the city, the connecting service was gradually reduced. Eventually only a shuttle train connected with the New Haven boats. After 1903 no special service connected with the Bridgeport Line because its wharf was within sight of the regular passenger station and the line carried few through passengers.[27]

Once the New Haven had attained a monopoly of the rail and water transportation in southern New England, it made some alterations in the established routes. In 1904 service via Stonington was abandoned. The Norwich Line took over most of the passenger traffic formerly moving via the Stonington Line. At the same time a daily-except-Sunday passenger service out of New Bedford was begun during the summer months,[28] which benefited travelers bound for Nantucket and Martha's Vineyard.

In Maine rail-water co-ordination existed only between the Maine Central Railroad and its water lines. From the beginning of the Mount Desert Ferry service a daily limited train with parlor cars operated between there and Boston. By 1914 there were two day parlor-car trains and one overnight train from Boston; from New York a daily through overnight train made the trip in twelve hours. The trains operated directly to the wharf, where two steamers waited. Five or ten minutes after the train arrived, the express steamer left for Bar Harbor, and shortly after that the local boat departed for Bar Harbor and points beyond. Similar steamer service connected with the trains for Boston and New York. Often travel was so heavy that the trains needed extra sections.

In 1901 the Maine Central began steamer service between Rockland and points in Penobscot Bay. Because the Eastern Steamship Company boats from Rockland operated in conjunction with their steamers out of Boston, travelers by rail had to wait overnight for the boat from Rockland to points in Penobscot Bay. These poor connections slowed the recreational development of the Penobscot Bay region. To stimulate rail travel, the management of the Maine Central decided to establish its own steamer service to connect with the company's Boston and New York trains. Two separate lines had to be established because one steamer could not make all the landings and still meet the trains. This service operated solely to cater to the summer tourist travel, whereas the Mount Desert service of the railroad was maintained on a limited basis during the winter months for the permanent residents.[29]

Without the boat trains the steamship lines on Long Island Sound could not have survived, for the through business was necessary to sustain the first-class service of these lines. The close co-ordination of boat trains and steamers belies the claim that steamer service deteriorated under railroad control. Indeed, the management of the Maine Central improved on the steamship companies by establishing service where no steamship company was willing or able to co-ordinate its schedule with that of the railroad.

Accommodations and Special Services

Of all the New England coastal lines the Fall River Line was the best known, and it set the unofficial standards by which the others were judged. Its steamers were the largest and most expensive, its furnishings the most luxurious, and its services designed to attract the best clientele. In 1896 the company arranged a special messenger service to meet the boats in New York and escort strangers, ladies, and children, as well as deliver messages, telegrams, or packages. Later, special stenographic services were available to those who desired to do business en route. When the wireless became available, passengers could send ship-to-shore messages. The *Commonwealth* contained a library that loaned the latest best sellers to passengers. Particular attention was paid to details such as serving only good-quality food, furnishing the best bar supplies, and attempting the utmost in cleanliness. Many steamers during those years were noted for the vermin found in the bedding, but not the Fall River Line. It invited its patrons to comment on anything they considered not up to the standards of the line.[30]

This attitude paid handsome dividends by increasing business, as can be seen by looking at the company ledgers and at the steamers built for the service. It also was reflected in the character of the clientele. The Fall River Line and the other Sound lines apparently did not attract prostitutes and others of low moral character such as were prevalent on the Hudson River night boats. The comment was frequently made that a woman alone could travel in complete safety on the Fall River Line.[31] Two examples illustrate the reputation of the Fall River service. Often during the summer all the staterooms on the Fall River steamers would be sold out. When the ticket agent suggested that staterooms might be available on the Providence Line many would ignore the suggestion because they would travel only on Fall River Line steamers, notwithstanding that the steamers then on the Providence Line provided the winter service on the Fall River Line. A resident of Plymouth, Massachusetts, put it more emphatically: "It is almost an epoch in the boy's life to go to New York by the Fall River Line. I çan remember it myself."[32] On the other first-class lines under New Haven control the standards remained at least as good as before the New Haven acquired them and were often better.

The Maine Central Railroad raised the standards of its steamer service as it completed new steamers. When the railroad constructed the *Moosehead* (1911) and the *Rangeley*

(1913), which each had a capacity of eight hundred passengers, it furnished the ships in fine San Domingo mahogany and provided special parlor staterooms, with maids and porters to cater to the desires of its first-class passengers. The permanent residents of Mount Desert Island alone would never have won these accommodations, and while they may have appreciated the luxury they enjoyed during the summer, they were less than happy about the winter service provided by the railroad. They maintained in a letter to the Interstate Commerce Commission that the winter service should operate beyond Bar Harbor, but the railroad countered that the added service would be "unremunerative for one boat." To operate a second one would be "unreasonable." The position of the railroad was sustained by the commission.[33]

A large percentage of the year-round passengers on the Sound lines demanded punctuality because of appointments or other connections they had to make. The companies went to considerable expense to obviate delays. The New Haven Railroad made it a regular practice to operate special trains to Newport if the boat from New York was running late. A wireless message from the captain was all that was necessary to have the train waiting at Newport. Whenever stormy weather, fog, or an accident forced a steamer into port, the captain notified the railroad, which at once dispatched a special train to take the passengers to their destination. This service was provided at no additional cost, and occasionally the railroad furnished a complimentary meal as well.[34] Without common ownership this service would have been impossible.

All first-class lines went to considerable expense to maintain reliable and punctual service. The Metropolitan Line converted its steamers to oil to enable them to operate on schedule, and the New England Steamship Company overhauled its steamers regularly to reduce the chance of breakdowns. The crews of these steamers were well trained in operating the ship and in caring for the needs of the passengers.[35] If one wanted transportation without these extras or could not afford the fare on a first-class line, there were low-fare lines from some cities.[36]

The charge that railroad control injured the passenger service on the first-class lines has no foundation in fact. If the testimony of the people best acquainted with the service can be trusted, the railroads merit praise for the standards they maintained.[37]

After 1890 the steamship lines, whether independent or controlled by railroads, could not compete with the railroads in speed. Their appeal rested on their luxury, lower fares, and the cleanliness of a sea voyage. Many took the advice given by a writer in 1911 who urged his readers to take a sail on one of the many steamship lines sailing from New York City. Such a voyage would temporarily get people away from the noise of the city and its streets, which were "filled with fast moving automobiles, with their nerve racking noises, their pungent odors, and attendant dust clouds."[38] These factors enabled the coastal steamship lines to compete successfully for passenger business until World War I. Thereafter, increased use of automobiles (despite their noises, odors, and dust clouds) revolutionized private and public transportation.

Freight Service

Freight service on the coastal lines under railroad control evolved into a highly complex and sophisticated system. The origins can be traced back to at least 1840, but the methods then employed bore only slight resemblance to those in use after 1900. Attracting and retaining the business of a large number of shippers, all with varying needs, required satisfactory conditions in regard to rates, speed and frequency of service, dependability, and the handling of freight. Only a meticulous balancing of these factors could satisfy shippers over a long period of time.

The Rate Structure

Few aspects of transportation are more complex and involved than freight tariffs. Passenger fares are relatively easy to understand, since passenger service is primarily a point-to-point operation over the most direct route or routes, and the fare varies with the distance between points. Freight tariffs are confined to no such simple formula. Because freight is of such variety and delivery time is sometimes less important than low rates, it is not uncommon that the longest and most circuitous routes offer the lowest rates. Such routes are usually called differential routes. Many of the longer coastal lines formed part of a differential route that carried freight at much lower rates than the faster and more direct all-rail route. Fortunately the rate structure of the coastal steamship lines between New York and New England was somewhat less complex than these.

In water transportation two methods of establishing rates were used. Bulk cargo rates were subject to bargaining, or agreement between the shipper and the shipowner or his agent. These rates were not published and varied from shipper to shipper. Rate fixing on goods carried on the regularly scheduled steamship lines between New York and New England followed the methods developed by railroads and resulted in rate structures similar to those of the railroads. As might be expected, the railroads and the steamship companies often co-operated in fixing rates. The general principle utilized was to charge what the traffic will bear. Because the water rates were not subject to government regulation, they were less influenced by the cost-of-service principle than were rail tariffs. According to one authority, "When entirely free from restriction, a carrier either by rail or water will fix its charges primarily in accordance with the value of the service, and only secondarily with reference to the cost of the service." The Interstate Commerce Commission tended to favor the cost-of-service principle.[39]

After Congress established the Interstate Commerce Commission the scheduled steamship companies followed railroad practices more consistently in setting their freight rates. They adopted the six railroad classifications as well as the practice of issuing commodity rates to the larger shippers. Where rail-water co-operation existed, through rates were issued; where it did not, both carriers usually charged the shipper the full local rates. In the latter case the shipper often had the additional inconvenience and expense of paying for the transfer of his freight from one terminal to another.[40]

In New England the through rail-water rates usually included terminal charges and marine insurance. Steamship companies did not have the same liability for damage to freight that railroads did. Thus, marine freight was usually insured. The insurance normally covered freight stored in terminals for up to seventy-two hours after its arrival. In New England as early as 1870 the Fall River Line included marine insurance in its rates, and in the 1880s the Stonington Line absorbed the cost of marine insurance. The Portland Steam Packet Company provided insurance after 1880, but some of the Maine companies did not follow suit until the formation of Eastern Steamship Company in 1901.[41] In the twentieth century only the local companies failed to adopt the practice.

After 1887 all joint rail-water rates had to be published and were under the control of the Interstate Commerce Commission. Port-to-port rates, until the passage of the Shipping Act of 1916, were free of regulation. After 1916 only the maximum rates had to be filed; this change did not seriously impair the bargaining power of the coastal lines and had only a slight effect on the port-to-port rate practices.[42]

Between the railroads and steamship lines in New England there was, after 1900, seldom any significant competition in rates. Adjustments were often made, but widespread rate wars were avoided. Some local competition did occur at certain Sound ports, but it seldom lasted more than a year or two. Only tramp steamers provided rate competition, and very few of them sailed in New England waters.[43]

Rate differentials were commonly granted to the weaker

lines, both on port-to-port traffic and on through freight. The Colonial Navigation Company between Providence and New York had such a differential on local traffic. The Central Vermont Railway enjoyed one on traffic from New York City to points in the Midwest.[44]

The establishment of individual rates, however, followed no consistent pattern. This is especially evident in an examination of the methods used and rates established in the 1870s and 1880s. At that time the New England coastal lines usually based their rates on comparable rail rates, but some rates were based on cubic footage of cargo. Many companies fixed their rate at the rail rate or lower, absorbing any cartage or terminal charges.[45] The Eastern Steamship Corporation adopted the following procedure: "It is not necessary for us to cut the rail line rate for we give better service than the railroads. We aim to meet their rates *i.e.* if the rail line rates are advanced, we advance ours, and likewise if we raise our rates, the railroads raise theirs."[46] Some independent steamboat companies had consultations with shippers who sought to get the lowest rates they could on port-to-port traffic; other steamship companies granted authority to agents who contracted with shippers for freight. Rates established by consultation or contract were not published. This practice gave large shippers a definite advantage. Accusations often were made against the railroads and steamship companies that they favored large shippers, and there was evidence that large shippers sometimes pressured transportation companies to grant them lower tariffs.[47]

The commodity or special rate is crucial to an understanding of the rate structure. The class rates often furnish little real evidence about transportation costs because of the large volume of traffic moving under the lower commodity rates. The tariff files of the Interstate Commerce Commission contain literally thousands of commodity rates on practically every article that moved in quantity. To trace these rates and compare them to others would be a prodigious task. In 1913 the noted railroad authority William Z. Ripley estimated that three-fourths of the business of American railroads was done under commodity rates. The percentage on the Sound lines was probably higher than that. Once these rates were issued, they became extremely difficult to cancel. Often granted to encourage new industries or to enable older ones to remain competitive, commodity rates usually became permanent features of the tariff structure. Uniform classification of goods was constantly being urged, but while appealing in theory, was virtually impossible to practice. Railroad officials viewed the agitation as an effort to give noncompetitive points all the advantages of competition without any of the annoyances.[48] Few places with lower commodity rates wanted to see them raised solely to rationalize the classification.

Freight Rates, 1880–1916

The inconsistencies of the old port-to-port steamboat rates were illustrated after the New Haven Railroad gained control of the Sound lines. The rail-water rate on cotton piece goods between Lowell, Massachusetts, and New York City was much lower than the all-rail rate. The arrangement dated from the earliest days of rail-water service on the Sound lines. When officials of the New Haven attempted to reorganize this inherited rate structure on a more reasonable basis, they had to keep this rate lower or come under considerable pressure from shippers and possibly lose the traffic to the Metropolitan Line. As a New Haven official so aptly stated the problem, "The reason why that low rate is in is because it has always been so."[49]

More chaotic were the tariffs on the port-to-port business of the New Haven Steamboat Company and the Bridgeport Steamboat Company. When these companies were taken over by the New Haven Railroad in 1900 and 1903, the port-to-port rates were written in manuscript, but the New Haven was informed by steamboat company officials that they were meaningless because "the actual rates were in the heads of the men connected with the docks of the company." Not only were the rates unpublished, but also, rebates of up to three cents per hundred pounds were granted to certain favored shippers. The New Haven Steamboat Company justified these practices on the grounds that only in this manner could the company compete with the Starin Line, a freight line between New Haven and New York. The rebates resulted in some rates being lower than the lighterage charges in New York, which were absorbed by the steamboat company.[50]

At Providence and Boston comparable conditions existed. A former agent of the Joy Line said that discrimination and rebating were general practice in Providence: "They were all doing it. We could not have gotten any business if we did not do it." In Boston David O. Ives of the Boston Chamber of Commerce agreed. He told how it was virtually impossible to get water rates stated for a short period, let alone on a long-term basis. Ives "had to knock around Boston and ask shippers who have the tariffs."[51] The New England railroads had already learned the pitfalls of discrimination and rebating; by 1900 these practices were much less extensive among them than they had been. East of New Haven, where railroad control of steamship lines had existed longer, rebating occurred far less frequently.[52]

Despite the instability in port-to-port traffic, through rates remained remarkably stable between 1870 and 1900, except for the years during the rate wars. The rates on cotton piece goods are an example. Piece goods had always moved under commodity rates that had been established when the mills first opened. From 1875 to 1879 the rate from Lowell to New York was thirty cents per hundred pounds. Then it dropped to nineteen cents, where it remained until 1897, when it rose to twenty-five cents. In 1902 it was restored to nineteen cents, which rate was in effect in 1910.[53] Other through rates generally followed this pattern, being higher in the 1870s and showing a decline thereafter until the turn of the century. The proportional or transshipment rates between Boston and New York, which were established in the late 1870s to allow the several routes between these cities to compete, underwent no change before 1916.[54] Some adjustments, especially on local rates, were instituted after the passage of the Interstate Commerce Act, but New England rates did not decline as much as those in other sections of the country.[55]

Beginning about 1900 freight rates throughout the country began to rise, but the exact amount is difficult to determine because a large proportion of the increase was the result of changes in classification and in the size of a minimum carload. In New England the commodity rates on goods moving to New York did not follow the upward trend. The tariffs filed with the Interstate Commerce Commission contain hundreds of new lower commodity rates issued between 1902 and 1907 to compete with the independent steamship lines that challenged the New Haven monopoly.[56]

The rate structure as it existed between 1900 and 1916 favored the rail-water routes to New York. For example, see the class rates given in Appendix A, table 13. These were in effect from 1900 to 1914, when a general increase occurred.[57] The sample commodity rates in table 14 indicate the favorable treatment accorded the larger shipper from inland points. As tables 15 and 16 indicate, the increases effective December 1914 made the rates higher from all points, but the impact was varied. The commodity rates on some articles remained below the class rates.[58] The class rates between New York and Portland via the Eastern Steamship Company likewise tended to be higher than the commodity rates. In September 1910 they were, for classes 1–6, 35, 30, 23, 19, 16, and 14 cents per hundred pounds. Cotton piece goods in bales or boxes were 15 cents per hundred pounds in any quantity; boots and shoes were 30 cents. Yet paper from Cumberland Mills, Maine, via the Maine Central Railroad and Eastern Steamship Company was 12 cents per hundred pounds, which was lower than any class rate. Between New York and Boston class rates by water were set as much as 4 cents higher than commodity rates because the commodity rates put certain items in a lower classification.[59]

Away from the port cities the class rates to New York over the New Haven Railroad were identical whether on all-rail or rail-water routes. West of New London and Willimantic, however, the commodity rates favored the rail-water routes by a large margin. The revenue lost by issuing commodity rates on items like cotton piece goods, woolens, and boots and shoes was made up through volume movements. These three items constituted approximately 75 per cent of the tonnage carried on the Norwich, Providence, Fall River, and New Bedford lines. The New Haven Railroad quoted no all-rail commodity rates to New York City on these articles.[60] (See table 16 in Appendix A.)

Some changes were made between 1870 and 1916 in the division of the through rail-water rates. In the mid-1870s the Old Colony Steamboat Company retained between 60 per cent and 80 per cent of the freight revenue. On the Norwich Line the division on Boston–New York tonnage had been fixed at 45 per cent to the boat and 55 per cent to the railroad. To stations on the Norwich & Worcester Railroad above Central Village, Connecticut, each retained 50 per cent. On freight between Central Village and Norwich the boats received 70 per cent and the railroad 30 per cent. According to an agreement signed in 1869 the Stonington boats kept 63 per cent of the Boston–New York revenue; in 1878 this figure was reduced to 55 per cent. In July 1913 the divisions on the Bridgeport, New Haven, and Norwich lines assigned 50 per cent of the revenue to the railroad and the same to the boats. On freight from points south of the Boston & Albany Railroad the Providence, Fall River, and New Bedford lines received 60 per cent of the rate and the railroad 40 per cent of the rate. On traffic from territory north of the Boston & Albany the share retained by the steamers dropped to 55 per cent.[61]

When the Interstate Commerce Commission investigated the operation of the Sound lines, its investigators charged that these divisions were unfair to the steamship lines because of the longer distances they carried the cargo and that they prevented independent companies from entering the trade.[62] Officials of the New Haven Railroad denied these charges. Considering the history of the divisions and the fact that water rates were usually lower than rail rates, these divisions seem fair. The later divisions also illustrate the reduction in bargaining power of the steamship lines.

The variety of articles shipped over these rail-water routes was enormous; westbound tonnage on the Sound lines of the New Haven included all forms of cotton textiles, woolens, leather and rubber footwear, paper and paper products, chemicals, machinery, brassware, hardware, fish, cranberries, candy, wire, rope, and soap. The flow of freight on the Sound lines was heavier westbound than eastbound, the reverse of tonnage movements on the railroads of New England. Eastbound traffic on the Sound lines consisted principally of groceries and foodstuffs, manufactured articles produced in New York City, and raw materials like cotton, wool, and leather.[63] On the lines in Maine canned goods from the packing companies there composed a large portion of the tonnage, along with sardines, cotton textiles, woolens, and paper. Most of these articles moved under commodity rates.[64]

How important were the favorable rates in this system? Shippers were almost unanimous in desiring favorable rates, but they claimed that rate stability was even more important. Stability permitted long-term planning, which benefited both producers and consumers.[65]

The Boat Trains

Favorable rates constituted only one aspect of the problem. Since only a few shippers were located close to the steamship terminals, transportation to the steamers became of vital consequence. Here railroad control of the coastal lines manifested its value. The co-ordination in passenger service has been described; in freight operations the value to the New England economy was incalculable.[66]

To tap the hinterlands of New Bedford, Fall River, Providence, New London, New Haven, and Bridgeport, the New Haven Railroad operated special freight trains to connect with the steamers to New York City. They operated on tight schedules and had the right of way over all but passenger trains. So that the boat trains could keep their schedules, the engines pulled well below their maximum tonnage rating. Engines normally rated at 1,260 tons in fast freight service carried only 1,000 tons; others might pull as little as 750 tons. The ratings varied according to the grades and type of engine, but all hauled well under their maximum rated tonnage for fast freight service. These trains enabled shippers to load their goods later in the day and to ship orders to their customers in New York on the day received instead of the following day.

The boat-train service was so demanding that one railroad man chided J. Howland Gardner, the vice-president of the New England Steamship Company, "Gardner, you are making us pull the wheels out from under our trains to get this boat train freight down to you." Because of these schedules, the trains could leave their starting points much later than would ordinarily have been possible. In 1915 the Fall River boat train from Boston left at 12:30 in the afternoon. The train from Worcester to New London departed from Worcester at 2:45 in the afternoon. Service from the south side of Providence did not leave until after 5:00. The boat trains connected with others at junctions such as Middleboro, Mansfield, Taunton, and Concord Junction in Massachusetts, and Putnam and Plainfield in Connecticut.[67]

The first boat-train service predated the Civil War, but the express schedules did not begin until sometime after the war. In the 1880s the schedules were gradually adjusted to suit better the needs of the merchants and manufacturers of New England. By 1889 the Norwich Line had an express boat train between Boston and the boat; the freight cars had passenger trucks and Westinghouse air brakes at a time when air brakes were uncommon in freight service.[68]

When the New Haven gained control of the Sound lines, its officials realized that there was considerable redundancy in the rail-water service. Under the pre-1904 tariffs shippers east of New London and Willimantic could route their goods via any of the Sound lines at identical rates. This condition, the traffic officials of the New Haven claimed, slowed the service because it complicated the routing of cars and necessitated the movement of many partially loaded cars. After studying these problems, the traffic officials decided to discontinue the Stonington Line and improve the thrice-weekly service from New Bedford as the businessmen there had been demanding.

Following an analysis of the movement of tonnage from inland points to each of the Sound lines, the capacity of steamers on each line, the delivery points in New York City, and the needs of various shippers, the New Haven in 1904 established a new routing system for the boat trains, which is shown on map 2. Traffic officials of the New Haven explained the new system to shippers and asked for their co-operation. Where questions arose, the situation was reconsidered and changed if necessary. Under the new arrangement most of the freight that had been sent on the Stonington Line now moved over the Norwich Line. The remainder was sent on the New Bedford Line. The freight from the Boston & Maine Railroad, which had been sent to New York via the Norwich Line, now went through New Bedford, where service was now daily except Sunday. These changes were possible because the Norwich and New Bedford steamers used the same pier in New York City. As the general freight agent of the New Haven said, the shippers only desired "that route which gives satisfactory service at a reasonable charge." New Haven officials denied the charges of federal investigators that these changes eliminated alternative routes for shippers. Many businessmen questioned the importance of being able to choose between alternative routes. A few businessmen did complain about the changes, but considering the overwhelming praise later given the service, these complaints were of minor importance.[69]

The savings accruing to the railroad were sizable. Eliminating the Stonington terminal and changing the boat-train schedule reduced expenses $100,000 annually, even though some additional men had to be hired at New Bedford. The Shore Line Division alone saved forty-eight freight handlers,

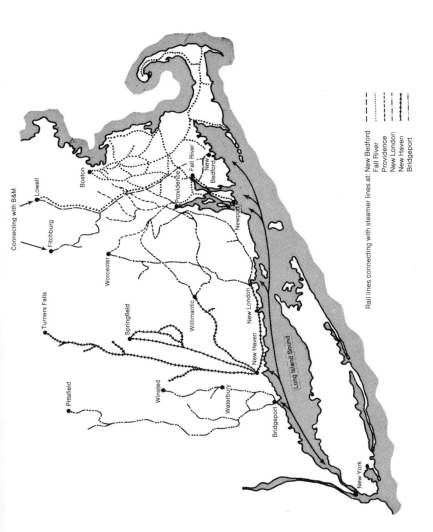

MAP 2. *Routing System of the New York, New Haven & Hartford Railroad and the New England Steamship Company, as Reorganized in 1904*

three clerks, and twelve other railroad and dock employees. The change permitted the abolition of two freight trains and the elimination of considerable mileage on other trains.[70]

About a year afterward some congestion occurred on the New Bedford Line, forcing the rerouting of some freight. The traffic department of the New Haven conceived the idea of contingent procedures for diverting traffic whenever certain Sound lines became taxed beyond their capacity. Since the Norwich and New Bedford lines landed at Pier 40, Hudson River, and the Fall River and Providence lines at Pier 19, Hudson River (after 1912 at Pier 14, Hudson River), freight could be diverted from one line to another of either pair without affecting the delivery in New York. If notification was received by 11:00 in the morning at the junction point of Mansfield that the boats on one line would be full that night, its boat trains could be diverted to the companion line. The shipper was probably unaware of this, for his goods would arrive the following morning as expected. Diversion of boat trains was practiced only between the New Bedford, Fall River, Providence, and Norwich lines. Before 1916 diversions seldom involved more than 130 cars in any month, and during some months there were none. This procedure meant that consignors and consignees could plan on prompt delivery under almost all traffic conditions, including the congested conditions that prevailed during World War I.[71] In their testimony before the Interstate Commerce Commission shippers were practically unanimous in their praise of the contingency plans made for diverting the boat trains.[72]

With the rail lines and boat lines under common control, the diversions involved no delays such as would be caused by rechecking the freight on the wharf and changing engines on the trains. Such delays were usually encountered on independent lines. In northern New England, industries and railroads were more widely dispersed, making diversion to places like Portland or Boston only an academic problem. In southern New England it was a real problem, one the New Haven Railroad handled well.

Approximately 70 per cent of the freight that was carried on the Sound lines of the New Haven was interchanged with the railroad.[73] Without excellent co-operation between the railroad and the steamship company, delays would have been unavoidable and chaos might have resulted.

Industries Dependent on the Sound Lines

Why did New England require this service? The reasons may be traced to the pre-Civil War years, when the first textile mills moved into Fall River, New Bedford, Providence, and the surrounding areas. Attracted by easy access to transportation facilities, textile production increased at a rapid pace until by the 1870s the whole of southeastern New England was blanketed by textile mills and finishing plants. At the same time boot and shoe manufacturers concentrated in eastern Massachusetts. By 1909 the state produced more boots and shoes than any state in the Union.[74]

The textile mills had been drawn to southeastern New England as much by the low cost of transporting raw materials by water to the mills as by the ready access to the New York market. By 1815 New York City had become the chief center for the distribution of imported fabrics, but its position in the distribution of domestic textiles was unimportant. Not until the Civil War did the city gain prominence as a market for domestic textiles, and then even merchants from Boston found it expedient to establish branches there. This change made access to the New York market crucial to the mills in New England, access provided by the Sound lines and their connecting railroads.[75]

The years after 1870 witnessed a remarkable growth in New England textile production and in the manufacturing of clothing in New York City. In 1909 New York City manufactured 38.4 per cent of the total dollar value of men's clothing and 69.3 per cent of the dollar value of women's clothing. The New England mills had to be able to supply the needs of these New York manufacturers or lose the business to textile mills in other sections of the country—especially the growing textile industry in the South.[76]

Similar growth occurred in other industries producing high-value products, such as boots and shoes, woolens, and paper products. In conjunction with cotton textiles and groceries, these goods constituted the largest percentage of goods moving west on the Sound lines. Northern as well as southern New England came to depend on the Sound lines. The cotton textile mills in New Hampshire shipped about one-third of their product to New York. The shoe shops and paper mills in Maine and New Hampshire likewise made extensive use of the rail-water routes.[77]

The Importance of the Rail-Water Service

What these shippers demanded was service. Before the Interstate Commerce Commission they testified almost unanimously that rates were of much less consequence than expeditious and reliable service. In order to remain competitive with other regions of the country that had lower manufacturing costs, they had to get their goods to New York rapidly and often, or be forced out of business. After 1900 the problem became more acute.[78]

When the Sound lines had been controlled by several railroads, many businessmen claimed, the situation had often been chaotic. Agents for the various lines would solicit traffic from shippers who could not always provide sufficient quantities for a carload. This meant extra handling and checking at transfer stations to make carload lots, and the possibility of split lots and delays in service. Few expressed any desire to return to these conditions.[79]

The Sound lines provided what amounted to express delivery at regular rates. Often they gave speedier service than the express companies. A typical example occurred when a mill in Fall River shipped one consignment by the Fall River Line and another the same afternoon by express. The con-

signment shipped via the Fall River Line arrived at its destination in New York City four or five hours before that sent
all-rail at express rates.[80] Points as far north as Nashua, New
Hampshire, had twenty-four-hour delivery to New York;
freight from Manchester reached there in thirty-six hours.
All-rail service from Nashua required at least three or four
days. From Taunton, Massachusetts, it took about four days
for freight to reach New York by rail; next-morning delivery
was normal via the Fall River and New Bedford lines. The
same situation existed in other sections of New England that
shipped goods on the Sound lines. All-rail delivery usually
took one to four days longer, and sometimes up to a week
longer.[81] In the winter of 1913–14 the New Haven Railroad
began an experimental all-rail service between Lynn, Massachusetts, and New York City that was supposed to handle
less-than-carload shipments as rapidly as similar shipments
moving on the Sound lines. The goal was never realized.
Some shipments required eight days, and none arrived in less
than four days.[82]

Why did rapid delivery become so important after 1900?
The marketing situation in New York holds the key. Retailers
and wholesalers preferred to keep only a minimum of stock
on hand because of high rents and the increasing frequency
of fashion changes. Yet delivery had to be guaranteed. The
rail-water service meant that a New York merchant could
telephone his factory or supplier in New England during the
morning and place his order. The consignor dispatched the
order on the boat train late that morning or early in the afternoon, and it arrived on the dock in New York the following
morning. In some cities near the coast, freight for the New
York boats was received until 4:00 or 5:00 in the afternoon.
The service was extremely dependable. One shoe manufacturer in Brockton said that of 170 shipments via the Fall
River Line only 7 failed to arrive the following morning.
Without such twenty-four-hour deliveries, he claimed, 50 per
cent of his orders could not have been secured. Other businessmen had similar experience.[83]

By 1900 many of the same industries that dominated the

New England economy were growing around the greater New York area and in northern New Jersey, and competing with New England companies for the New York market. It was the rail-water service that kept New England competitive, for the rail lines to New York City could not handle the traffic so quickly.[84] The problem was clearly stated by the general freight agent of the New Haven Railroad: "The ability of the carriers to provide service for the fellow that has a geographical disadvantage comparable with what the man may have at the more advantageous geographical location, enables the New England manufacturer . . . to compete in those markets."[85]

Rail-water co-ordination on the Sound lines was most prevalent on westbound traffic, because of the need for rapid service and because tonnage was heaviest in this direction. Although most eastbound traffic did not require such prompt delivery, it was carried on boat trains that connected with the steamers from New York. The New Haven steamer lines were the only New England coastal lines on which traffic was considerably heavier westbound. All the others generally carried more traffic eastbound.[86]

Compared with the lines controlled by the New Haven, the freight service of the independent steamship lines was far less dependable. After 1912 many shippers criticized the service of the Metropolitan Line, which was then owned by the Eastern Steamship Corporation. From Lynn the service to New York over the Metropolitan Line required seventy-two hours whereas via the Fall River Line shippers had second-morning delivery. During the months when the passenger service was not operating, the steamers left at about 10:00 in the morning, which was an inconvenient time for shippers. The Metropolitan Line also had a reputation for indifference in settling claims. The S. D. Warren Company in Cumberland Mills, Maine, less than ten miles from Portland, sent an average of 24,500 tons of paper annually to New York City in the years 1914 to 1916. Of this, 20,000 tons went via the New Bedford Line and only 1,500 tons via the Maine Steamship Company. The remainder went by rail.[87]

Many New England shippers claimed that they were quite willing to pay higher rates for this service than they were being charged. They had a valid point: because the goods shipped on the Sound lines were high-grade, high-value articles, the cost of transportation assumed less significance.[88] After 1910, however, as rates increased, the narrowing of the gap between costs and profits forced many textile companies to consider abandoning New England for the South. It is true that those who in 1915 and 1916 urged the Interstate Commerce Commission to allow the New Haven Railroad to retain its steamship lines were basing much of their case on opinion and fear of the unknown. Nevertheless, the number favoring the New Haven outnumbered those opposed by fifty to one. This support came despite the financial mismanagement of the New Haven Railroad under the presidency of Charles S. Mellen. The attitude of most New England businessmen was summarized best in this statement: "It has taken years and an enlightened management to work their [rail-water] service up to its present standing, and we want it continued."[89]

Providing this service did not give the railroad a large return on its investment. In 1913 only the Fall River Line had an operating ratio below 80 per cent, and in obtaining this figure no provision was made for depreciation or interest. In computing these ratios no allowance was made for the operation of the boat trains and other railroad expenses incurred as a result of the co-ordinated rail-water service.[90] Because of the dispatch required, many of these railroad activities had higher operating costs than regular railroad service.

In rates, schedules, and service, passengers on the railroad-controlled steamship lines fared well. The passenger service on the Fall River and Providence lines was unexcelled. The Maine Central Railroad likewise operated an unprofitable first-class ferry service that no small independent company could or was willing to provide. To accommodate the passengers, the limited boat trains deposited and loaded them only a few steps from the steamers. No doubt independent companies could also have done this, but in New England examples of such co-operation after 1870 are sparse.

The rail-water freight service enabled New England industry to survive longer than it would have against competition from other regions where manufacturing costs were lower.[91] This, in turn, kept the whole New England economy prosperous and kept the labor force employed. Twenty-four- to thirty-six-hour delivery at regular freight rates cannot be viewed as a detrimental effect of railroad control. The boat trains and terminals were operated and maintained at a cost considerably higher than other railroad facilities. The result was that New England goods could reach New York City as rapidly in 1905 as they did thirty years later.

The rail-water service permitted merchants to maintain lower inventories in New York, where rents were high and warehouse space at a premium. New England manufacturers could retain their markets because they could fill orders on short notice. The constant demand of the shippers was "service, prompt and stable."[92] Rates before 1912 remained secondary. Two facts made this situation possible: the high value of New England manufactures and the unique concentration of complementary markets and manufacturers in the New York area. Within this framework the Sound lines continued to function for one principal reason: the peculiar topography of the city of New York. By 1880 the Sound lines had become the only way to dispatch freight to New York from New England.

6. Terminals and Freight Handling, 1881–1916

In 1917 a witness before the Interstate Commerce Commission, when asked about the ability of the railroads to handle the traffic brought to them, said that the business of a railroad is "not measured by the amount of business they can put over their line, but the business they can digest, or the amount of business they can digest in their terminals."[1] In this answer he emphasized a vital fact: a transportation system can be only as efficient as its terminals.

In spite of the long maritime tradition and extensive railroad network in the United States, during the late nineteenth and early twentieth centuries there was generally poor coordination between railroads and steamships. Terminals formed "the weakest link in the water [transportation] system," and the organization of harbors was generally "faulty."[2] The older port cities suffered severely from a failure to adopt a general scheme of development that would ensure a free interchange of traffic between all interior lines of communication and the water terminals. During the early history of the ports of Boston and New York few could have foreseen the development of the railroad and its revolutionary impact on transportation routes. Almost all the older ports that continued to handle a significant percentage of coastwise and foreign commerce suffered from poor co-ordination and wasteful terminal practices. These conditions resulted from poor planning, topographical features, failure to adapt to changing conditions, lack of foresight or of money, or a combination of these and other factors. No port in the eastern half of the country suffered from these maladies more than New York; yet upon its markets and its prosperity depended a large proportion of the industries in New England.[3]

Topographical Problems

The Port of New York

In 1915 New York City was the most important industrial center in the United States, and the value of its manufactures exceeded that of any state in the Union except Pennsylvania. For firms depending upon foreign markets, it was the country's leading port of export. But reaching the port by land from New England had been easier before the Civil War than it became after the war, as a result of developments that began in the 1840s and 1850s.[4]

The rivers and bay that make such a magnificent harbor also split the port of New York into several distinct areas and complicate communication between its component parts— Manhattan, Brooklyn, Staten Island, and the New Jersey docks. Surrounded almost entirely by the East River and the Hudson River, the island of Manhattan was cut off from easy access by rail except from the north, where the New York Central and New Haven railroads crossed the Harlem River (see map 3). New Jersey and Staten Island are separated by river and bay from Manhattan and Brooklyn. To overcome these obstacles, the railroads acquired tugs, car floats, lighters, and barges to move freight and railroad cars between the terminals in the separate land areas of the port.[5]

Although the New York Central Railroad and the New Haven Railroad entered Manhattan from the northern end of the island, in 1915 only the former was carrying rail freight

MAP 3. *Port of New York,*
Manhattan Sector, around 1880

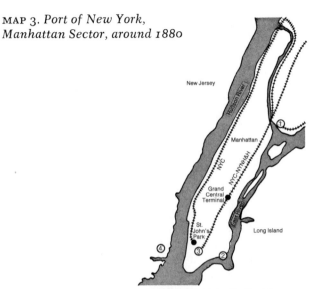

1 New Haven Railroad Harlem River Terminal
2 Pier 50
3 Centre Street Station
4 Pennsylvania Railroad Terminal

over that route. In 1849, when the New York & New Haven
Railroad was completed, it entered New York City over the
rails of the New York & Harlem Railroad, and its terminal
was near the south end of Manhattan, on Canal Street. But already difficulties were being encountered: between Twenty-
sixth Street and the Canal Street station all trains had to be
drawn by horses because city ordinances prohibited the use of
steam locomotives in that area.[6]

In 1850 the New Haven Railroad secured a block of land
south of Canal Street, bounded by Centre, White, Elm, and
Franklin streets. On this site it constructed a brick freight station. From the beginning its efficiency must have been less
than ideal because of the need to use horses south of Twenty-
sixth Street. Additional complications arose in 1857, when
the city of New York prohibited steam locomotives below
Forty-second Street. Now all freight cars to the Centre Street
station had to be moved 2.75 miles by teams of horses. Ironically, that same year the New Haven and the New York &

Harlem railroads had constructed a new passenger station at Twenty-sixth Street and Fourth Avenue. This was in use until 1871, when Grand Central Station was completed.[7]

As the city grew, the Centre Street station became inadequate, forcing the management of the New Haven to seek additional facilities for handling its freight. In 1869 a solution was found by leasing the financially troubled Harlem River & Port Chester Railroad. The New Haven, in November 1873, completed a double-track line between its main line at New Rochelle and the Harlem River. In the previous month a perpetual lease of the Harlem River & Port Chester Railroad had been signed giving the New Haven extensive wharf facilities and water rights in New York Harbor. The New Haven management admitted to its stockholders that it expected no profits from the lease for several years, but claimed that the lease would prevent any hostile interest from constructing a parallel line into New York. The lease would also enable the New Haven Railroad to increase its freight business between New York City and New England, since it was impossible to handle much more freight business at the Centre Street station. The company quickly moved to improve and expand the tug, barge, and wharf facilities inherited from the Harlem River & Port Chester Railroad.[8]

The car float operations in New York were centered at Pier 50, East River, at the foot of Montgomery Street. A large transfer yard and float bridges were constructed at the Harlem River, and car floats transferred cars between the yard and Pier 50 (see map 3). The Centre Street station remained in operation, but its operating expenses were very high. A team of horses could handle only one car at a time, and by 1885 the station was handling an average of one hundred cars daily on its eight tracks. In December of that year the New Haven decided to close the congested Centre Street station and move all its local freight operations to Pier 50.[9]

Several factors must be considered in understanding the difficulties encountered by the New Haven. It was throughout the nineteenth century primarily a passenger railroad; until the 1890s freight traffic provided a much smaller percentage of revenue than did passenger traffic. This meant that the conservative management did not believe it could justify the expense of constructing large freight facilities on Manhattan, and there are some indications that during the 1870s the management actually discouraged freight business. A second point was that the city of New York did not view railroads very favorably after the Hepburn Investigation in 1879. It would probably have been impossible to get a franchise to build a rail line to the southern part of Manhattan with sufficient land to permit the expansion of the freight handling facilities as business increased. A third point was cost. By the 1880s Manhattan already had been built up as far north as 125th Street, making construction at grade out of the question. The entrance to Grand Central Station was through a tunnel, and any lines south of the station would have had to use tunnels or elevated tracks to avoid congesting further the streets of the city. Operating the line below Forty-second Street with horses would have been uneconomical. No other means of locomotion was possible because the electric locomotive had not been perfected. Thus, in 1885 the only choice was to abandon the freight line to Centre Street and enlarge the pier stations on the East River. This left only the New York Central & Hudson River Railroad with freight lines to Manhattan.[10]

By the 1880s the pattern for handling package and merchandise freight in New York was becoming fixed. The New Haven Railroad and the New York & Northern Railroad used car floats to handle all freight destined to New York City proper. The New York Central Railroad was using its freight line to St. John's Park as well as car floats. For through traffic between New England and the southern and western states the New Haven used its own car floats and the New England Transfer Company to carry cars the twelve miles between the Harlem River Terminal and the terminals of the trunk line railroads on the New Jersey shore across from Manhattan. The trunk line railroads likewise had extensive fleets of tugs, car floats, barges, and lighters that they used to transfer freight to their pier stations on the west side of Manhattan and to interchange freight with other railroads and private terminal companies.[11]

The operating costs of these facilities were high. By 1893 the New Haven was leasing Piers 45, 46, 49, 50, 51, and 51½ (later renumbered 36–42) on the East River to accommodate one hundred to two hundred cars a day that were being loaded and unloaded. Equally significant was the extra time required to handle cars. Loading the cars, assembling the floats, moving them to the Harlem River yards, and then making up a train meant early closings at the Pier 50 complex to insure an early arrival of the cars in New England. On westbound all-rail shipments it meant early departures from New England. To move a car float between the Harlem River and the yards of the Pennsylvania Railroad at Harsimus Cove in Jersey City required two to four hours, not including the time to load and unload the car floats.[12]

In the 1880s congestion in New York was already a concern of those interested in efficient terminal operations. One author believed that terminal operations were "the key to the solution of many of the problems relating to transportation," and that co-operation, not competition, was the proper long-term solution.[13] In addition, progressive and effective operation of terminal facilities depended upon prompt freight handling. As the city increased in population, the difficulties multiplied.

The New York dock commissioners submitted a variety of plans to eliminate the congestion at the pier stations; none was ever adopted.[14] By the 1890s the terminal facilities in New York for handling package freight were rapidly becoming inadequate, but by then the cost of rectifying their inadequacies was too great for any single company or public agency to assume.

The city of New York had once owned about 95 per cent of the waterfront on Manhattan, but after 1798 the city gradually relinquished title to these areas. Not until 1870, when the Department of Docks was organized, did control by the public again become the goal. By 1900 the city had regained most of the waterfront, but its supervision was negligible because of its policy of granting long-term leases to the tenants.[15] Nevertheless, any reorganization of the port had to be approved by the city because of its ownership of the wharves and the property at the bulkhead line. After 1910 leases were issued only for ten-year periods, with the privilege of renewal provided the lessee made permanent and extensive improvements to the piers. The city could, before the expiration of the lease, repossess the property upon payment of an appropriate amount toward the cost of improvements made by the lessee.[16] The post-1910 policy permitted realistic planning toward reconstructing the waterfront and improving the port, but, in fact, no major changes occurred before World War I.

The failure to adopt a comprehensive plan for rationalizing rail and water facilities left the coastal steamship lines as the primary mode of transportation between New England and New York City. Their terminals on Manhattan Island enabled them to function as "practically lighterage lines" from the railheads at the Sound ports to the New York piers. The steamers in effect took the place of lighters and car floats that otherwise would have been necessary. In addition, their several piers provided a variety of terminals in New York City, giving shippers and the railroad a flexibility otherwise impossible.[17]

Following the Civil War each Sound line had begun to handle more of certain articles than others, depending on the hinterland it served and the location of its New York terminal. The Fall River and Providence lines used Piers 18 and 19, Hudson River (after 1912 they moved to Piers 14 and 15), to handle a part of the textile trade, boots and shoes, and similar articles. Pier 40, Hudson River, where the Norwich and New Bedford lines docked, serviced the dry goods trade and the jobbing centers. The Connecticut River business and that from New Haven and Bridgeport was suited to East River deliveries. Map 4 shows the location of the various ter-

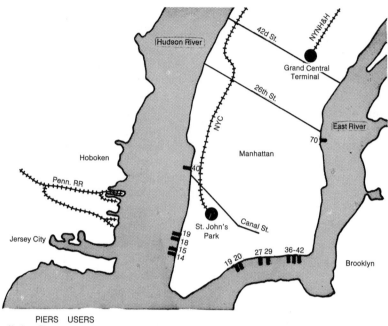

PIERS   USERS
Hudson River:
14, 15   N.E.S.S. Co., Fall River and Providence lines
18, 19   Eastern Steamship Corp.
    40   N.E.S.S. Co., New London (Norwich) and New
         Bedford lines

East River:
19, 20   Hartford & New York Transportation Co.
    27   N.E.S.S. Co., Bridgeport and New Haven lines
    29   Central Vermont Transportation Co.
36-42   N.Y., N.H. & H. R.R., car float and lighterage
         terminal
    70   N.Y., N.H. & H. R.R. and N.E.S.S. Co.,
         lighterage deliveries and passenger station

MAP 4. *New York Harbor, Showing Manhattan Piers of the
New England Steamship Company, Other New England Coastal Lines,
and the New Haven Railroad, 1916*

minals of the New Haven Railroad and New England Steamship Company.[18]

The control exerted by the railroads serving New York on the New York waterfront became an issue of growing concern. West Street was almost monopolized by the pier stations of the railroads with terminals across the Hudson River in New Jersey.[19] Interchange between these railroads and steamship lines was confined to lighters, which proved slow and expensive. Experts suggested many solutions to remove the railroad pier stations from West Street. In 1897 the New York City Department of Docks urged the construction of a marginal railroad with spur tracks to the piers and a large transfer vessel to move cars between New York and New Jersey. This would eliminate the need for the extensive car float and lighter fleets. The plan also called for the terminals of all the Sound lines to be moved to the East River. It was claimed by the members of the Department of Docks that having all the Sound lines on the East River would be more suitable for the passengers. The planners did admit that the problem of freight deliveries under this proposal needed additional investigation.[20] Implementation was never undertaken.

In 1911 Calvin Tomkins, the dock commissioner of the city, completed a comprehensive plan for the whole port. He desired to remove the railroad pier stations from West Street, thus ending their domination of the area and opening the waterfront to marine interests, and to improve communication among the piers, railroads, and barges and lighters. To accomplish this a marginal railroad was to be constructed along West Street and freight tunnels built under the Hudson River to connect the marginal railroad and the New Jersey terminals of the trunk line railroads. New freight classification yards in New Jersey were to be constructed to serve the proposed freight route under the Hudson River.[21] The plan had merit, but like its predecessors, was never carried out.

Several factors worked against change. Inertia was a major obstacle. Many groups were satisfied with the status quo and saw no need to change; those favoring changes could not agree on a plan. The outbreak of World War I and the sudden demands it placed on the port of New York doomed any immediate implementation of radical changes. The use of the motor truck during the war also made obsolete some of the prewar proposals and wrought changes in the flow of freight traffic. In addition, the rivalry between New York and New Jersey was an important obstacle in the way of change.

What emerges is that the city of New York required prompt delivery of goods from New England because of the shortage and high cost of warehouse facilities in the city. The New England railroads could not furnish this type of service because of the necessity of rehandling freight cars through the yards and onto the car floats, and then the slow trip to the pier stations on Manhattan. In contrast, steamer freight remained untouched after leaving New England ports until it was unloaded on the piers; unloading the steamers was faster and more efficient than unloading freight cars on car floats. The congestion at the pier stations that existed in normal times strengthened the opinion of shippers that the railroads in New York City were not capable of expeditiously handling their goods. Without the coastal steamship lines in World War I the congestion would have been even worse.

Soon after the turn of the century the congestion at the New York terminals forced the New Haven Railroad to handle most of its through freight to the southern and western states over the Poughkeepsie Bridge route of the old New England Railroad.[22] This change, however, did not eliminate the congestion at the local New York yards and pier stations. Because of the eminence of New York City as a center for garment manufacturing and the export trade, as a jobbing center, and a major population center, each year there was more freight destined for local markets or export. The Sound lines could deliver merchandise freight more efficiently than the railroads. Until the 1920s, when long-distance trucking over an adequate road system was available, no other transportation could match the railroad-controlled steamship lines for speed and convenience between New England and New York City.

New England Ports

Some of the New England ports also had topographical problems that contributed to their dependence on the Sound lines or that otherwise shaped their patterns of handling freight. Of these the port of Providence was probably the most important. The Boston & Providence Railroad and the Providence & Worcester Railroad had terminals on the peninsula between the Providence and Seekonk rivers, convenient to the wharves of the Providence Line and other coastal lines at Fox Point. However, by an accident of history the Boston–New York main line lay at some distance from these terminals. Connections with the New York, Providence & Boston line to New York (later part of the Shore Line route between Boston and New York) were quite difficult because of a hill between the wharves and the main line. A track did traverse the city streets, but as rail passenger traffic increased, the switching of cars through the station to the spur track at street level to Fox Point became impossible except in movements involving only a few cars.[23]

In the 1890s, because of increasing congestion in the area, the city ordered the grade-level railroad track discontinued. The only all-rail connection left between the main line of the New Haven and the wharves on Fox Point was through the junction at Valley Falls, Rhode Island, and thence down the east side of the Seekonk River, and across the river to the wharves. From Union Station to Fox Point via Valley Falls was over fourteen miles, whereas through the tunnel that was constructed in 1908 it was three miles. Yet the tunnel did not solve the freight problem, because its chief purpose was to accommodate the heavy passenger traffic through Union Station.[24]

After 1908 a special switching service was operated between the main line and Fox Point for certain industries near the Union Station complex. It had to be timed precisely to avoid delaying four passenger trains leaving Providence between 4:45 and 5:30 in the afternoon. Additional freight service through the tunnel for other industries was impossible because of the heavy passenger traffic. The Union Station complex handled about 330 trains a day, of which 120 moved through the tunnel. Since freight for the boats had to be delivered before 5:20 in the afternoon, there was no way to accomplish additional switching without hindering the passenger schedules at Union Station. Thus, of necessity, boat-train service for shippers located west of the Union Station went to New York via the Norwich Line.[25]

Another handicap of the Providence terminal was the approach to the Fox Point wharf. Almost all of the half mile of track between the yards where the boat trains arrived and the wharf were on city streets. To switch the cars from the yards to the wharf required twenty to thirty minutes under the most favorable conditions. Officials of the New Haven claimed that if the railroad had not had to operate on such a precise schedule to the boats, it would have been able to save $1,000 a week.[26]

The difficult terminal situation made Providence especially susceptible to the advantages of motor trucks. Their use could extend the distance over which it was economically feasible to haul goods to the steamers and circumvent the rigidity of the rail schedules. It could also reduce the time in transit from the factory to the wharf. In 1916 truck service extended as far as Boston and Worcester; many local Providence firms used trucks to haul their shipments to Fox Point.[27] Trucks also speeded delivery of goods shipped by steamer from New York to New England points.

The Colonial Navigation Company and the Bay State Line, which was controlled by the New Haven, had no direct rail connections in Providence. Instead, they used trolley and interurban lines to bring freight to their docks. The trolley and interurban companies had special cars to collect freight in Providence and surrounding towns. The system worked well and was similar to the boat-train service of the Providence

Line. As motor trucking became more common, the Colonial Line and the Bay State Line used it to secure better connections and compete with the Providence Line for traffic on more advantageous terms.[28]

Fall River had a topographical problem as well. The city was built on the east side of the Taunton River and Mt. Hope Bay, and upon a long, steep ridge paralleling the waterfront. The Watuppa branch railroad, between Fall River and New Bedford, did not cross the ridge to connect with the lines along the shore. Mills along this branch would have been severely handicapped had the New Bedford Line not existed. They would have had to send their consignments to New York either by a circuitous rail route or via the Fall River Line and an uneconomical wagon haul to the Fall River Line dock. For that matter, New Bedford itself was not favorably located for efficient rail service to New York.[29]

Newport was in a similarly inconvenient location, and the boat service afforded the Newport fishing industry a particular advantage. All the Fall River Line steamers stopped there to load and discharge passengers, and fishermen would telephone the New York and Boston fish markets in the afternoon to compare prices. If New York quoted a better price, the fish were sent on the New York boat. If Boston was paying more, the fish went by train to Boston. The all-rail service from Newport to New York was liable to the same delays that affected the rest of New England, delays to which perishable fish could not be subjected. Between 250 and 2,100 barrels of fish a day were shipped from Newport, depending upon the catch. The flexibility provided by the Fall River Line was a valuable asset to the city.[30]

The remaining New England ports had fewer problems arising from topography. Boston lacked good co-ordination between its railroads because of its lack of car float facilities to interchange cars between the New Haven yards and those of the Boston & Albany Railroad.[31] The coastal steamship lines docked along Atlantic Avenue, where some wharves had limited rail connections via the Union Freight Railroad. Congestion on Atlantic Avenue, however, limited the amount of service the line could furnish. Steamship companies without any rail connection were restricted in the amount of through business they could secure, and they had to provide for the transfer of goods from rail freight stations to the wharves at an average cost of between four and ten cents a hundred pounds.[32] Nevertheless, the need for special rail-water co-operation was less pressing because so much of the traffic requiring this co-operation moved via the Sound lines. Where such service was needed, it could not be furnished. The Metropolitan Line carried a great deal of freight that did not require next-morning delivery in New York. Normally it could not compete with the speedy transport furnished by the Sound lines; an exception was the freight carried on the passenger steamers, but these operated only about five months of the year.[33]

One of the best ports for rail-water connections was Portland. Franklin Wharf, terminus of the lines of the Eastern Steamship Company and the Maine Steamship Company, was located only a short distance from the yards of the Grand Trunk Railway; a marginal railroad encircled the city, connecting with all its railroads. At Franklin Wharf itself the methods of handling freight were not efficient, but the rail connections were excellent. These connections enabled the Grand Trunk to interchange a large amount of freight with the Boston and New York steamship lines.[34]

The charge was often made that the railroads controlled, by lease or ownership, so much of the waterfront in ports of the United States that they could effectively shut out any competition by water. At the same time railroads could dictate the flow of traffic, as the New Haven did by routing almost all of its New England export traffic to New York instead of to Boston.[35] The co-ordination at a port between rail and water lines in package freight movements seems to have depended upon how much the railroads desired to interchange this freight. Where railroads controlled the steamship lines or desired such an interchange, terminals were adequate for the traffic handled. Elsewhere this freight had to travel by other routes or tolerate poor facilities and connections.

Freight Handling

The expeditious handling of the package freight and general merchandise sent on the coastal lines required railroad yard facilities at the Sound ports and fairly extensive freight handling facilities at the New York piers. Since no bulk cargoes moved via the coastal steamship lines, mechanical freight handling did not appear until the twentieth century.

The railroad terminal between India Point and Fox Point in Providence was the most extensive one maintained by the New Haven Railroad, for it served the Merchants & Miners Transportation Company as well as the Providence Line. The facilities were increased in size as the tonnage shipped on the Providence Line and the other coastwise lines grew. In 1903 the New Haven expanded the facilities so as to reduce the amount of switching done on India Street. The new yard had a capacity of ninety cars and a double-track drawbridge to prevent delays. Railroad tracks ran down the wharves at Fall River, New Bedford, Providence, and New London, reducing the distance that freight had to be moved between the freight cars and the steamers.[36]

Loading the freight on the steamers required large numbers of stevedores because of the short time between the arrival of the boat trains and the departure of the steamers. Joint ownership of the railroad and steamship lines made it unnecessary to recheck the freight as it was transferred from freight car to boat or vice versa. To check the freight would have required valuable time and slowed loading.[37] Each railroad terminal from New Bedford to New London had a gang of 100 to 150 men who were joint employees of the New Haven Railroad and its subsidiary, the New England Steamship Company. So too were the freight agent and the office force.

The stevedore force could load freight on the steamers at the rate of fifteen to twenty cars an hour. At New York the longshore force was still larger, ranging from 165 at Pier 28, East River, to 350 at Pier 14 and Pier 15, Hudson River. During 1915 and 1916 the force at Piers 14 and 15 handled between 14,000 and 20,000 tons of freight each week for the Providence and Fall River lines.[38]

The arrival of a boat train at the terminal signaled the beginning of an incredible amount of hustle and activity. The stevedore force would grab their hand trucks, break the seals on the car doors, and put down ramps across the space between the platform and the cars. Then a steady stream of men and hand trucks moved back and forth between the cars and the freight deck of the steamer. Each man knew his job well. On the steamers the freight was stacked rapidly according to the delivery point in New York City. Everyone knew that not a moment could be wasted, for other boat trains were soon due to arrive. The stevedores had to empty these cars in time to have the tracks clear for the next train. This process was repeated with each boat train, and most of the activity was concentrated in a three- to six-hour period.

Handling freight in this manner was expensive. In 1917 New England Steamship Company officials stated that it cost $1.42 per ton to move the textile tonnage between its New England terminals and New York City. This figure included stevedoring, wharf labor, clerical labor, and terminal charges including rental. It excluded transportation charges—that is, anything for the use or operation of the steamers—as well as interest on the plant used in the operations. On textiles from Lowell to New York the steamship company received as its proportion of the through rate $1.32 a ton, which was ten cents less than its costs. Because these high costs were associated with efficient handling, the shippers patronized the service. Some shippers who had been using the Metropolitan Line switched to the Fall River Line solely because of the inefficiency of the dock operations of the Metropolitan Steamship Company.[39]

The methods of handling package and merchandise freight

changed little until about 1910. The two-wheel hand truck was standard, but its use required a large number of men whenever speed in stowage and unloading was necessary. Then came the perfection of the battery-powered electric truck. In 1911 several railroads in the New York area tried out the electric trucks, as did the New England Steamship Company. The railroads rejected them for use at their Manhattan pier stations, claiming that they could not be efficiently employed in loading freight cars on car floats. The fact that they cost about a thousand dollars apiece may have been equally significant.

When the New England Steamship Company moved the terminus of the Fall River and Providence lines from Piers 18 and 19 to Piers 14 and 15, it had electric trucks ready to handle cargo at Pier 14. An estimated 90 per cent of the freight handled at the new terminal complex moved over Pier 14. The company had twenty-one electric trucks at Pier 14 in 1913 and thirty by 1916; their use made Pier 14 one of the most efficient freight stations on Manhattan. In 1918 the installation was valued in excess of fifty thousand dollars.[40] The savings in labor were astonishing. A one-ton-capacity electric truck displaced five men, whose wages aggregated fifteen dollars a day. It could negotiate grades impossible for a man with a loaded hand truck, and it traveled three to four times faster. At rush hours one hundred fewer stevedores were required to move the same amount of freight. Electric trucks helped relieve the congestion so prevalent at the pier stations along West Street. Time studies proved that by careful arrangement of the terminal and the use of electric trucks several minutes could be saved on each delivery.[41]

What was most remarkable, however, was the fact that New England Steamship Company pioneered the use of these trucks. Throughout the New York City area there seemed to be general apathy among railroad officials toward using mechanical appliances for handling merchandise freight, despite the fact that reaching the last freight car on the outer car float often involved a round trip of more than a quarter of a mile. That was a long, time-consuming walk for a man with a hand truck, when an electric truck could travel three or four times faster with perhaps four times as much freight. Given such conditions, the railroad pier stations could not handle freight as rapidly or as efficiently as could the coastal lines.[42] In spite of protestations that electric trucks could not be utilized efficiently at their New York pier stations, railroad officials did come to approve their use when faced by wartime congestion and pleas from Washington.[43]

The New England Steamship Company had several advantages over the railroad pier stations. Pier 14 was the widest pier in lower Manhattan, being 125 feet wide, compared to an average of between 80 and 90 feet for the other piers. This extra width permitted vastly superior organization. Unlike other coastal lines that stowed freight in the holds of their steamers, by means of elevators, the steamers of the New England Steamship Company stowed freight on the main deck. This enabled a roll-on–roll-off movement of trucks, whether hand or electric, and less rehandling of the freight. In the morning, when the steamers were unloading, freight could move directly from the freight deck to the waiting delivery trucks or into designated areas for later pickup by the consignee. When deliveries were made to the boat in the afternoon, freight moved from the delivery vans to waiting electric trucks, which carried it without rehandling directly to the freight deck of the steamer. Only at the busiest times was this not done. These methods were efficient and fast; they eliminated rehandling and so reduced breakage; and they received the praise of truckers, who were very conscious of the losses incurred by inefficient freight handling and terminal organization.[44]

Compounding the terminal problem at New York and to a lesser extent at the Sound ports was the desire of shippers to hold their freight as late as possible in the afternoon before delivering it to the terminal, and to pick up incoming freight as early as possible in the morning. This resulted in long lines at the discharging and receiving platforms in New York City and made rapid handling of freight mandatory in order to maintain the schedules and reduce waiting. Again the

Sound steamers had the advantage, because stevedores could load and unload the hand and electric trucks on the steamers themselves without rehandling, and they had a shorter distance to haul the cargo between the platform and the steamer freight deck.[45]

The tonnage the steamers could handle was considerable. Between 1903 and 1912 the Sound lines under New Haven control carried an average of 1.3 million tons of freight a year. On the basis of about 15 tons per carload this would have required over 86,000 freight cars a year, or 238 a day. Using a figure of six tons per car, the figure quoted for merchandise freight, it would have required 215,000 cars, or 590 cars a day, to handle this tonnage.[46] To add this to what already moved all-rail through the Harlem River float bridges to New York would have placed an intolerable burden on the railroad facilities. To add the freight carried on the Metropolitan Line, the Central Vermont Transportation Company, and the Maine Steamship Company would have been impossible.[47] In 1917 the New Haven railroad delivered a daily average of 150 cars by rail to the Harlem River yards for transfer by car floats to Brooklyn and its Pier 39 complex (Pier 50 before renumbering) on Manhattan. The New England Steamship Company steamers delivered five hundred or more carloads daily. To have forced this to the rail lines would have required fifty to sixty more car floats, for which dock space was unavailable on the island of Manhattan.[48] These averages occurred during the wartime congestion, but complaints about congestion were heard even in 1913 and 1914, when traffic was slightly subnormal. New England shippers for many years had been critical of the poor rail service to New York. What the addition of five hundred or more cars a day would have done to service over the New Haven Railroad is left to the reader's imagination.

In addition to its large pier stations, the New England Steamship Company provided free lighterage service within the lighterage limits of New York Harbor. In 1916 the company had two transfer steamers, seven tugs, twenty-six lighters, and thirty-three barges. The steamship company did not interchange freight with the trunk line railroads at Jersey City, but it did with the coastwise lines in New York City and with the railroad pier stations on Manhattan. In 1912 the expenses for lighterage were $135,154.41, and in 1913 they were $124,263.18.[49]

These facilities were over and above those the New Haven Railroad maintained to move cars and less-than-carload freight between its Harlem River terminal and other points in the port. The New Haven interchanged cars by means of car floats with the Pennsylvania Railroad, the Central Railroad of New Jersey, and the Lehigh Valley Railroad. Interchange with the Erie Railroad and the Delaware, Lackawanna & Western Railroad was via the Poughkeepsie Bridge route. In 1897 an average of 1,429 cars a day were interchanged via car floats; in 1913 the average had risen to 2,100 cars a day.[50]

Railroad ownership of the Sound lines provided an alternative routing, and a necessary one. Given the terminal problems in New York City, no other solution was feasible before the motor truck. The New Haven claimed that if it were forced to dispose of its steamship lines, it would do its utmost to move as much traffic as possible over its rail lines and to secure the required terminal stations in New York to handle this tonnage. Whether it could have done this in a satisfactory manner is doubtful.[51]

Terminal Operating Costs

Terminal costs in New York City were high, and they came under criticism by many transportation experts. More lightering was done in New York Harbor than in any other harbor in the country. Under the existing conditions no other method appeared possible. The average cost to the railroads for lightering freight between their rail terminals and destinations within the lighterage limits ranged from thirty-four cents per ton for the New York Central Railroad to seventy cents per ton for the Pennsylvania Railroad. The cost to the New England Steamship Company was probably closer to thirty-four cents because its delivery points and its piers were nearer to each other than were those of the Pennsylvania Railroad. However, this would not include the cost of rail movements between the yards and the piers, which was considerable.[52]

Terminal expenses were a major item in the budget of a transportation company. In 1882 the Old Colony Steamboat Company had leased its Hudson River terminal at Pier 28 (later renumbered Pier 19) for $45,000 a year, which at that time was a record. In 1915 Piers 14 and 15 alone had a rent of $175,000 annually. In 1908 the annual rental of all the New York piers used by the New England Steamship Company totaled $206,868.58; by 1916 it had risen to $292,814.50. After 1910 all the leases granted by the city of New York had escalator clauses whereby the second ten years of a lease cost more than the first ten years.[53] In 1885 the president of the Old Colony Steamboat Company testified that pier expenses in New York were in excess of $100,000 annually and that it took 20 per cent of the freight revenue just to pay these expenses. By 1916, however, it is likely that pier expenses were an even higher percentage than in 1885.[54]

Each year the terminal expenses increased, and it was this cost spiral that eventually forced the coastwise lines out of business. In 1917 the Interstate Commerce Commission warned the railroads that they would have to face the issue of increasing terminal costs and take account of it in their rate structures. The steamship lines were gradually encountering similar difficulties.[55]

The steamboat lines under New Haven control circumvented the congestion at the port of New York, and they provided a flexibility not otherwise available. In New England too they provided shorter routes and faster service from places like Providence and New Bedford, where topographical features put these cities at a disadvantage in reaching New York City by rail. Although the service was expensive to operate, it served the uncommon requirements of New England industry. Without the service, these industries would have been unable to remain competitive as long as they did.

The whole service hinged on the unique concentration of manufacturing and commercial markets in New York. Had these markets been dispersed, there would have been no need for the co-ordinated rail-water service, since the tonnage would not have been sufficient to support its continuation. The New Haven Railroad fostered its utilization and was especially progressive in the operation of the terminals in New York City. It did for its steamship lines what it was unable to do for its rail lines: it provided terminals capable of dispatching efficiently the maximum tonnage the boats could carry. Nothing more could have been asked.

7. The New Haven Monopoly, 1899–1907

IN 1899 the New Haven Railroad controlled the New Bedford, Fall River, Providence, Stonington, and Norwich lines, giving it a virtual monopoly of the Sound traffic from these points. Little public opposition had been expressed in southern New England to the near-monopoly of the New Haven, but there were some observers who were unhappy about the situation. In addition, certain officials of the New Haven regarded the circumstances in some areas as unfavorable to the railroad.

In 1897 Charles S. Mellen, then second vice-president of the New Haven, had expressed concern about the fact that the company was losing so much business to the local steamship lines running between New York and places like Port Chester, Stamford, Norwalk, Bridgeport, New Haven, and Hartford. He estimated that $900,000 annually in gross revenue was lost to these lines, and he believed that the railroad ought to enter its own vessels into these ports to get some of the traffic. He proposed conferences with local businessmen to get their good will and then their shipments. He also noted that rates could be established at low levels. Any return was worthwhile, Mellen believed, as long as the revenue was sufficient to warrant operating the lines.[1] Mellen was to employ similar tactics when he became president of the New Haven in 1903. His goal was complete monopoly for the New Haven.

Although not all of Mellen's ideas were pursued, his suggestions concerning the operation of fighting lines were adopted when independent steamship lines invaded New Haven territory. The tactics were ruthless but, for the New Haven, successful.

Competition at Providence

Hardly had the New Haven attained dominance east of New Haven when it was challenged at Providence by two new competitors. On 21 March 1899 the Joy Steamship Company, headed by F. M. Dunbaugh, commenced operation of a semi-weekly freight service between Providence and New York with the steamer *Rosalie*. On 12 June Chester W. Chapin, Jr., entered the New Haven Steamboat Company in a daily passenger and freight service between Providence, New Haven, and New York with the steamers *Richard Peck* and *Shinne-cock*. Chapin's challenge was by far the more formidable of the two, for his Narragansett Bay Line used two modern steamers (the *Shinnecock* under charter), and had a new steamer, the *Chester W. Chapin*, under construction. Both companies received a favorable reception from shippers and travelers in Providence and for a while each earned satisfactory revenues.[2]

Not content with one route, in July F. M. Dunbaugh entered the Joy Steamship Company on the all-water freight route between New York and Boston, challenging the monopoly long enjoyed by the Metropolitan Steamship Company.[3] Nothing like these activities had occurred in New England since the rate war that ended in January 1881.

The selection of Providence as the point to challenge the New Haven was logical because of its size and the availability of enough business to support a second line. Moreover, the port had no winter passenger service. This gave the New

Haven Steamboat Company and later the Joy Line a free field during the seven months of the year when the Providence Line carried only freight. During the summer of 1899 the three lines enjoyed good business, but the competition forced the Joy Line to reduce its freight rates on 20 July. Many outside of the New Haven Railroad organization admired the "pluck" of the competitors.[4] Meanwhile, the management of the New Haven Railroad responded to the challenges. Because the Narragansett Bay Line of the New Haven Steamboat Company presented the more serious threat, it came under attack first.

Just why Chester W. Chapin, Jr., decided to challenge the New Haven Railroad is not clear, but his move had the appearance of a serious effort, especially with the construction of the new propeller *Chester W. Chapin*. Chapin was reported to have been unhappy because the railroad was diverting high-class freight away from his company at New Haven.[5] The Providence Board of Trade welcomed the line and was pleased to have passenger service restored during the winter months. From June to December 1899, on business between New York and Providence, the Narragansett Bay Line received $65,212.23 in passenger revenue and $49,652.29 from freight. The passenger fare was $2.50 one way and $4.00 round trip. The one-way fare was fifty cents lower than the fare on the Providence Line.[6] Unlike many of the steamers employed by later competitors of the New Haven Railroad, the *Richard Peck* and the *Chester W. Chapin* were new, first-class steamers, which attracted a respectable class of traveler. The Joy Line could not boast such fine accommodations for its clientele.

New Haven Railroad officials were increasingly concerned about the situation at Providence, but they were unsure how to respond to the new competitors. Sources close to the railroad said that as soon as the *Chester W. Chapin* was completed, the New Haven Steamboat Company would eliminate the stop at New Haven and begin direct service between Providence and New York. Chapin was apparently willing to abandon the traffic between Providence and New Haven. The

New Haven Railroad, which owned Belle Dock in New Haven, the terminus of the New Haven Steamboat Company, was in a somewhat embarrassing position because of this and because of the through business it interchanged with the steamers at New Haven. John M. Hall, then vice-president of the railroad, felt that the steamboat company had had its way for too many years and that the actions it was then taking could not be ignored. One solution he proposed was the establishment by the New Haven of a steamboat line to compete with the Narragansett Bay Line.[7]

By early in 1900 the pressure for some sort of settlement was increasing and the situation approached a climax. On 9 February 1900 the directors of the New Haven Railroad voted the following resolution: "That the Committee heretofore appointed on the relations between this Company and the New Haven Steamboat Company be and they are hereby authorized to cause proper notice to be served terminating the tenancy of the New Haven Steamboat Company, at Belle Dock in the City of New Haven, if they deem it advisable to do so." On 10 March 1900 it was reported that the New Haven Steamboat Company had decided to construct still another twin screw steamer to run with the *Chester W. Chapin* on the Narragansett Bay Line.[8] Whether true or not, the report probably spurred the executives of the New Haven Railroad to take quick action to eliminate this troublesome competitor.

On 14 April, at a special meeting of the standing committee of the board of directors, it was voted to accept the result of the negotiations of the special committee on the purchase of the New Haven Steamboat Company. The railroad agreed to pay $140 a share on the condition that all or most of the stock could be secured. The railroad also agreed to purchase from Chester W. Chapin, Jr., the Lonsdale Wharf property in Providence. The agreement was favorable to the steamboat company, since the price paid for the stock was $40 above par.[9]

The official explanation of the purchase was given in the annual report of the railroad: because of the strategic location of the New Haven Steamboat Company, its easy accessibility to New York City, and the interchange of traffic between the two companies, it was considered a valuable asset to the railroad.[10] Another explanation saw the sale as a triumph for Chester W. Chapin, Jr., whose object, it was said, was to force the railroad to buy him out. He died just before the final agreement was made. A short time later the directors of the New Haven Steamboat Company passed a resolution which read: "the view of the directors [is] that they were cognizant of the pleasure which it would have given Mr. Chapin if he could have known that his line had been acquired by the New Haven Railroad Company."[11]

Whatever Chapin's motives were, the New Haven Railroad could not completely ignore the competition, unless it wished to encourage others to undertake similar actions. After purchasing the steamboat company, the railroad suspended the Narragansett Bay Line. This was a disappointment to the businessmen of Providence, who had long been restive under New Haven domination. What disturbed them most was the power of the New Haven and its ability to dictate its own terms. The victory of the railroad—or perhaps that of Chapin —drew protests from those favoring independent steamship lines, but their protests had little impact.[12] It had become evident that the management of the New Haven would not tolerate competition that threatened its monopoly in southern New England.

The competition between the Narragansett Bay Line and the Providence Line of the New Haven Railroad had been so intense that it had forced F. M. Dunbaugh to suspend temporarily the Providence service of the Joy Line. His slower and older steamers could not compete with the flyers of the other two lines. After the Narragansett Bay Line ceased operations, Dunbaugh, on 15 May 1900, re-established a thrice-weekly service between Providence and New York City that now also carried passengers.[13] The New Haven, freed of the Chapin challenge, could now concentrate all its efforts on this competitor.

The railroad did not hesitate very long. On 11 July the

Massachusetts began a new "excursion service" between Providence and New York at a fare of one dollar each way. In a letter to Edward G. Buckland, the attorney of the New Haven in Providence, John M. Hall, now president of the New Haven, explained that the company had only "yielded to the urgent demands of the people of Providence for cheap rates during the summer season." If questioned about the new service, Buckland was to state that the railroad was "simply trying an experiment of cheap rates during the season to see whether they are appreciated by the people or not, and to give the people of Providence an opportunity to go to New York and back if they so desire, at a low rate." Hall noted that the New Haven was able to inaugurate this new service because the company had a vacant dock and steamers it could not otherwise use. He further instructed Buckland to "avoid any allusion to the Joy Steamship Company, and of course any statement that may indicate that we are putting on this service to in any way interfere with their enterprise." This was the first overt move against the Joy Line. But it had only slight effect and did not seriously injure the thriving business of the line.[14] Yet those aware of the attitude of the New Haven management knew that further efforts would be made.

During the autumn the *Rhode Island* continued the operation of the New Haven excursion line—sometimes known as the New Line. The Joy Line operated three nights a week; these happened to be the same nights the New Haven scheduled its thrice-weekly winter service. The reaction of Providence businessmen was less than friendly: "if that grasping company [the New Haven] really considers that Providence is entitled to a low-priced service every other night during the winter to New York, it would have its sailing the evenings not first established by the Joy Line." This tactic the Providence Board of Trade considered "contemptible." The directors of the railroad at that time had no desire to buy the Joy Steamship Company and did not care to prevent others from doing so. But they did have a fixed policy of harassing the line into submission.[15]

In January 1901 Dunbaugh began a daily service on the Providence and Boston lines of the Joy Steamship Company. Both did a thriving business. As a result the company had to build additional freight sheds on its East River pier in New York.[16] Seeing this business going to a competitor did not please the management of the New Haven, and it continued its efforts to check the Joy Line. In May 1901 it declared open war by establishing a new low-fare fighting line between Providence and New York using the steamers *Rhode Island* and *Connecticut*. The so-called cheap line charged only fifty cents for the one-way fare, compared to one dollar on the Joy Line and three dollars on the Providence Line. By using older steamers the New Haven could compete with the Joy Line on its own terms. Again the Providence Board of Trade criticized the railroad for its tactics. What concerned the board was that if the New Haven emerged victorious, Providence would once again find itself "at the mercy of what has been termed a 'gigantic monopoly.'"[17]

The expanding business of the Joy Line forced Dunbaugh to expand his fleet by the purchase of older steamships from Maine companies. He purchased the *Tremont* and for a short time chartered the *Penobscot*. Between 1902 and 1904 he purchased two side-wheelers from the Eastern Steamship Company.[18] Attempts to charter other steamers were thwarted whenever possible by the New Haven. Late in the summer of 1901 Dunbaugh was trying to renew the charters on the *Martinique* and the *Cocoa*, which were owned by the Florida East Coast Railway. The general traffic manager of the Metropolitan Steamship Company wrote to Percy R. Todd, second vice-president of the New Haven Railroad, to request that the railroad use its influence with Henry M. Flagler to persuade him not to renew the charters. Todd replied that he was quite willing to do all he could and that President Hall had already written Flagler about the *Martinique*. Earlier in the summer Captain Horatio Hall of the Maine Steamship Company had refused to agree to the charter of the *Manhattan* by the Joy Line. Both the Metropolitan Steamship Company and the New Haven were grateful to Captain Hall. Percy Todd, to express the gratitude of the railroad, sent Hall an annual pass good on all New Haven rail and water lines. Captain Hall raised the price of chartering the *Penobscot* by two thousand dollars.[19]

Early in 1902 the Metropolitan Steamship Company and the New Haven continued their joint harassment. They applied pressure on the American Sugar Refining Company and other companies in an attempt to have them stop their shipments over the Joy Line. The attempt was successful. In August 1902 the management of the refining company ordered its plants "not to ship via the Joy Line." In return, the New Haven and the Metropolitan Line gave the company a rate reduction on all sugar shipped from New York. The new rate matched the Joy Line rate.[20]

Still not content, New Haven officials moved to sever the agreement of the Joy Line with the Dyer Transportation Company, which carried Joy Line freight between Providence and Fall River. Dyer served the Merchants & Miners Transportation Company as well, but the New Haven was concerned only with the Joy Line. Recognizing that the New Haven could ruin him, Captain Dyer, owner of the company, had no desire to fight the railroad. The Joy Line had been chartering one of his boats for twenty-five dollars a day. Percy Todd, representing the New Haven, decided that it would be better to pay Dyer not to operate his vessels for the Joy Line than to buy him out. If the New Haven should do the latter, Todd feared that the Joy Line would begin its own service. The cost of operating one of Dyer's boats was ten dollars a day. On 29 January 1902, two days before the Joy Line charter terminated, the New Haven agreed to pay Dyer ten dollars a day for keeping one boat idle. After three weeks Dyer could again use the vessel, but he could carry no Joy Line freight. If, in the interim, the Joy Line secured a boat elsewhere, the charter was to be terminated. All payments to Dyer were made through the office of Edward G. Buckland, the New Haven Railroad attorney in Providence, so that they could be kept confidential and not easily connected with the railroad. This agreement remained in effect until 11 October 1902.[21]

Between January and October 1902 rates dropped precipitously. Both the Joy Line and the two New Haven lines cut freight rates and granted rebates.[22] By September steamship men were of the opinion that Dunbaugh's Joy Line could not be making money on its freight and that the passenger business to Boston and Providence was what enabled the company to continue its freight operations. During July the Metropolitan Steamship Company and the New Haven Railroad had used spies to see how the Joy Line was doing. The figures showed that the Providence Line with its higher fare carried about 4,300 fewer passengers than the Joy Line. The so-called New Line, or cheap line, of the New Haven carried half again as many at fifty cents each. During the same period the Joy Line was carrying about fifty or sixty tons of freight a day each way, whereas its steamers had a capacity for about three hundred tons. At the same time, because of the rebates it granted, freight on the Providence Line increased twenty thousand tons in one year.[23]

These are examples of the pressure that the executives of the New Haven exerted on competitors. They used their connections with other railroads and under certain conditions would co-operate with a competitor like the Metropolitan Steamship Company to check new competitors. These tactics, when they later came to public attention, were evidence for the critics of the railroad and served to support arguments for divorcing the steamship lines from the railroad.

By August 1902 Dunbaugh was ready to come to an accommodation with the New Haven, for he could no longer fight against the greater resources of the railroad. The New Haven preferred to keep the Joy Line an independent operation to preserve the fiction of competition, and negotiations began concerning the proposed agreement. Dunbaugh agreed to withdraw all agents of the company at interior points and to cease the solicitation of freight for the Providence steamers from Boston and interior points. In return, the New Haven agreed to grant the Joy Line a two-to-five-cent differential on low-grade freight and to withdraw its fighting line—the New Line—for the duration of the agreement and discontinue winter passenger service out of Providence. Passenger fares were fixed at $3.00 for the Providence Line and $1.25 one way and $2.50 round trip for the Joy Line. All these negotiations were conducted in a highly secret manner, with only the officials of the Joy Line, the New Haven, and the Metropolitan Line being aware of the situation. Dunbaugh agreed to confine the operations of the Joy Line to Boston and Providence and to send no freight west of New York City on through rates. He remained as president of the Joy Steamship Company.[24]

The agreement was signed on 3 October 1902 and was to be effective for one year beginning October 19. The New Haven suspended operation of the New Line on 11 October, under the pretense that because of the strike of anthracite coal miners, coal was scarce and too expensive to allow continued operation of the line.[25] Thus ended the competition of independent steamship lines at Providence. The restoration of freight rates to the level existing before the competition displeased Providence businessmen, but their protests brought no change. Edward G. Buckland planned to get into the newspapers an "emphatic statement" that the New Haven did not directly or indirectly control the Joy Line. Officials of the Metropolitan Steamship Company did not desire to negotiate a similar agreement with the Joy Line, but did view favorably the one signed at Providence.[26]

The agreement between the New Haven and the Joy Line worked well during the next couple of years and resulted in increased revenue and business for both companies. Freight was so heavy that the Providence Line had to divert some of it to the Fall River Line.[27] The New Haven had succeeded in retaining all the through business, while giving the Joy Line a portion of the local business in Boston and Providence. Yet it had temporarily retained the fiction of competition at these points to blunt any criticism of its monopolistic position.

Extension of New Haven Control

While it was fighting the Joy Line, the New Haven Railroad acquired the New London Steamboat Company. This company operated a service between New London, Watch Hill, and Block Island, but more significant was the fact that it also operated, under charter, the boat service connected with the Central Vermont Railway. Whether this was the principal reason that the New Haven purchased the company is unclear, although it probably was an important consideration.

Before 1896 the Central Vermont Railroad had owned and operated its own steamers between New London and New York. In 1896, when the railroad entered receivership, its steamers were inadequate to handle the freight traffic of the railroad and their seaworthiness was suspect. Unable to replace them because of its financial difficulties, the railroad decided to charter new steamers from the New London Steamboat Company. The steamboat company at the time was owned by the directors of the New London Northern Railroad and the officers and directors of the Central Vermont Railroad. To provide the funds necessary to construct two modern freight steamers, the company issued $300,000 in bonds and about $100,000 in preferred stock.

When the Central Vermont Railroad emerged from receivership in 1899 as the Central Vermont Railway, a ten-year contract was signed that specified the exact terms of the charter. Two freight steamers, *Mohegan* and *Mohawk*, were to be used solely for Central Vermont business. They were lettered "Central Vermont Line." Additional steamers were to be furnished if necessary. For this the Central Vermont paid fifty cents for each ton of freight carried. It also loaded and unloaded the freight, paid all wharfage, rent, soliciting, and other expenses not directly connected with operating the steamers. The steamboat company paid all insurance, which was payable to the railway.[28]

Soon after the affairs of the Central Vermont were again on a solid foundation, Charles M. Hays, president of the

Grand Trunk Railway, which had had an interest in the Central Vermont since 1885, asked the president of the New London Steamboat Company if he wished to sell his company to the Grand Trunk. The price asked was unsatisfactory to Hays, and he decided that the Central Vermont should build its own new and modern steamers, then allow the contract between the two companies to lapse in 1909. When the Grand Trunk refused to purchase the New London Steamboat Company, its president sold the corporation to Stevenson Taylor, who was acting for the New Haven Railroad. On 13 April 1901 Taylor turned over to the New Haven enough stock to control the steamboat company; by September the remainder was in the hands of the New Haven.[29]

Little change was evident after the New Haven gained control. New Haven officials did endeavor to induce Hays to discontinue the Central Vermont steamer service and send its tonnage on the Norwich Line of the New Haven. The New Haven offered to allow the Grand Trunk to placard the New York piers as its own, and it offered the Grand Trunk a larger share of the New England business. All efforts of the New Haven were fruitless. The unusual relationship continued until 1909, when the contract expired.[30]

During the decade between 1899 and 1909 the Central Vermont Railway became part of a differential route on westbound tonnage between New York and the Central Freight Association territory in the Midwest. Sugar formed a large proportion of this tonnage, which did not require fast service.[31] Such traffic appeared quite lucrative to the management of the New Haven Railroad.

The final acquisition by the New Haven during this period was 11,378 shares of stock of the Bridgeport Steamboat Company, purchased in 1903 at a cost of $321,950. Only 662 shares remained outside of New Haven control.[32] With this purchase all the important Sound lines between New England and New York City, except the Hartford & New York Transportation Company, were under the direct or indirect control of the New Haven Railroad.

A hiatus of over two years occurred while the railroad reorganized its steamship properties and concentrated its attention on other aspects of New England transportation. Between 1892 and 1903 the New Haven had come a long way; it remained to be seen what course the company would now pursue. In 1903 the picture was somewhat obscure because of the return of Charles S. Mellen. He had just been elected president of the New Haven to fill the vacancy caused by the retirement of John M. Hall.

Charles S. Mellen

Mellen had been a vice-president of the New Haven until 1897, when, through the influence of J. Pierpont Morgan, the directors of the Northern Pacific Railroad elected him president. As president he had improved the earnings of the Northern Pacific and had showed himself a fighter in his efforts to check the moves of James J. Hill of the Great Northern Railroad. Mellen had also kept on good terms with J. P. Morgan, and Morgan's opinion counted for a great deal— especially since he was a director of the New Haven.

With the New Haven being challenged by competitors, trolleys as well as steamboats, on all sides, the choice of a man of Mellen's background seemed a judicious one. The fact that Morgan favored Mellen further buttressed the move. Mellen had the aggressive attitude needed to meet the new competitors on their own terms, but he had other qualities that were to result in grave difficulties for himself as well as the New Haven. He lacked tact and was often abrasive in his dealings with those who disagreed with him or questioned his motives and goals. Once he was convinced of the merit of an idea, few could persuade Mellen that another course of action might be more prudent. These qualities eventually brought upon Mellen the censure of much of the press of the region.

The management of the New Haven needed some changes, for it had tended to be too conservative in its attitudes toward change. Mellen, while vice-president, had chafed under the attitudes of President Charles P. Clark and others who Mellen believed were too complacent. But, as we shall see, Mellen went too far in abandoning caution.

Upon Morgan and Mellen rested the responsibility for the course the New Haven followed during the next ten years. Morgan wanted to bring New England transportation under the control of the New Haven, thus bringing about greater efficiency, he believed, and therefore benefiting the stockholders and the residents of the region. Mellen was selected to carry out this plan.[33]

New England received Mellen with an open mind, ready to judge him on his performance. Even in Providence, where the New Haven was not the most popular institution, he had a favorable reception.[34] The company faced several formidable challenges, and the handling of these challenges would dictate the reaction of the public. Electric interurbans were being constructed and projected throughout New Haven territory, where they were taking a considerable amount of the passenger and less-than-carload freight traffic from the railroad. The coastwise scene was temporarily quiescent, but here too the railroad had to be constantly on guard. Mellen had to preserve the business of his railroad without raising the specter of monopoly. In this he ultimately failed and in the process brought financial ruin to one of the most prosperous railroads in the United States.

The Formation of the New England Navigation Company

Since 1898 the steamboat lines had been operated by the marine district of the New Haven while all the companies retained their corporate existence. As the acquisitions multiplied, the arrangement became cumbersome, and the directors decided to form a new company in which all the steamship lines could be merged and operated under one management. This program was undertaken in 1904, soon after the railroad had reorganized the boat-train schedules and discontinued the Stonington Line. For the purpose a corporation called the New England Navigation Company was organized.

As an operating subsidiary, the New England Navigation Company differed in no major respect from those organized by other railroads. Only a careful reading of its charter would have made a perceptive lawyer or banker aware of the possibilities for which the company could be used. The charter had been approved on 14 May 1901 by the General Assembly of the state of Connecticut, in the name of the Colonial Commercial Company. The original capital stock totaled fifty thousand dollars. The company had to retain an office in New London, although additional offices could be established wherever necessary. Its books were to be open to the stockholders, and an annual statement of financial condition was to be issued to the stockholders. A change in name required a vote of two-thirds of the directors. The activities in which the company could engage included manufacturing; mining; trading; mercantile business; loaning money; acting as trustee; and owning, operating, or developing real and personal property, including the securities and franchises of other corporations. Only the operation of steam and street railroads and public utilities was prohibited.[35]

Formal organization of the Colonial Commercial Company took place in New London on 13 May 1903, with the necessary three directors present. From then until 19 July 1904 the company remained dormant. On the latter date the directors voted to increase the number of directors to five, and at the meeting a completely new board was elected. They were Charles S. Mellen, H. M. Kochersperger, John G. Parker, Augustus S. May, and Edward G. Buckland. All were officials or directors of the New York, New Haven & Hartford Railroad. For $52,000 they purchased all 500 shares of stock of the Colonial Commercial Company, of which 496 were held by Mellen. On 18 October they voted to change the name to New England Navigation Company.[36] How innocent the name sounded. Like an iceberg it did not reveal the dangers that lurked in one clause of the charter, which gave the company authority to hold, develop, buy, and sell the securities of other corporations. Such activity would very soon become the primary function of the New England Navigation Company. For the moment, however, it undertook the merger and liquidation of the various steamship companies owned by the railroad.

The New Haven had hired Stevenson Taylor, a marine engineer and naval architect who had long been associated with the Sound lines, to appraise the steamship companies.[37] At the meeting on 18 October 1904 the Navigation Company purchased them at a price equal to the appraised value. The price of the Bridgeport Steamboat Company was $300,000, and the Navigation Company assumed its funded debt of $100,000. It purchased the property of the New London Steamboat Company for $90,000. For the New Haven Steamboat Company it paid $496,000 less the funded debt of $349,000. The Providence & Stonington Steamship Company cost $2,035,000 less the funded debt of $200,000. The Norwich & New York Transportation Company was purchased for $675,000. To provide funds for these transactions the Navigation Company issued 34,000 shares of $100 par value stock to its five stockholders. At a meeting on 10 December 1904 the directors of the New Haven Railroad approved the sale of the steamship companies to the Navigation Company. Payment to the railroad was in capital stock of the New England Navigation Company. Transfer of title took place between 13 December 1904 and 1 January 1905.[38]

The most valuable steamship property owned by the New Haven was not included in the original transaction. The New Haven directors approved the sale of the Old Colony Steamboat Company in 1904, but the Old Colony stockholders did not take favorable action until 21 December 1905. The price of the company was $5,320,689, which was paid to the railroad in stock and debentures of the New England Navigation Company. Actual consolidation of the Old Colony Steamboat Company with the Navigation Company had taken place on 1 July 1905.[39] Thereafter all operations were conducted by the New England Navigation Company. This completed the transactions and ended some historic companies; the oldest was the New Haven Steamboat Company, which dated from the earliest days of steam navigation.

Consolidation brought no significant change in operation. Bookkeeping became less complicated, and all steamer earnings, which in 1903 had been included with rail earnings, were now reported separately.[40] The public, however, was less well informed because the charter of the New England Navigation Company required an annual statement only to the stockholders. The only stockholder was the New Haven Railroad.

The transactions that could be hidden were many. The New England Navigation Company soon became the vehicle by which the New Haven financed the purchase of trolley lines, power companies, the stock of other corporations, and new rail construction. It also used the Navigation Company to buy stock in the Boston & Maine Railroad. Although they are beyond the scope of this study, it was these transactions, many of which were of questionable value, that finally brought the censure of federal and state authorities on the railroad and its management.[41]

Competition at Fall River

The agreement between the New Haven Railroad and the Joy Line had restored stability to the Sound lines; its renewal in December 1904 indicated a continuation of satisfactory relations. The following month, however, a group of businessmen met in Worcester, Massachusetts, to form the Enterprise Transportation Company, with an authorized capital stock of $600,000, of which about $400,000 was issued. The company was headed by David Whitcomb, and all the directors except one were members of the Whitcomb family. The Whitcombs planned to operate a steamboat line between Fall River and New York.[42] For this purpose they purchased several old steamers, including the *Frank Jones* from the Portland, Mt. Desert & Machias Steamboat Company, the *Kennebec* and the *St. Croix* from the Eastern Steamship Company, and the *Warren*. The first passenger trip was made on 1 June 1905, and the first freight trip on 1 July 1905. Service was daily in summer and six times a week in winter.[43]

In May the New Haven was aware of the impending developments, and the correspondence files contain several letters about the threat posed by the Enterprise Transportation Company. The general manager of the new company, George Brady, had been discharged three years earlier from New Haven employment and later by the Joy Line. Brady was active in soliciting business for the new company, perhaps animated by a dislike of his former employer. The New Haven arranged to have agents keep watch on the traffic of the Enterprise Line so that if it made serious inroads on New Haven business, the railroad could "take such steps as may be deemed necessary to checkmate the same."[44]

The Whitcombs set the New York–Fall River fare during the summer at two dollars; the Fall River Line charged three dollars. In spite of the refusal of the New Haven to join with the Enterprise Line in making through rates, the latter sought to gain a share of the Boston–New York traffic. To do this the Whitcombs had to purchase rail tickets between Boston and Fall River, which they gave to passengers who held tickets.[45]

As early as June opinion among New Haven officials favored bankrupting the Enterprise Line rather than buying it outright. To do this, the New Haven appointed Stevenson Taylor, who had appraised the steamship properties, to begin negotiations for the purchase of the Joy Steamship Company from F. M. Dunbaugh so that it could be used as a fighting line. On 9 December 1905 the directors of the New Haven authorized the New England Navigation Company to purchase the stock of the Joy Steamship Company from Dunbaugh for the sum of $775,000. Two checks totaling this amount were drawn on 16 December 1905.[46] This transaction was not made public, for the Joy Line served as a useful cover to enable the New Haven to fight the Enterprise Line without affecting the quality of service on the Fall River Line.. The Dunbaugh management of the Joy Line remained unchanged.

Throughout 1905 New Haven officials had been assessing the impact of the Enterprise Line on railroad traffic; spies had been sent to the Enterprise Line pier in New York to learn how much freight the line carried. Agents of the Enterprise Line had been actively seeking business among large shippers in Fall River by setting rates 20 to 45 per cent below those of the Fall River Line, and the New Haven had become increasingly concerned over the possibility of a permanent loss of freight and passenger business to the new line.[47] As a result, in November railroad officials considered reducing the winter fare between Boston and New York via the Fall River Line from three dollars to two dollars. They decided against it so as not to injure the reputation of the Fall River Line.[48]

The purchase of the Joy Line provided a better weapon. In February 1906 the Joy Line reduced its Boston–New York fare to $1.75 to match that of the Enterprise Line. During the winter of 1906 the New Haven advanced the Joy Line $130,000 to purchase a steamer for the Fall River trade. With the steamer *Santiago* the Joy Line began freight service between Fall River and New York in June 1906. In October the New Haven abrogated the 1904 traffic agreement with the Joy Line so that the management of the latter would have a free hand in fixing rates. Between January and July 1906 the New Haven credited over $560,000 to the account of the Joy Steamship Company, a company that many believed was still owned and operated by F. M. Dunbaugh.[49]

Besides paying subsidies to the Joy Line, New Haven officials used their influence and connections to prevent the Enterprise Transportation Company from securing through rates with the railroads serving New York City. This forced the Whitcombs to bring two complaints before the Interstate Commerce Commission. The commission supported their position, but at that time it lacked authority to compel railroads to establish through rates with water lines. The two cases made clear that the Enterprise Line was being discriminated against in spite of statements to the contrary by officials representing the railroads serving New York City.[50]

The evidence presented to the Interstate Commerce Commission illustrates that many shippers liked and used the service offered by the Enterprise Line. The freight and passenger business provided a reasonable revenue for the company. In the spring of 1906 the Enterprise Line had an average revenue of one thousand dollars a day. Its low overhead expenses enabled it to undercut the rates of the Fall River Line.[51]

To men like Charles S. Mellen the situation demanded more aggressive action. In the middle of 1906 Mellen told Stevenson Taylor that he had made up his mind that a "cheap line" was required on the Fall River–New York route because the New Haven could not afford to reduce the rates on the Fall River Line. He asked Taylor to organize and manage a new corporation to carry out this task and promised to provide the necessary steamers. Taylor was to manage the company as his own. He accepted the offer and with his associates organized the United States Transportation Company on 4 October 1906. The New England Navigation Company sold the steamers *Rhode Island* and *Connecticut* to the new company for $650,000 and authorized the advancement of funds so that the United States Transportation Company could pay for the steamers. Taylor organized the new company under Connecticut laws with a charter granting very broad powers. In Mellen's words, "Practically the only object of the United States Transportation Company" was "to fight the Enterprise Line for Fall River business to a finish." In this task it succeeded.[52]

Between 1 January 1907 and 31 August 1907, the United States Transportation Company spent $190,956 renovating and repairing the *Connecticut* and $85,872 on the *Rhode Island*. Because of these extensive repairs, including new boilers for the *Connecticut*, the steamers were not ready for service until June 1907. As soon as the *Rhode Island* and the

Connecticut were ready, the Joy Line discontinued its Fall River service. The United States Transportation Company was known to be an ally of the New England Navigation Company, and a growing number of people suspected that the Joy Line also had intimate ties with the New Haven. Competition between the United States Transportation Company and the Enterprise Line was vigorous throughout the summer of 1907. This resulted in a steady decline in freight rates. Yet business remained good, giving all the lines from Fall River considerable tonnage, but less than satisfactory revenue.[53]

Since the Whitcombs faced alone the animosity of the New Haven system, the ultimate fate of their Enterprise Transportation Company was never in doubt. The panic in the autumn of 1907 brought the final blow. In November the company entered receivership with its liabilities in excess of $500,000, of which half were then payable or overdue. The receiver, Hollis R. Bailey of Boston, sold the *Kennebec* to the United States Transportation Company for $125,000. The directors of the New Haven, on 18 December 1907, authorized the transfer of this amount to the United States Transportation Company, which handled the actual transaction.[54]

Again the New Haven had triumphed by a combination of subterfuge and ruthlessness; within a few months all competition at Fall River ended, leaving the field to the Fall River Line. In March 1908 the United States Transportation Company was sold to a recent New Haven acquisition, the Hartford & New York Transportation Company, which discontinued its operation.

Two More New Haven Acquisitions

While the competition raged at Fall River, the New Haven Railroad was acquiring two more steamship lines: the Hartford & New York Transportation Company and the Maine Steamship Company.

The Hartford & New York Transportation Company dated from 1877, when it had been organized as a joint stock company to conduct barge and towing operations on the Connecticut River. In the 1880s it entered the passenger business between Hartford and New York City. The company had a checkered career, with good and bad years. Never a very prosperous concern, it normally earned a modest return for its stockholders. In 1895 Charles Goodrich, president of the company, offered to sell its passenger service to the New Haven Railroad. The offer was refused, whereupon Goodrich contracted for the construction of a new passenger steamer to furnish the required nightly service. Nevertheless, because the Connecticut River was icebound about three months each year, the Hartford Line was handicapped in competing with the New Haven. After 1900 Goodrich realized that without a large amount of new capital the company could not remain competitive. By the year 1905 it could not, out of its own revenue, provide enough money to modernize and replace its aging equipment.[55]

The freight carried by the Hartford Line was primarily package freight, general merchandise, early produce, and foodstuffs moving port-to-port. Over 90 per cent of the tonnage carried by the barge line of the company consisted of coal for points on the Connecticut River. It was the profits from the barge line that carried the company; the steamships earned hardly any profit.[56]

The first tangible expression of interest by the New Haven Railroad in the Hartford & New York Transportation Company came in September 1905, when Charles S. Mellen suggested to his board of directors that it appoint a special committee to check into the possibility of buying all the property of the Transportation Company.[57] Negotiations lasted from October 1905 until September 1906. Then the directors of the New Haven authorized Mellen to propose an exchange of two shares of railroad stock for five shares of Hartford & New York Transportation Company stock. Goodrich accepted the offer; between October 1906 and 1 April 1907, 7,985 shares of railroad stock at two hundred dollars a share were exchanged for 19,976 shares of the Transportation Company at a value of eighty dollars a share.[58]

With the purchase of this company the New Haven succeeded in its effort to control all the coastal steamship lines within its territory except for the Metropolitan Line and a few local lines at ports along the Sound. Unlike earlier acquisitions, the Hartford & New York Transportation Company remained independent, in order to serve as the operating company of the "cheap lines" that were used to eliminate competition.

The Maine Steamship Company also came under New Haven control, in December 1906 and January 1907. In 1906 the railroad made known its interest in this prosperous company. It was a Maine corporation, but its entire capital stock was owned by the Maine Steamship Company of New Jersey, which had been incorporated in 1901. By December 1906, through involved and *sub rosa* transactions, the New Haven had purchased all the stock of the New Jersey company for $400,000; it received the certificates in January 1907. Then the New Haven board of directors authorized the United States Transportation Company to purchase the stock. Stevenson Taylor carried out these instructions and became president of the Maine Steamship Company.[59]

The Liquidation of the Fighting Lines

On 31 October 1907 the New England Navigation Company sold the Joy Steamship Company to the United States Transportation Company for $1,019,756. This price was determined after a credit of $300,000 had been allowed from the sale of the Boston–New York line to Charles W. Morse, who now controlled the Metropolitan Steamship Company. During the time the New England Navigation Company owned the Joy Line it had accumulated a deficit of $151,610.48, not including interest or taxes. During the summer of 1907 the federal government was questioning the legality of the ownership of the Joy Line by the New Haven Railroad. The directors of the railroad, on 30 October 1907, decided it was not advisable to sell the Joy Steamship Company so as "to eliminate its control by this company." On 31 October 1907 the property and assets of the Joy Line were taken over by the United States Transportation Company.[60]

The following March the United States Transportation Company was purchased by the Hartford & New York Transportation Company. For this purpose the latter increased its capital stock from $750,000 to $2,750,000. Stevenson Taylor and the other directors of the United States Transportation Company were replaced by officials of the New Haven Railroad. This, in Mellen's view, would make it possible to liquidate the company whenever necessary because of the ease with which a quorum could be gathered.[61] After March 1908 the United States Transportation Company existed in name only.

On 18 December 1911 a new corporation known as the Hartford & New York Transportation Company was incorporated under Connecticut laws for the purpose of acquiring the property, rights, and franchises of the old Hartford & New York Transportation Company as well as the United States Transportation Company. On 31 December 1911, the transactions were completed. The Hartford & New York Transportation Company continued to operate the "cheap lines" that its predecessor had taken over from the Joy Steamship Company. The Providence service now operated under the name Bay State Line. The freight service between Bridgeport and New York, which the Joy Line had begun in the spring of 1906 to meet threatened competition, continued as the Merchants Line.[62]

The history of the transactions of the Joy Steamship Company and the United States Transportation Company will probably never be completely clear because their records are confusing and incomplete. When the New England Navigation Company acquired the Joy Line, Mellen ordered the Joy Line books destroyed because the general offices at New Haven supposedly lacked space to store old records. The accounting methods used by the United States Transportation Company were questioned by Price, Waterhouse & Company when its accountants examined the books in May 1908. In a letter to H. M. Kochersperger, vice-president of the New Haven Railroad, the accounting firm concluded: "We believe that you are aware of the wretched manner in which the books have been kept during the nine months under review, changes of system having been so frequent that three general ledgers have been installed during the period."[63]

In 1907 the New York, New Haven & Hartford Railroad was the only railroad in New England that still owned any passenger-carrying coastal steamship lines. In 1905 the Maine Central Railroad had sold the *Frank Jones* and discontinued the operation of the Portland, Mt. Desert & Machias Steamboat Company. Completion of the Washington County Railroad in 1900 had taken most of the traffic away from the steamboat company, and with only one steamer it could not provide adequate service to compete with the railroad. In addition, the International Division of the Eastern Steamship Company served some of the ports served by the *Frank Jones*. Thus ended the only remaining long-distance passenger line in New England owned by a railroad other than the New Haven.[64]

The New Haven had achieved its domination of the coastal lines in southern New England at a very high price. Not only had the financial costs been high, but also the company had lost a considerable amount of good will among the people of New England. This loss of good will would haunt the railroad and in the end defeat the ambitions of J. P. Morgan and Charles S. Mellen. What the New Haven had done along the coast of New England it was also doing in the interior of the region as it purchased trolley and interurban companies. In these transactions it was employing even more reckless financial methods.

Between 1905 and 1907 a most serious challenge was made by Charles W. Morse to the New Haven's coastal monopoly. Because of his unique qualities, ambitions, and financial strength, the struggle between Morse and the New Haven for the control of New England's coastal steamship business was on an unprecedented scale. The outcome would decide the fate of the New England coastal steamship lines.

8. Challenges to the New Haven Monopoly, 1906–12

ON THE evening of 15 September 1905 four men gathered at the Hotel Manhattan in New York City. They were Charles S. Mellen, Charles F. Choate, George M. Miller, and George J. Brush, and they comprised the subcommittee on water lines of the board of directors of the New York, New Haven & Hartford Railroad. The men discussed a proposal drawn up by Mellen for the handling of the steamship lines controlled by the railroad, and drafted an outline for the operations of the steamship lines that was followed as long as the lines continued in existence.[1]

Mellen wanted to establish a cheaper service of the type operated by the Joy Line and use it to prevent competition. To do this, he urged the purchase of the Hartford & New York Transportation Company, which would retain its corporate identity. This was soon accomplished, as described in the previous chapter. He also urged the establishment of lines between New York and the ports of Norwalk, Stamford, and Port Chester. Steamers were being run to these ports which, Mellen believed, interfered with the "railroad's traffic." This proposal was never implemented.

Of greater importance were Mellen's proposals to counter

the establishment of a new express passenger service between Boston and New York by the Metropolitan Steamship Company, hitherto a freight carrier only, and recently purchased by Charles W. Morse. Mellen proposed meeting the competition on its own ground, so to speak, and recommended that the New Haven construct three express freight steamers, costing around $500,000 each, to operate between New York and Providence or Fall River as well as on the outside route to Boston. The committee approved this recommendation and authorized the drawing of plans for three twin-screw freight steamers. Thus was the die cast for the last important struggle for the domination of the New England coastal steamship business.

Charles W. Morse

The man who was challenging the New Haven was Charles W. Morse. Coming from modest beginnings, he had amassed a considerable fortune in the ice business in Maine, and in 1899 had put together the American Ice Company, a trust noted for its corrupt promotion and business methods. From this he turned to banking and shipping.[2]

The Morse Consolidation

The first line to come under Morse control was the Kennebec Steamboat Company, which operated steamers on the Kennebec River and between Bath and Boothbay Harbor. By the end of March 1901 Morse had acquired 1,400 of the 2,500 shares outstanding. His reported purchase price for the one hundred dollar par stock was fifteen dollars a share. The second line he acquired had originally been operated by the Eastern Steamboat Company. Morse was also reported to have an option on a controlling block of stock of the Boston & Bangor Steamship Company, a report denied by the management.[3]

But Morse had already formulated a plan to consolidate the companies operating steamers between Boston, Portland, and New York, and on 8 October 1901 the Eastern Steamship Company was organized under Maine laws. This company was the result of the merger of four profitable properties: the Kennebec Steamboat Company, the Boston & Bangor Steamship Company, the Portland Steamship Company (formerly the Portland Steam Packet Company), and the International Steamship Company. Acquiring these four companies was not as difficult as it might seem, since they were owned by families or a small group of investors, had a nominal capitalization, and had little outstanding debt. The Boston & Bangor was the only one of the companies that was capitalized at more than $300,000; it had $600,000 stock outstanding. Morse had acquired ample financial resources through his American Ice Company and could make attractive offers. He paid $1,730,505.57 for the four companies. The Eastern Steamship Company had an authorized capital stock of $3,000,000 and the same amount in bonds, of which $1,750,000 was issued to pay Morse for the properties. The excess capitalization was needed for building new steamers and acquiring and improving new property.[4]

The reaction of Maine businessmen to the consolidation was a mixture of regret at the loss of local control and anticipation that service and facilities on the lines would soon be improved. It was rumored that Morse was anxious to extend his control to the Maine Steamship Company.[5]

The Eastern Steamship Company proved to be a profitable venture. This was to be expected, since each of the four companies that merged had been earning an average of between 3 and 8 per cent annually. The merger brought an immediate saving of $100,000 a year, which, the management claimed, would have been larger had not the price of fuel risen because of the coal strike in 1902. Within a few years officials of Eastern indicated that the company would be able to pay a 4 per cent annual dividend after deducting all expenses and setting aside sufficient funds for building a new steamer annually. In 1903 and 1904 the company earned annual dividends of 3 per cent and in 1905 and 1906, 4 per cent. Early in 1905 the Eastern Steamship Company purchased the Portland & Rockland Steamboat Company. This gave Eastern a virtual monopoly of Maine business, for the Maine Central Railroad had discontinued the Portland, Mt. Desert & Machias Steamboat Company.[6] Only the Maine Steamship Company was outside the combination. Yet Morse had visions of still greater consolidations, and he continued building his shipping empire. He financed this expansion out of the earnings of the steamship companies and with the backing of several New York banks of which he had gained control.[7]

To strengthen his position in New England, the most suitable property for Morse to control was the Metropolitan Steamship Company, still owned principally by the Whitney family. The company did a prosperous business and had a modern fleet of four steamers. Because its vessels carried no passengers the public was not well acquainted with its operations. Its reputation among shippers, however, was first-rate, and it was considered one of the best-paying lines serving New York. When Morse purchased the company from the Whitneys in the spring of 1905, he acquired four steel freighters plus two ancient wooden ones and some lighters. The floating property was assessed at $461,333. The outstanding capital stock was carried on the books at $500,000. Total capital and property was valued at $1,223,836. For this Morse paid Henry M. Whitney $1,500,000. Calvin Austin, whom Morse made president of the Metropolitan Steamship Company, reported that Morse and Whitney talked only twenty minutes before Whitney agreed to sell.[8]

A few days after the sale Morse formed a new corporation of the same name under Maine laws with a capital stock of $3 million and himself as principal stockholder.[9] The old Metropolitan Steamship Company, incorporated originally in New York and later (1884) in Massachusetts, was dissolved. Morse sold the new stock for $18.33 a share, which netted him $550,000; $1 million in bonds were also sold for ninety-five cents on a dollar, which netted Morse another sizeable profit. The total profit to Morse was $1,500,000. Simultaneously he announced that the Metropolitan Steamship Company would build modern express turbine passenger liners capable of averaging twenty-five knots for service on the outside route between Boston and New York.[10]

By 1906 no one could doubt Morse's ultimate purpose: control of all the major steamship lines operating along the Atlantic and Gulf coasts. In February 1906 he added the Clyde Steamship Company; between that date and the spring of 1907 he acquired the New York & Texas Steamship Company (Mallory Line), the New York & Cuba Mail Steamship Company, and the New York & Porto Rico Steamship Company. Morse also purchased the Hudson Navigation Company, the Citizens Steamboat Company of Troy, and Murray's Line of Troy (a barge line). These companies, along with the Eastern Steamship Company and the Metropolitan Steamship Company, owned ninety-seven steamers, sixty lighters, eight tugs, and six barges.[11]

After acquiring these companies Morse reincorporated them in Maine with greatly increased capital liabilities. The New York & Texas Steamship Company became the Mallory Steamship Company, and the other companies retained their former names. On 1 January 1907 Morse incorporated in Maine the Consolidated Steamship Lines as a holding and operating company. In April and May it took over the majority of the capital stock of the Eastern, Metropolitan, Clyde, and Mallory steamship companies and in June the majority of the stock of the New York & Cuba Mail Steamship Company and the New York & Porto Rico Steamship Company of Maine. The Hudson Navigation Company and the Citizens Steamboat Company of Troy remained outside the combination.[12]

Consolidated Steamship Lines issued $60 million in capital stock (all common) and the same amount in bonds. A call went out to each stockholder of the constituent companies asking them to exchange their stocks at one hundred dollars par value for the same number of shares of Consolidated Steamship Lines at one hundred dollars par, plus the same amount in bonds of the Consolidated. Total assets of the six constituent companies was about $45 million, including the floating equipment, docks, warehouses, and leases, but not the good will. Against this amount stood $120 million in stocks and bonds of the Consolidated plus $24,797,000 of first mortgage or underlying bonds actually issued by the six constituent companies and $2 million in stock not held by Consolidated Steamship Lines.[13] Despite the striking difference in value between the real assets and the amount of capital stock and bonds outstanding, a direct relation between them is difficult to make because of the size of the consolidation. Also, the capitalization was measured by the par value of the stock, which was often far above its real worth. Another factor was the size of the consolidation. Because of its extensive control of coastal and foreign routes, it might generate more business than the total of the companies as independent corporations. Nevertheless, given the fact that the fixed obligations of the Consolidated Steamship Lines totaled annually more than $3,600,000, any financial crisis or sudden reduction in business would have a disastrous impact on its ability to meet these obligations.[14]

The Battle for Control

The pyramiding that Morse accomplished is remarkable. Anyone who could engineer such an amalgamation within this brief period of time merited careful watching. His near monopoly made him suspect in many circles, and nowhere more than among the officers and directors of the New Haven Railroad. They saw his consolidation as a threat to the prosperity of the New Haven coastal lines as well as the railroad itself. Although difficult to measure, another factor of importance was J. P. Morgan's dislike of operators and speculators who challenged his interests. How much Morgan had to do with Morse's eventual downfall is uncertain, but it was probably considerable, for Morse was not only disrupting many New York banks, but also challenging the New Haven, for which Morgan had a special regard.

Despite the impressive collection of steamship lines under Morse's control, several important ones remained outside his consolidation. Two independent companies, the Maine Steamship Company and the Hartford & New York Transportation Company, were purchased by the New Haven before Morse could make a bid. So striking had been Morse's aggrandizement that when Charles C. Goodrich, president of the Hartford & New York Transportation Company, was approached by a representative of the New Haven Railroad about selling out, he was convinced that the gentleman was representing Morse.[15] But the sparring had only begun. Morse, to be certain of controlling the trade north of New York City, had to get control of either the New England Navigation Company or the Merchants & Miners Transportation Company. The latter served Boston, Providence, Philadelphia, Baltimore, Norfolk, and Savannah. Without one or, preferably, both companies he could not exercise the absolute control that he desired.

The New Haven management was aware of the situation and had already taken steps to check Morse. As early as March 1905 the New Haven had had Stevenson Taylor check into the financial condition of the Boston & Philadelphia Steamship Company—also known as the Winsor Line. By January 1907 negotiations were in progress for its purchase. The ostensible reason for purchasing the Winsor Line was to gain control of the waterfront property in Providence between Fox Point and India Point, which was owned by the steamship company. In fact, the purchase was part of a larger plan to check Morse. On 6 February 1907 the New Haven offered $185 a share for a majority of the stock. The offer was accepted, and the New Haven acquired 14,810 out of 15,000 shares at the price offered, plus a $9.25 per share commission to Kidder, Peabody & Company. The purchase was completed on 25 April 1907, with the final price totaling $2,775,000.[16]

In the midst of these negotiations it was announced that Morse had offered $20 million for the steamship properties of the New England Navigation Company, which at the time had an outstanding capitalization of $5 million. Charles S.

Mellen was the only one of the New Haven directors who favored the sale, but he later changed his vote to make the refusal unanimous.[17] Since J. P. Morgan viewed speculators like Morse with a jaundiced eye, Morgan would likely have refused to sell no matter what Morse offered for the steamship lines. Morgan's position was the decisive one. As Mellen aptly stated it: "Wherever Morgan sits on a board [of directors] is the head of the table, even if he has but one share."[18]

In 1914 Mellen testified before the Interstate Commerce Commission that President Theodore Roosevelt had urged that the New Haven refuse to sell its steamship properties to Morse because of Morse's proposed monopoly. Roosevelt in return promised, said Mellen, that during his administration, unless the laws were changed, he would give the New Haven no trouble regarding its ownership of steamship lines.[19]

Refusing Morse's offer, the directors of the New Haven committed themselves to fight him for control of the largest independent coastal line serving New England, the Merchants & Miners Transportation Company. This was one of the oldest companies on the Atlantic coast. It had started operation in 1854 with two steamers on the route between Boston, Norfolk, and Baltimore. In 1873 the company inaugurated the Providence-Baltimore service; in 1876 it added the Baltimore-Savannah line; and in 1900 the Philadelphia-Savannah line. Its fleet of seventeen steamers was modern, and most of them carried passengers and freight. Like the other coastal lines, it handled primarily package freight, merchandise, and some raw materials like cotton and wool. The company had been paying regularly an annual 8 per cent dividend on $2 million worth of capital stock.[20] Whoever controlled this company could effectively dominate the routing of a large amount of traffic between New England and the South. If the New Haven gained control, the Morse combination would be denied a large proportion of traffic along the Atlantic coast, would be subject to raids on its traffic, and would be unable to establish unilaterally its own freight tariffs.[21]

When the New Haven refused Morse's offer for the New England Navigation Company, it was already in a strong position in the bidding for the Merchants & Miners Transportation Company. Merchants & Miners and the New Haven had a common bond in their opposition to the Enterprise Line, which had been threatening both. Charles S. Mellen had also kept the Merchants & Miners officials informed of the progress of the negotiations for the purchase of the Boston & Philadelphia Steamship Company. Mellen was explicit in stating that the New Haven was not attempting an invasion of their territory. He even offered to sell the Winsor Line to Merchants & Miners because the routes of the Winsor Line were complementary to the existing services of the Transportation Company. The proposal was made more attractive by offering it to the Merchants & Miners Transportation Company without profit. Only the Providence wharf would be retained by the New Haven.[22]

Three other factors aided the New Haven in its bid for Merchants & Miners. First, purchasing the Merchants & Miners Transportation Company would protect the existing division on traffic between New England and the South. Second, a considerable amount of the Providence traffic of Merchants & Miners was interchanged with the New Haven; if Morse should gain control, this interchange might be impeded. Third, the management of the Merchants & Miners Transportation Company, according to Joseph C. Whitney, president of the company, "did not believe in Mr. Morse's plans at that time, and we did not care to enter his combination." Whitney favored the purchase of the Winsor Line, which the New Haven was quite willing to sell in return for a traffic agreement and one-half the stock of Merchants & Miners Transportation Company, which would be purchased by the New England Navigation Company. Any division of Merchants & Miners stock would not take place until the capitalization of the company was increased from $2 million to $5 million. In addition, the New Haven would retain the Providence and Fall River terminals of the Winsor Line.[23]

Whitney accepted the New Haven offer, partly because his company was experiencing a shortage of capital that made it difficult to increase its facilities for handling properly the increasing traffic. The New Haven could supply this capital. Transfer of all the securities and properties took place between 1 May and 13 May 1907. To avoid the charge of monopoly, representatives of the New England Navigation Company and the Merchants & Miners Transportation Company drew up an agreement to place the stock of the latter in trust. On 21 May a formal agreement was signed between the New England Navigation Company and Nathaniel W. James, representing the other stockholders. The agreement placed the 25,000 shares owned by the Navigation Company in trust in a Baltimore bank. The Navigation Company could nominate directly only four of the nine directors. No matter how its control was restricted, the fact remained that again the New Haven had checked Morse's plans.[24]

During the first five months of 1907 the New England Navigation Company and the New Haven Railroad had acquired control of three more steamship companies: the Boston & Philadelphia Steamship Company, the Maine Steamship Company, and the Merchants & Miners Transportation Company. The New England coastal steamship lines were now separated into two opposing combinations, each determined to increase its share of business at the expense of the other. After the New England Navigation Company announced that it was going to purchase the Merchants & Miners Transportation Company, a rate war seemed "virtually unavoidable."[25] These two combinations certainly could have coexisted; after 1917 they did so with little difficulty. But given the nature of the three dominant personalities in 1907 —Morse, Mellen, and Morgan—open conflict was practically inevitable. Like European imperialists they enjoyed the prestige and power that accompanied empire building. The cost of creating such systems was of secondary importance; winning the game had precedence. They would brook no interference or challenge to their plans.

The Battle for Patronage

The arena of a particularly fierce and direct contest between the two forces was steamer service between Boston and New York. When Morse purchased the Metropolitan Steamship Company in 1905, he announced that the company would begin to provide passenger as well as freight service on the outside route. It would build modern turbine passenger liners capable of averaging twenty-five knots.[26] Just three and a half months later occurred the meeting of the New Haven subcommittee on water lines at the Hotel Manhattan, and its decision to build express freight steamers. The New Haven had been willing to tolerate and on occasion co-operate with a freight line between Boston and New York, but to see this line threaten its monopoly of the passenger service was too much.

The Metropolitan Steamship Company's first public announcement regarding the construction of the two passenger liners, the *Harvard* and the *Yale*, came in August 1905. The news was received favorably throughout New England, and many observers predicted that the new steamers would capture a fair share of the Boston–New York traffic. During the winter of 1905–6 Mellen and Morse held a meeting at which they discussed the matter of the impending outside passenger service. According to Calvin Austin, Mellen expressed his displeasure about the service, but did not, as was later claimed, threaten to ruin the line.[27]

For his part, Morse was determined to compete with the best service offered by Mellen's New England Navigation Company. When he signed the contract for the two turbine liners with Charles M. Englis, he instructed Englis "to build the ships so that they would be beyond any class of ships heretofore constructed for the reason that this route was a new undertaking and it would be necessary to put vessels there of the class of vessels of the New York, New Haven & Hartford Railroad." No estimate could then be made about the cost. Throughout their construction changes in specifications were made, and the steamers were not completed until the autumn of 1907. Because of Morse's desire to get them into operation as soon as possible they were put in service between New York and Boston with some of the joiner work and painting unfinished. The completion of this work took place during the layover in New York. The final cost of the *Harvard* and the *Yale* was $1,225,000 apiece,[28] which indicates Morse's determination to pursue a desired end whatever the cost.

Meanwhile, three express freighters were being built for the New England Navigation Company. Throughout 1906 and early 1907 there was much speculation about where these new freighters would be used. In February 1906 a statement appeared in the press to the effect that a new outside freight line between Boston and New York would be started using the three steamers. In May 1907 rumors were rife of a deal between Morse and the New Haven to avert a rate war; it was said that Morse would not use the *Harvard* and the *Yale* on the New York–Boston route and that the New Haven would not begin its proposed freight line between these ports. Instead, the new freighters, the *Old Colony*, the *Massachusetts*, and the *Bunker Hill*, would be used on the Fall River and New Bedford lines. This seemed confirmed when the *Massachusetts*, the first of the three to be completed, began operating in freight service on the Fall River Line.[29]

The rumors of an agreement to prevent a rate war had some foundation in fact. On 14 March 1907 Charles W. Morse and Charles S. Mellen had met in Grand Central Station to discuss their differences. At this conference Mellen agreed to sell to Morse the Boston–New York line of the Joy Steamship Company, and the two men agreed to establish identical rates between Boston and New York. Finally, Mellen agreed not to begin the proposed freight line between New York and Boston until Morse put the *Harvard* and the *Yale* in service. Both agreed to confer again before the *Harvard* and the *Yale* began regular service. In early April the New Haven sold the Boston–New York line of the Joy Steamship Company to Morse for $350,000. Morse discontinued its operation. On 3 April, at a conference in New York City, officials of the Metropolitan Steamship Company and the New England Navigation Company agreed on identical freight rates between Boston and New York and other points served by both companies.[30]

If a truce had been made, it was only for a regrouping of forces. Sale of the Joy Line to Morse would enable the New Haven to devote all its resources and energy to the completion of the three new express steamers it was building. Clearly Mellen wanted to be prepared to meet the threat of the *Harvard* and the *Yale* on equal terms. Neither of these men seem to have placed much trust in the other. During June the *Harvard* and the *Yale* were being rushed to completion. The *Yale* was ready first and on 29 June sailed from the wharves of W. & A. Fletcher Company in Hoboken, New Jersey, for Boston. During the summer, while the *Harvard* was being readied, the *Yale* ran between Boston and St. John, New Brunswick, and was a "huge success." The *Harvard* was ready in September, and the New York–Boston service began on 28 September 1907, with the *Yale* leaving from India Wharf in Boston and the *Harvard* from New York. The *Yale* was sold out twenty-four hours before leaving time, and the *Harvard* carried about five hundred passengers. The 292-mile run around Cape Cod took between fourteen and a half and fifteen hours. Each vessel sailed at 5:00 P.M.[31]

The Metropolitan Line continued passenger service until early November, when the *Harvard* and the *Yale* were laid up for the winter. In spite of their success, their operating expenses were high—four thousand dollars a day. Once again rumors circulated, this time indicating that the two steamers would be sent to the Pacific coast. These rumors had some basis. Representatives of Seattle businessmen had approached officials of the New Haven Railroad regarding the removal of the *Harvard* and the *Yale* to the Pacific for service between Seattle and San Francisco. They would pursue the matter only on the condition that the New Haven invest a considerable amount in the scheme. Mellen answered this proposal in his characteristic manner: "I would not . . . put up a dollar on any scheme such as outlined."[32]

The Collapse of the Morse Consolidation

In October 1907 reports were heard that Morse had once again offered to buy the New Haven steamship lines and had been refused.[33] Despite all his activity Morse was on the brink of disaster, for he had overextended his financial resources. In mid-October a panic hit, which forced several of the Morse banks to close and placed the Consolidated Steamship Lines in financial jeopardy. In November the stockholders of the constituent companies decided to take the operation of their companies out of the hands of the Consolidated Steamship Lines. They appointed H. R. Mallory, H. P. Booth, and one other to take over the active management of the separate lines. In an attempt to restore public confidence in the Consolidated Steamship Lines, the directors and managers representing Morse were replaced. These efforts, however, proved fruitless.[34] On 1 January 1908 the company was forced to pass the payment of interest due on its $60 million in collateral trust bonds. The management said that because of the prevailing financial conditions it had been forced to devote its earnings to paying for new steamers recently completed or under construction. On 4 February 1908 the Consolidated Steamship Lines entered receivership. According to current quotations the entire $120 million in stocks and bonds was worth $6 million, or five cents on the dollar. The Metropolitan Steamship Company had been unable to meet its obligations even before this, and its creditors had attached the *Harvard* and the *Yale*.[35]

After the receivers had been appointed, a committee of bondholders drew up a plan of reorganization, which was submitted on 30 June 1908. It divided the holdings into two parts. The four southern companies became the constituent companies of a new combination called the Atlantic, Gulf &

West Indies Steamship Lines. The Eastern Steamship Company and the Metropolitan Steamship Company remained outside this combination.[36]

The Metropolitan Steamship Company

While the Morse lines were struggling with financial crises, the New England Steamship Company, the recently created operating company of the New Haven steamship lines, was preparing to enter the outside Boston–New York route in January 1908. Although there were some doubts as to whether the New Haven would actually carry out this plan, especially after the panic, Calvin Austin, president of the Metropolitan Steamship Company, intended to counter the threat. He learned from New Haven officials that they were planning to use the 1899 tariff for all freight, despite the rate agreement of the previous April. In mid-November 1907 he announced the reduction of freight rates to the 1899 tariff, effective December 1, and increased the number of weekly sailings of his freight steamers. Benjamin Campbell, a New Haven vice-president, wrote to E. F. Atkins, a member of the Boston Business Men's Association, assuring him that Austin's action would not change the intentions of the New England Steamship Company.[37]

In order to mask as much as possible the actual purpose of the new line and to maintain the fiction that its primary purpose was to meet the wishes of the businessmen in Boston, Charles S. Mellen, through Campbell, requested the Business Men's Association to say in a formal resolution that "the [New Haven] line shall receive the good will and earnest support of the various business houses which the association represents." On 11 December such a resolution was passed, and the secretary was instructed to notify the members about the new line and recommend "the new service to their support and patronage."[38] Next, Campbell asked Atkins to have his committee suggest a name for the line that could be used in all its advertising. When no immediate reply was forth-coming, Campbell telegraphed Atkins asking him if "Boston Line" or "Boston Merchants Line" would be acceptable. Atkins replied without delay that the latter would be "very acceptable." On 17 December Campbell notified Atkins by letter that this would be the official title of the line.[39]

On 3 January 1908 the steamer *Bunker Hill* and the dock facilities of the Boston Merchants Line were open for inspection by Boston businessmen who would use the line. R. T. Haskins, Boston freight traffic manager, had arranged to surprise the guests by having a band from one of the Fall River Line steamers to entertain them and serving refreshments.[40] The whole affair was a masterful job of public relations.

After the line had been operating for about three weeks, Louis D. Brandeis, a leading critic of the management of the New Haven Railroad,[41] charged that the Boston Merchants Line was established only to drive the Metropolitan Line out of business. Campbell again wrote Atkins assuring him there was "absolutely no truth in the charge made by Mr. Brandeis. The New Haven had no designs upon the Metropolitan Steamship Company, and never has had." The service was begun "wholly upon its merits and purely as a business proposition." The New Haven, Campbell continued, was utterly indifferent to the future course of the Metropolitan Steamship Company.[42] The letter had all the cordiality and apparent candor that could be expected, but only someone oblivious of recent events could have believed Campbell's assurances, especially in the light of the actions of the New Haven against the Joy Line and the Enterprise Line.

The effect of the new service on the business of the Metropolitan Line was severe. Calvin Austin said several years later that the line "put the Metropolitan out of business very fast." Brandeis was only one of many who were critical of the Boston Merchants Line. Others commented unfavorably on the greed of the New Haven. Nevertheless, the New Haven management seemed willing to allow the Metropolitan Line a share of the business. Neither engaged in further rate cut-

ting, and Calvin Austin announced publicly that his company would not reduce rates.[43]

During the next three years occurred some of the most in-
tricate financial maneuvering ever seen in New England.
Steamships were transferred from one company to another,
new companies were formed, and others were dissolved. By
the spring of 1908 J. P. Morgan and some of his allies had
already reached positions from which they could exert considerable influence in the affairs of the Metropolitan Steamship Company. Charles W. Morse, because of his financial
mismanagement of the several steamship lines and banks,
was forced out of the Consolidated Steamship Lines. With
him went much of the spirit and drive that had characterized
the activities of the company in the years before 1908. In the
autumn of that year he was sentenced to imprisonment for
his corrupt financial activities. Settling matters between the
Metropolitan Steamship Company and the New Haven was
easier once Morse was removed.[44]

In the spring of 1908 concerted efforts were begun to
transfer the *Harvard* and the *Yale* to the Pacific coast. The
Metropolitan Steamship Company continued to operate the
two steamers during the summer seasons of 1908 and 1909,
when they did a fair business.[45] In October 1909 the assets of
Metropolitan Steamship were sold to a new corporation organized expressly for this purpose and known as the Metropolitan Steamship Company of New Jersey. In the meantime,
negotiations on the *Harvard* and the *Yale* were still continu-
ing, and by the spring of 1910 final arrangements had been
made to terminate the service of the two steamers. The negotiations and the resulting arrangements were subject to the
approval of the New Haven management and J. P. Morgan.
On 15 March 1910 the Metropolitan Steamship Company of
Maine was organized; it was controlled by the New Haven
Railroad through some of the subsidiary companies of the
railroad. The Maine company immediately purchased the
four freight steamers and other floating equipment of the
Metropolitan Steamship Company of New Jersey, except for

the *Harvard* and the *Yale*. On 19 March Mellen announced the discontinuance of the Boston Merchants Line, explaining that it had failed to earn operating expenses and that the Metropolitan Steamship Company, having recently been reorganized, was now capable of providing a satisfactory daily service; no longer was there need for two competing lines.[46]

Although the public was unaware of the complicated transactions behind this announcement—the details were not made public until the investigations of 1913 and 1914—rumors were widespread that the departure of the *Harvard* and the *Yale* was imminent.[47] However, during the season of 1910 they again served New England, operated by the Metropolitan Steamship Company of Maine under lease from the Metropolitan Steamship Company of New Jersey. In September, after two and a half years of negotiation, the two steamers were leased to the Pacific Coast Navigation Company. On 1 and 2 October 1910 the *Harvard* and the *Yale* made their last revenue trips between Boston and New York. Within a few weeks they were on their way around Cape Horn to the Pacific. Again the New Haven had succeeded in eliminating a competitor.[48]

President Mellen assured the mayor of Boston that the city would not be without passenger service during the 1911 season. In November 1910 the New Haven announced that the express freighters *Bunker Hill, Massachusetts*, and *Old Colony* were being rebuilt to carry passengers and that they would be ready for service by June 1911.[49] The rebuilding of each vessel cost between $424,000 and $433,000. It was paid for by the Hartford & New York Transportation Company, which had purchased the three freighters from the New England Navigation Company for $600,000 apiece.[50] The alterations necessitated an increase in the capital stock of the Transportation Company, which was made possible by use of funds from the New England Navigation Company. During the season of 1911 the Hartford & New York Transportation Company operated the three steamers; like the *Harvard* and the *Yale*, they had high operating expenses. Later Charles C. Goodrich, president of the Transportation Company, said that steamers of this type could not be used profitably in the New York–Boston service because of the short season and the high operating cost.[51] Plans were being readied, however, to place the conduct of this service in the hands of others.

During the autumn of 1911 the reorganization of the Eastern Steamship Company was begun, and in December a satisfactory plan was agreed upon. A new company, known as the Eastern Steamship Corporation, was chartered in Maine to take over the properties of the Eastern Steamship Company, the Metropolitan Steamship Company of Maine, and the Maine Steamship Company. The directors of the New Haven were quite happy to be rid of the Metropolitan Steamship Company, as long as it was in friendly hands. In order to get rid of it, Mellen had to throw in the highly profitable Maine Steamship Company. As Mellen stated it: "if we threw in that orange [Maine Steamship Company], we could dispose of the lemon [Metropolitan Steamship Company]." The new Eastern Steamship Corporation issued $3,075,000 in common stock, $3 million of 6 per cent preferred stock, and $5,700,000 in bonds. Each holder of twenty shares of Eastern Steamship Company stock with a par value of $2,000 received $1,000 par value of the new common stock, $1,000 par value of the new preferred stock, and $1,000 par value in new 5 per cent bonds of the Eastern Steamship Corporation. Calvin Austin was elected president of the new company.[52]

During February 1912 all assets and property of the Maine Steamship Company—which then owned the *Bunker Hill*, the *Massachusetts*, and the *Old Colony*—were sold to the Eastern Steamship Corporation. In payment the New England Navigation Company received 20,000 shares of Eastern common stock, 15,000 shares of preferred stock, and $2,500,000 par value in bonds. This gave the Navigation Company 35,000 shares out of a total of 91,500 shares in the new corporation.[53] Although the New Haven never seems to have exercised an active voice in the management of the Eastern Steamship Corporation, its interests were always a prominent factor in policy decisions.

Despite the large New Haven interest in the new corpora-

tion, the Boston Chamber of Commerce favored the reorganization because it believed that better service would be furnished between Boston and New York. The Chamber of
Commerce did not, however, like what it considered the excessive capitalization—to support this capitalization might
necessitate an advance in rates.[54] This view was prophetic,
for within a short time the company was in financial difficulty.

This long involved battle to end independent competition
marked the last time that the New Haven attempted to drive
out a competitor by bankruptcy or purchase. When confronted by a new challenge at Providence in the spring of
1910, it used other methods to bring the same result.

The Southern New England Railway

When President Charles M. Hays of the Grand Trunk Railway, which controlled the Central Vermont Railway, had an
opportunity to purchase the New London Steamboat Company in 1901, he declined because he thought it would be
preferable for the Central Vermont to control its own steamers between New London and New York. When the contract
with the New London Steamboat Company expired in 1909,
he organized the Central Vermont Transportation Company,
a wholly owned subsidiary of the Central Vermont Railway.
It operated two freight steamers in connection with the railroad and interchanged traffic only with the railroad.

Like the New Haven Railroad, the Central Vermont "found
it very troublesome" when the steamers were not under absolute railroad control. When a railroad controlled its own
steamers, no problems arose over schedules, maintenance of
the steamers, divisions of the rates, and other similar factors
which can affect business relationships. In addition, the hinterland served by the Central Vermont Railway did not supply many passengers or much high-grade freight. This made
the route unattractive to an independent company.[55]

The Central Vermont Transportation Company handled heavy westbound traffic as part of a differential route to the West in conjunction with the parent Grand Trunk Railway; for most of the relatively few shippers located on the Central Vermont Railway who required New York City delivery of their products, the railroad gave next-morning or second-morning delivery at Pier 29, East River. Little local New London or Norwich traffic moved over the Central Vermont boat line because of its poor facilities for handling team deliveries and the limited amount of traffic between these points and New York.[56] The Central Vermont differential route to the West was of minor significance to most New England manufacturers, since it was not as easy for them to use as other all-rail differential routes.

In general, little notice was paid the Central Vermont until 1910, when the Grand Trunk announced that it was going to construct a new railroad from Palmer, Massachusetts, on the Central Vermont Railway, to Providence. It was to be called the Southern New England Railway. A new steamship line would handle traffic between Providence and New York City. The announcement was enthusiastically received in Providence, which had long been restive under the New Haven monopoly. Almost every businessman in Providence favored the new line. The Rhode Island General Assembly approved the charter; the only opposition came from the New Haven and its supporters. The enthusiasm in Providence was not shared in Boston, since Boston was being bypassed.[57]

The background of the Southern New England is complex. A possible explanation for its construction involved the differential route between New England and the West. The New Haven Railroad and the Canadian Pacific Railway formed a differential route which competed with that of the Central Vermont and the Grand Trunk. The American trunk line railroads forced the New Haven to give up the route with the Canadian Pacific, but the Grand Trunk feared a renewal of the Canadian Pacific–New Haven alliance. It decided to insure its own connections. First the Grand Trunk secured its own water line to New York by the formation of the Central

Vermont Transportation Company. The second step was the building of the rail-water route through Providence. A. W. Currie, who wrote a history of the Grand Trunk, claims that the Southern New England was probably the idea of Charles M. Hays. Hays had tried since 1904 to get access to New York City by obtaining trackage rights over the New York Central and the West Shore railroads or by negotiating agreements with other railroads serving the city; when these efforts failed he made an unsuccessful bid for the New York, Ontario & Western Railroad, which the New Haven took over a few months later. Hays became convinced that only a rail-water route would succeed.

No matter how well justified the new route might have been from an operational standpoint, it was a challenge to J. P. Morgan and the New England monopoly of the New Haven, and thus an exceedingly hazardous enterprise. Throughout 1910 and 1911 the New Haven blocked the Southern New England wherever and however it could, but the popularity of this challenger of the New Haven removed all the obstacles the latter could devise. The state of Rhode Island alone spent $500,000 in and around Providence to provide terminal facilities and wharves for the Southern New England. In May 1912 grading work began with a force of over two thousand men.[58]

While preparations were being made to begin the construction of the railroad, plans were readied for the steamers. In April 1910 the Central Vermont Transportation Company signed a contract with Harlan & Hollingsworth Corporation to construct two combination passenger and freight steamers to operate between Providence and New York. They were to have a speed of twenty knots and carry seven hundred passengers and five hundred tons of freight. These steamers, the *Manhattan* and the *Narragansett*, cost $1,665,253, which the company paid by increasing its capital stock from $200,000 to $1,000,000. It also issued bonds. In November 1913 the ships were delivered complete except for their interior furnishings.[59]

Despite these auspicious beginnings the construction of

the rail line ceased on 12 November 1912; it was resumed intermittently thereafter, but never completed. "Stringency in the European money market" was the official reason for the suspension, but rumors were already circulating that New Haven and Grand Trunk officials were negotiating a traffic agreement. This was confirmed a few weeks later.[60]

Several factors influenced the decision to suspend construction of the Southern New England Railway. Perhaps most important was the death of Hays on the *Titanic*. When he died, the Grand Trunk management showed little enthusiasm for taking on such a determined foe as the New Haven. In addition, the railroad was encountering serious financial difficulties. The Grand Trunk stockholders had never been informed of the details of the venture, and upon Hays's death the board of directors in London began to realize how deeply enmeshed the railroad was in the conflict with Morgan and the New Haven.

The management of the New Haven had showed its determination in September 1911, when the Boston & Maine Railroad, now controlled by the New Haven through the Boston Railroad Holding Company, canceled all through rates with the Central Vermont Railway. This meant a loss to the Central Vermont of about $100,000 annually and forced the rerouting of considerable traffic between New England and New York City that formerly had moved over the Boston & Maine and the Central Vermont. Many shippers were angry about this, because the change meant slower service for industries located along the Boston & Maine.[61] The cancellation made a profound impression in Canada and in London.

A third factor was the attitude of the Canadian government. Ottawa questioned the potential diversion of traffic from Canadian to American ports over the Southern New England. Its concern was natural, since the Canadian government was then subsidizing the construction of a Grand Trunk extension to the Pacific so that Canadian exports and imports could be handled exclusively through Canadian ports. Hays might well have gone ahead with the Southern New England, but his successors had little desire to incur the wrath of Ottawa. Nevertheless, the Grand Trunk management continued to deny that the Southern New England was dead. Construction work continued sporadically until 1916. World War I ended the project.[62] During the war the United States government expropriated the steamers *Manhattan* and *Narragansett;* after the war the Canadian government nationalized the Grand Trunk Railway.

A congressional investigation of the affair, however, served to confirm the suspicions of most New Englanders that collusion had ended the project. When Charles S. Mellen was indicted by a federal grand jury for his role in an agreement with the Grand Trunk to halt further construction, there seemed to be no doubt that this was the reason for the demise of the Southern New England project. But without the guiding spirit of Hays the project had slight chance for success.[63]

The Colonial Line

In June 1910, while the New Haven was concentrating on blocking the Southern New England Railway, another local steamship line commenced operation between Providence and New York City. The Colonial Navigation Company was headed by F. M. Dunbaugh, who had organized the Joy Steamship Company. This time the harassment of Dunbaugh by the New Haven was minor compared to its earlier efforts against him. In part this was the result of a law passed in 1910 that was designed to end the use of fighting lines like the United States Transportation Company. The law provided that in order to restore rates that had been reduced to fight a competing water line, the railroad had to get permission from the Interstate Commerce Commission.

The Colonial Navigation Company had two steamers that it operated in a daily year-round passenger and freight service to New York. Most of its business was local, because the New Haven refused to establish joint passenger and freight rates with the company. By 1913 the Colonial Line had enough business to purchase two more steamers. That same year the company brought a complaint before the Interstate Commerce Commission charging the New Haven with discrimination for its refusal to establish joint freight and passenger rates with the company. In 1910 the commission had been granted power to decide such matters. Not until 1918 did the commission sustain the charge of the Colonial Navigation Company and order the New Haven to enter into joint rates with it.[64]

In a way the order of the commission was really an anticlimax, for the New Haven and its many affiliated companies had long since ceased to dictate to New England. Dry rot had set in well before 1912, but everything seemed to culminate in that and the following year. The great days of the New Haven were over, and by the end of 1913 all New England knew it. Instead of chastising the railroad, New England now had to come to its rescue.

Weaknesses of the New Haven Monopoly

The cause of the eventual collapse of the New Haven monopoly was not any drastic reduction in business, but rather the inability of New England to supply enough business to enable the New Haven and its subsidiaries to meet their fixed obligations. In building the New Haven monopoly, cost had been of minor concern; this attitude resulted in inflated capitalizations that eventually overtaxed the whole system. In addition, Congress had just passed the Panama Canal Act of 1912, which forbade railroads to own any water lines after 1 July 1914 unless the Interstate Commerce Commission found to be operated in the public interest. This placed the New England Steamship Company and the Hartford & New York Transportation Company operations under a cloud and added to the uncertainties confronting the transportation system of New England. Many criticized this provision in the new law, but in the preceding few years such a furor had arisen over the large proportion of coastal tonnage controlled by railroads that Congress felt constrained to pass the act.[65]

While the New Haven was acquiring its steamship lines, it was also enlarging its trolley and interurban holdings and gaining control of the Boston & Maine Railroad and through it the Maine Central Railroad. The New York, Ontario & Western Railroad and the Rutland Railroad were controlled through stock ownership, and the New Haven had a ten-year working agreement with the New York Central Railroad to divide the profits or losses of the Boston & Albany Railroad.[66] By 1912 the New Haven had amassed a transportation system the like of which the region has never seen. The cost, however, was far too high.

On 30 June 1903, the year Charles S. Mellen became president of the New Haven, the capitalization of the railroad was about $79 million in stock, and the bonded debt was about $14 million. On 30 June 1912 the amount of stock outstanding was $179,726,200, and the bonded debt totaled $242,053,041. Of this increase, $136 million was spent for improvements to equipment or property, while the remainder was expended outside actual railroad operations. The New England Navigation Company underwent similar increases in its capitalization and indebtedness. On 30 June 1906 its capital stock was placed on the books of the New Haven at $5,948,000 (par value $5 million) and the bonded debt was $2.5 million; on 30 June 1912 outstanding stock totaled $56,917,399 (par value $53 million) and the bonded debt was $4,275,000 plus over $7 million in short-term notes held by the New Haven. This increase reflected little significant addition to the physical assets of the company. Most of the additional capital had been used to finance the acquisition of railroads, power companies, trolley lines, and steamship lines, and the construction of some new rail lines and steamers.[67]

The Navigation Company had undergone several changes in which it alternated between being just a holding company and being a holding and operating company. It operated the steamship lines until April 1907, when it sold them to the

Consolidated Railway Company, which in May merged with the New York, New Haven & Hartford Railroad Company to form a new company called the New York, New Haven & Hartford Railroad Company. In June this company leased the steamship lines to a new operating company called the New England Steamship Company, and on 29 September 1907 the railroad sold them outright to the steamship company. The New England Steamship Company operated the water lines until 31 January 1908, when it sold them back to the New England Navigation Company. The Navigation Company continued to operate the steamship lines until 30 June 1912, when they were again sold to the New England Steamship Company, which had been revived as an operating company. These sales became very involved as funds were transferred from one company to another, and each transaction permitted the issuing of new securities on which someone made a profit. They in part explain the increased capitalization of the New England Navigation Company.[68] Each increase meant that a larger amount of fixed charges had to be met each year. Throughout these years the actual operation of the steamship lines remained basically unaffected.

The whole issue of the New Haven monopoly became bound up with state rivalries and politics.[69] The most controversial point was New Haven control of the Boston & Maine, which Louis D. Brandeis and those supporting his position watched with growing hostility. Before long they viewed suspiciously everything the New Haven owned, controlled, or operated, regardless of its merits, including the steamship lines.[70] Many aspects of the financial manipulation of the steamship lines could be questioned. For example, in June 1908 there suddenly appeared in the accounts of the New England Navigation Company an entry of $3,506,250 under the label "good will." Another example was the sale by the United States Transportation Company to the Navigation Company of the steamers *Rhode Island* and *Connecticut* for $932,000 in March 1908. In August 1910 they were sold for scrap, with the New England Navigation Company receiving $9,000 for the *Rhode Island* and $8,500 for the *Connecti-*

cut.[71] Some justification might be found for an entry of good will, which was a real asset of the Fall River Line, but not for the rapid change in value of the two steamers.

Yet the people of New England were split over the issue of New Haven control, despite the ruthless methods sometimes employed by the Mellen-Morgan management. Some of the division was the result of regional rivalry. In Maine the Boston & Maine–New Haven merger was favored because the state felt that the New Haven might provide better service than the Boston & Maine had. In Portland, businessmen were convinced that Boston was preferred over Portland. Railroad magazines saw many benefits in the consolidation, as did other more general publications.[72] In Massachusetts itself, where the issue had to be settled by the legislature, the state was sharply divided into two camps. When the merger did not bring the benefits its proponents claimed it would, those supporting Brandeis gained the dominant positions.

To a stranger traveling over the New Haven system in 1912 its achievements were impressive, but unrest was growing because of its shortcomings, especially on the rail lines. Only the operation of the steamship lines escaped the general criticism, primarily because they allowed shippers to circumvent the congested terminals on the rail lines. The investigations that lasted from 1913 to 1916 were to prove this conclusively. The deteriorating economic situation during 1913 and 1914 was to bring a crisis to the New Haven system. The trolley lines had been purchased at the peak of their prosperity; by 1912 the automobile already was beginning to reduce their revenues.

All this, combined with several serious accidents and questionable financial practices, brought the issues to a head, and the Interstate Commerce Commission began an official investigation of rates and service in the New England area. This marked the beginning of the end of the New Haven monopoly.

9. The Decline of the
Coastal Lines, 1912–56

WHEN CHARLES S. MELLEN testified before the Interstate Commerce Commission in the spring of 1914, he was asked if he had consciously planned to secure a monopoly of transportation in New England. He answered affirmatively and added: "I came pretty near doing it." He also remained convinced that such a monopoly would benefit the region.[1] Yet whatever benefits the monopoly might have brought to the area, the Mellen management had effectively alienated most of New England by the methods it used in obtaining this monopoly. The management seemed so insensitive to public opinion that friends of the New Haven were sometimes hard pressed to justify its actions and policies.

The Investigations of the New Haven Railroad

The monopoly was supposed to bring better service and lower rates to New England and thus enable its businessmen to meet competition from the rest of the country. However, during 1911 and 1912 "numerous and persistent" complaints were made to the Interstate Commerce Commission regarding New England railroads, especially their freight service.

As a result, the commission opened the New England Investigation, with hearings beginning in May 1912.[2] The investigators heard many shippers testify that rates had increased on the coastal lines after the New Haven had gained an interest in them. Others found service slower and subject to unexplained delays. Many also protested the discontinuance of through service over the Boston & Maine and the Central Vermont.[3] Witnesses also made public some of the financial affairs of the railroad, about which Louis D. Brandeis had raised questions as early as 1907. Brandeis, who had represented the Boston Fruit & Produce Exchange in the hearings on freight service, later appeared in his own behalf to attack the financial dealings and raise doubts about the veracity of the New Haven management.[4] The testimony of the accountants working for the commission and the testimony of New Haven officials, including Mellen, showed that funds had been misused. The evidence made clear some of the dangers of banker management of railroads.[5]

Eventually the New England Investigation was to conclude that passenger service in New England was excellent. However, it did not deal with the question of safety. A series of accidents to New Haven passenger trains during the last three months of 1912 heightened public criticism of the maintenance policies of the railroad and its continued use of wooden passenger cars. Then in December 1912 Mellen and some officials of the Grand Trunk Railway were indicted by a federal grand jury on charges of violating the antitrust laws in halting the construction of the Southern New England Railway. And in the spring of 1913, with the death of J. P. Morgan, Mellen lost his principal supporter. Confronted with these troubles, with declining earnings, and with the hostility of most of the press in New England, Mellen and those closest to him had no choice except to resign. By July 1913 Mellen, who was president of the New Haven, Boston & Maine, and Maine Central railroads, had announced his resignation from all three. He was replaced as president of the New Haven by Howard Elliott, who had been president of the Northern Pacific Railroad. In the summer of 1913 the reaction in railroad circles toward Mellen was fairly sympathetic. Many believed that the basic difficulty lay in his personality. He was called "the last of the railway czars," but his policies were considered basically correct.[6]

With the change in the upper echelons of the New Haven management, public hostility toward the road lessened. Howard Elliott gave the Interstate Commerce Commission complete co-operation. Mellen became rather embittered. In an interview published in the *Boston Post* on 9 November 1913 he claimed that he had had nothing to do with the financial policies of the New Haven. Charles A. Prouty, a member of the commission, observed that this was an example of what happens "when thieves fall out." While testifying before the commission in 1914, Mellen placed much of the blame for the collapse of the New Haven on J. P. Morgan.[7]

Because the New England Investigation had revealed considerable misuse of New Haven funds, the United States Senate in February 1914 passed a resolution ordering the Interstate Commerce Commission to conduct a new investigation of the New Haven. The resolution granted the commission authority to examine the records of the entire New Haven system, authority it had not had in the New England Investigation. This time several directors and others involved in the financial transactions testified. Some of the testimony was probably of doubtful authenticity, but in connection with evidence gathered by agents of the commission from the New Haven files, it showed the mismanagement and corruption that took place between 1903 and 1913. The entire story will probably never be known, for with the death of J. P. Morgan only Mellen's account of these years was heard. Projects like the New York, Westchester & Boston Railroad were of doubtful value from the beginning; their purchase and construction costs were all out of proportion to their value to the New Haven. The tactics the New Haven management used to build this monopoly were similar to those employed against the Joy and Enterprise lines. The only difference was that it cost far more to accomplish these ends in the rail and trolley acquisitions.[8]

In June 1914 the Interstate Commerce Commission published its report on the financial transactions of the New Haven, and it was greeted with muted enthusiasm by some and near hostility by others. Many feared that the report would impair further the already shaky financial position of the New Haven system, while others believed that the commission had taken the testimony too much at face value. Some of the same persons who had been sympathetic toward Mellen when he resigned in 1913 now changed their opinion. The *Commercial and Financial Chronicle* stated that "Mr. Mellen cannot get rid of his responsibility by shifting the blame upon others [sic] shoulders; least of all on a dead man [J. P. Morgan]."⁹ The *Railway Age Gazette* likewise altered radically its previously favorable opinion of Mellen and his place in New England railroad history.¹⁰ Despite the criticism of Mellen and his testimony, the commission came under fire for its report on the New Haven. Critics claimed that the commission had "sensationalized already known facts," accepted a large amount of testimony at face value, and undertaken its examination of the New Haven a few years too late.¹¹

The criminal trial of the New Haven directors, charged with violating the antitrust act of 1890, lasted from mid-October 1915 to early January 1916, and resulted in a verdict of innocent for six and a divided jury on the remaining five directors. This trial concluded the financial investigation and prosecution of criminal charges brought by the government against the New Haven and its former management, but additional private suits lasted several more years. Mellen himself escaped prosecution. In spite of these proceedings, the primary concern of the new management was restoring the financial health of the New Haven. The railroad passed its dividend in 1914 for the first time in years; it did not pay another until 1928.¹²

Perhaps the most serious fault in building the New Haven monopoly was the almost complete absence of any sense of public responsibility on the part of the Mellen management. This was quite evident in its efforts to eliminate water competition; it was more apparent in the methods used to secure the Boston & Maine Railroad.[13] In many instances railroad officials seemed determined to secure, maintain, and extend the monopoly whatever the cost in money and in the loss of good will. The loss of public support, more than anything else, insured that the slightest faltering in the fortunes of the monopoly would bring the wrath of all New England upon the Mellen regime.

The Dismemberment of the New Haven Monopoly

Financial collapse of the New Haven system accompanied the partial dismemberment of the monopoly ordered as a result of the antitrust action brought by the Department of Justice.[14] The traffic agreement between the New Haven and the New York Central Railroad was canceled on 1 February 1914. A week earlier all New Haven representatives had been withdrawn from the boards of directors and managements of the Boston & Maine and Maine Central railroads. The Department of Justice ordered the sale by 1 July 1914 of the stock of the Merchants & Miners Transportation Company, and within three years from that date the sale of the stock of the Eastern Steamship Corporation. In the interim the New Haven could not exercise the voting rights that this stock conferred. The trolley lines in western Massachusetts and in Vermont were to be sold within five years of 1 July 1914. The trolley companies in Connecticut and Rhode Island were given managements that were independent of the railroad, but the New Haven did retain its financial interest in these companies. These trolley investments in southern New England were to be disposed of as soon as possible, but this provision was never carried out.[15]

When the Interstate Commerce Commission opened its investigation of the steamship lines controlled by the New Haven, the Merchants & Miners Transportation Company and the Eastern Steamship Corporation were not included in the New Haven petition. The Merchants & Miners stock was sold at a loss of over $3.5 million. The Eastern Steamship Corporation was already in financial difficulty because it had been unable since 1913 to earn its fixed charges.[16]

The Investigation of the New Haven Boat Lines

The Interstate Commerce Commission investigation of the New Haven steamship lines, referred to as "Steamer Lines on Long Island Sound," began in 1914. Almost from the beginning widespread support was evident for railroad operation of the lines of the New England Steamship Company and to a lesser extent for the Hartford & New York Transportation Company.[17] Against this support were aligned the attorneys of the commission and the Department of Justice. The attorneys for the Department of Justice concentrated their argument on the issue of monopoly. They claimed that "the continued operation of these lines" would "exclude, prevent, or reduce competition within the meaning of this [Panama Canal] Act." The Department of Justice did not oppose operation by the New Haven of the New Bedford, Martha's Vineyard & Nantucket Steamboat Company, the line to Block Island, the Newport & Wickford Steamboat Company, or the ferry between New Bedford and Fairhaven. In their presentation the United States attorneys took slight notice of the fact that the New Haven originally was far more interested in the railroads that owned or controlled the steamboat lines than the steamboats themselves.[18] In discussing the independent companies purchased outright by the New Haven, the circumstances of the purchases were seldom made completely clear. Some of the companies, like the Narragansett Bay Line, were apparently started solely to force the New Haven to buy them out.

Adrian H. Boole, one of the attorneys for the Interstate Commerce Commission, had long been hostile toward railroad ownership of steamship lines. He termed the policy of permitting this "a pernicious one" because it created "monopoly in transportation."[19] Throughout the hearings Boole continually returned to the issue of competition and claimed that divorcement of the Sound lines from New Haven control would bring a return of competition. He apparently ignored evidence indicating that in the past, competition between steamship lines themselves and between steamship lines and railroads had brought instability to New England transportation. Faced with competing industries in other regions of the country, New England businessmen could afford no instability in transportation. In his investigation of the files of the New Haven and its controlled companies, Boole found considerable damaging evidence on the tactics employed by the Mellen regime to eliminate competitors, but hardly anything disparaging about the service on the lines operated by the New England Steamship Company. Boole did not represent the official position of the commission; he was employed to look up the facts, and his testimony was that of a witness for the commission. Nevertheless, he and Alexander H. Elder, the other attorney for the commission, placed most of their emphasis on the restoration of the pre-1880 type of competition, a form of competition which most businessmen in New England using the Sound lines testified they did not wish restored.[20]

When the second stage of the hearings on the steamer lines opened, in February 1916 in New York City and a few days later in Boston, attorneys representing over two hundred firms throughout New England and in the New York City area asked permission to intervene on behalf of the New Haven. Their pleas were granted.[21] From the outset the New Haven maintained that the rail-water service dated from the earliest days of New England railroad operation and that the Sound lines had long been owned by or dependent upon their railroad connections. Representatives of the railroad and the New England Steamship Company testified on matters of service, safety, co-ordination and co-operation between the railroad and the steamship lines, the high quality of the steamers, and the need for the service on the part of New England shippers. They emphasized one point again and again: if divorcement were ordered by the commission, the railroad would do its utmost to send as much traffic as possible to New York by rail so that it could retain the maximum amount of revenue for itself.[22]

All the interveners, who represented the Boston Chamber of Commerce, the Providence Chamber of Commerce, the Merchants' Association of New York, the New York Produce Exchange, the Connecticut Chamber of Commerce, the Fall River Cotton Manufacturers' Association, the New England Paper & Pulp Traffic Association, and many more individual corporations and trade associations, testified to the excellent quality and dependability of the rail-water service.[23] Few expressed any hostility toward the Mellen management, and all appeared far more interested in a continuation of the existing service than in punishing the railroad for its recent sins. Most were quite emphatic in stating their belief that good service was far more essential to the citizens of New England than the often illusory benefits that competition might bring.[24] They were supported by many newspapers and periodicals within and without the transportation business.[25]

The opposition to the New Haven was barely heard above those favoring the railroad. Considering the dearth of opposition it was surprising to find two vocal antagonists at Providence. They seemed at least as concerned with the misconduct of the Mellen regime as with the importance of rail ownership of the Sound lines. It is perhaps significant that neither was in a business that required prompt and dependable delivery to New York City and both could team or truck their shipments to the docks. One of them, William H. Harris, Jr., charged that the New Haven had considerable influence in the Providence Chamber of Commerce and that many shippers in the city were afraid to testify before the commission because they feared retaliation by the New Haven. The Chamber of Commerce emphatically denied these charges. Those from other sections of New England opposing continued New Haven operation of the Sound lines were less hostile than the gentlemen from Providence. One opposed such ownership on principle because he represented a group favoring public ownership of utilities.[26]

Despite these complaints, the evidence presented by Adrian H. Boole, and the opposition of the Department of Justice, the majority of the Interstate Commerce Commission ruled on 10 July 1918 that the New Haven Railroad could continue to operate its steamship lines and car float services in New York Harbor. It concluded that the steamship lines were "being operated in the interest of the public and are of advantage to the commerce and convenience of the people." The commission noted that under the then wartime conditions independent ownership and operation of the steamship lines was impossible because of the disruption it might cause. Should these conditions change, however, the commission reserved the right to reopen the investigation and review its decision to grant the New Haven petition for continued operation of its steamship lines.[27]

The Central Vermont and Maine Central Boat Lines

The Central Vermont Railway and the Maine Central Railroad also had to petition the Interstate Commerce Commission for permission to continue the operation of their steamers. The Central Vermont, like the New Haven, had the support of the shippers who utilized its service. The differential route to the West was especially valued. Adrian H. Boole again represented the commission, and he took the same negative position in the matter of railroad ownership. Boole maintained that the railroads were not aggressive enough in securing traffic, a charge that was denied by the representatives of the Central Vermont. Despite the relatively minor objections of Boole, the commission unanimously agreed that the Central Vermont Transportation Company was being operated in the public interest. It also granted permission for the Transportation Company to operate steamers between Providence and New York in connection with the Southern New England Railway.[28]

The Maine Central application encountered little difficulty except from a few local residents on Mount Desert Island who desired better winter service. Again Boole represented the commission, and this time he attacked the railroad for discontinuing the service of the Portland, Mt. Desert & Machias Steamboat Company. Here too the commission approved unanimously the continued ownership and operation of the Frenchman's Bay and Penobscot Bay services. Had the Maine Central withdrawn its steamers, equivalent service would have been unavailable.[29]

The Reorganization of the Eastern Steamship Corporation

The New Haven and Boston & Maine railroads were not the only New England transportation companies that encountered financial difficulties in 1913 and 1914. During this period the Eastern Steamship Corporation failed to earn its fixed charges, and in October 1914 receivers were appointed. The receivers were unable to solve its financial difficulties. Thus in September 1916 the Maine courts ordered the sale of the assets of the corporation.[30]

The receivership of the Eastern Steamship Corporation forced a change in the federal court ruling that the New Haven Railroad could not use the voting power of its Eastern stock. In April 1916 the United States District Court for the Southern District of New York ruled that the railroad could participate in the reorganization of the Eastern Steamship Corporation because it was deemed essential that the New England Navigation Company, owner of a large amount of Eastern Steamship Corporation debentures, be protected from serious loss. Any interest in the new corporation emerging after the reorganization was to be subject to the same provisions, as were the holdings of the Eastern Steamship Corporation.[31]

The sale of the properties of the Eastern Steamship Corporation took place on 4 January 1917 and brought $3,366,000. The purchasers assumed the liabilities of the liquidated corporation. On 23 January 1917, in Kittery, Maine, the new owners held the first directors' meeting of a company styled Eastern Steamship Lines, Inc. This corporation had an authorized capital stock of $6 million, and it operated all the services of the liquidated company.[32] During the first year and a half of its existence it sold to the federal government for war service the *Bunker Hill*, the *Massachusetts*, and the *Old Colony*, and the four freight steamers that had formerly belonged to the Metropolitan Steamship Company. The government paid for these seven steamers more than they had originally cost the Eastern Steamship Corporation. Their loss meant considerable curtailment of regular service, including the suspension of the Portland–New York line and most of the service on the lines in Maine.[33] On the positive side, the sale of these steamers at such favorable prices enabled the new company to emerge from the war in excellent fiscal condition.

On 14 July 1919 the directors of the Eastern Steamship Lines authorized the purchase of 18,750 shares of Eastern preferred stock owned by the New Haven Railroad. It was purchased outright for $890,625.[34] Thus ended the last vestige of New Haven control that had originated in the fight with Charles W. Morse and the battle over the *Harvard* and the *Yale*.

The Coastal Lines during World War I

The last great era for the New England coastal steamship lines came during World War I. They proved their value by circumventing the unbelievable congestion in the port of New York, where facilities for handling merchandise and package freight were utterly inadequate. Many railroads had to place embargoes on freight consigned to the port, but even then freight cars backed up scores of miles waiting for ships to load their contents.[35] The congestion that had periodically plagued the port long before the war now reached crisis proportions. The situation in New York and elsewhere finally forced the federal government to take over the operation of the railroads of the country. The Interstate Commerce Commission acknowledged the value of the steamship lines in this situation. The congestion at New York was one of the principal factors influencing its favorable decision on New Haven ownership of the Sound lines. During the war the co-ordination was especially important.[36]

Ironically, it was these same conditions that speeded the acceptance of a quite new mode of transportation that was to revolutionize the whole transportation industry. Many businessmen utilized the motor truck because they could not obtain delivery by rail. Once they realized the flexibility motor trucks offered, many abandoned or greatly reduced their shipments by rail. By 1916 the truck was used in New England for hauling freight as far as fifty miles; in local hauling its use had been extensive for several years. During 1917 and 1918 the overtaxed railroads welcomed any relief from the congestion and they themselves used trucks to move freight. The success of these movements by railroads and shippers made acceptance of motor trucks far more rapid than otherwise would have been possible.[37] Only the most skeptical could doubt that these vehicles were the wave of the future. The motor truck was something that neither the railroads nor the steamship lines could successfully fight. In its early stages it was especially well adapted to the carriage of the type of merchandise and package freight that comprised more than half the tonnage carried on the steamers.[38]

Added to the problem confronting the steamship lines was the increased use of the automobile. Those lines carrying a large number of tourists were most susceptible to encroachments by the automobile. New England, with the short distances between its towns, was ideally suited to automobile travel. In 1914 and 1915 the Boston & Maine Railroad reported that passenger revenues in the resort regions served by the railroad had been reduced by the increased use of the passenger automobile and the jitney.[39]

The Coastal Lines in the 1920s and 1930s

The decade of the 1920s was a time of trouble for New England railroads and steamship lines. The movement of freight via the Sound lines, which had seemed so promising in 1915 and 1916, had deteriorated rapidly by 1920, when the federal government returned the New England railroads and the steamship lines of New England Steamship Company to their owners. For railroads and steamship companies the period between 1920 and 1940 was one of continual readjustment to new forms of competition. These companies vainly attempted to retain a reasonable share of the freight and passenger business that was being lost to trucks, busses, and automobiles.

The problem facing the coastal lines and the railroads was twofold: first, they faced the competition of bus lines and unregulated trucks as well as the increased use of the automobile; second, the truckers were competing with the railroads and steamship lines for a smaller amount of tonnage, as many long-established manufacturing firms either closed down or moved outside of New England. The railroads and steamships had additional handicaps because of the short distances between New England markets, the reasonably good network of roads in the region, and the flexibility the motor truck gave to the shipper. In 1921 the steamship lines of the New Haven Railroad carried almost 50 per cent less freight (over one million tons less) than in 1917. During the rest of the decade the decline of tonnage continued, though not as rapidly.[40] Freight revenue remained relatively high until 1921, but this only reflected rates that were much higher than before the war. After 1921, freight rates declined, as did the percentage of high-grade freight carried on lines of the New England Steamship Company. In an attempt to keep the boats loaded the Sound lines began interchanging a considerable amount of freight with the railroads at New York City. Before the war, because of the large amount of local and export freight carried by the steamers, they had carried very little freight of this type. Other freight formerly carried by the Sound lines of the New Haven now moved via Eastern Steamship Lines or the Central Vermont route.[41]

To aid in the competition for traffic, the New Haven Railroad organized the New England Transportation Company as a wholly owned subsidiary of the railroad. It was authorized to perform highway service for the transportation of passengers, freight, mail, and express. Begun in August 1925 as a bus operation, the company inaugurated truck service in 1929. Common ownership enabled the close co-ordination of highway service with the rail and water lines. Trucks and busses also were substituted for unprofitable rail service, thereby saving the railroad substantial expense. In 1930 the substitution of busses for trains had saved the New Haven approximately $1.2 million a year. The use of trucks by the New England Transportation Company had brought back to the railroad some of the less-than-carload freight previously lost to independent truckers.[42]

Added to the troubles of the New Haven and its water lines was the loss of a large number of through Boston–New York passengers to Eastern Steamship Lines, which had constructed two new steamers for this route to replace the *Bunker Hill* and the *Massachusetts*. The steamers used the Cape Cod Canal, and during the 1920s this became a very popular route. The loss was felt most by the Fall River Line. Except for 1923, when a shopmen's strike on the New Haven Railroad forced many passengers to the steamship lines, and 1927, when a sizeable increase was noted, the decline in the number of through and local passengers traveling on the water lines of the New England Steamship Company was steady. Only the summer passenger service on the New Bedford Line ran counter to this trend, primarily because the steamers connected with the boats to Martha's Vineyard and Nantucket. Both islands were growing in popularity as summer resorts.[43]

The management of the New Haven took other measures in an attempt to arrest the decline in freight tonnage. Between 1916 and 1930 the New England Steamship Company spent over $218,000 on mechanical freight-handling equipment to improve the speed and efficiency of loading and unloading the steamers. The company installed the equipment at the Sound ports as well as the piers in New York City. Nothing helped. By 1930 it was no longer necessary to operate a separate freight steamer on the Fall River Line. The passenger boat could now handle all the tonnage. The New London (Norwich) Line was operated after October 1929 with one steamer instead of two.[44]

In spite of claims that Eastern Steamship Lines was taking passengers and freight from the Sound lines of the New Haven, it too was feeling the impact of the decline of New England industry—especially in textiles—and the use of the motor truck and automobile. The cotton trade to Boston and Portland dropped sharply in 1926 and 1927; after 1924 the service between Rockland and Bar Harbor was operated at a "very substantial loss." In 1927 Eastern abandoned service on the Kennebec River.[45]

In 1931 Eastern Steamship Lines founded its own trucking subsidiary to provide pickup and delivery service for less-than-carload lots from various shippers for forwarding on the steamers. Although it may have slowed the rate of decline, it could not check the decline in traffic, especially on the shorter routes like that between Portland and Boston. Eastern Steamship Lines had its most profitable years in 1929 and 1930. Thereafter a deterioration of revenues and business set in, and within a few years the company abandoned several lines.[46]

All the coastal lines were being hurt by increased operating costs, particularly in terminal expenses. Unlike the railroads, the steamship companies had to bear the cost of handling all their tonnage, and during the 1930s the wages and overtime paid to longshoremen rose substantially. Added to this were increases in the price of fuel and supplies, and increased wages and overtime pay to operating personnel. Because the coastal lines competed directly with the railroads and unregulated trucks, they could not raise their rates, for these rates already were close to or identical with those of the competition. Any increase would have been more than offset by a permanent loss of business.[47]

Retrenchment and Abandonment

In effect, the only solution for the independent and railroad-controlled coastal lines was retrenchment. In 1920 the New England Steamship Company discontinued passenger service on the New Haven and Bridgeport lines. Next to go were the redundant operations. The Newport and Wickford Line ended service in 1925 and the Merchants Line to Bridgeport in 1926. This was followed by the abandonment of the Bay State Line to Providence in February 1931. Despite the refurbishing of the steamers, business continued to decline on the Hartford Line, forcing its suspension in the autumn of 1931. The New London (Norwich) Line followed in 1934. The death knell of the Sound line service operated by the New England Steamship Company came in July 1937, when a series of strikes occurred on several of its steamers. The parent New Haven Railroad was already in receivership when the trustees announced that all steamship service between New England and New York City was being suspended. Only service between New Bedford and the offshore islands was continued. In 1946 the New England Steamship Company sold its remaining steamers to an independent company and surrendered its certificate of convenience and necessity to the Interstate Commerce Commission. The once mighty fleet of the New Haven Railroad sailed no more.[48]

The other New England coastal lines acted in a similar manner. The Maine Central Railroad discontinued its steamer service in April 1931. Eastern Steamship Lines ended service on the Portland-Boston line in 1932. Service between Bar Harbor and Rockland was discontinued in 1934 and that between Boston and Bangor in 1935. The company suspended all passenger service between Portland and New York in 1936, although a weekly summer service was operated in 1939 because of the New York World's Fair.[49]

With the outbreak of war in Europe in 1939 and the resulting demand for shipping by the federal government, it was only a matter of time before the vessels of the coastal lines would be chartered or purchased for war service. Thus, between 1940 and 1942 the remaining New England coastal lines, except for the Central Vermont Transportation Company, ceased operations. The Colonial Navigation Company made the last passenger run between Providence and New York in March 1942. It was the last in New England.

In spite of assurances that service would be restored after the war, the outlook for the coastal lines in 1946 was bleak. Operating and terminal costs were prohibitive, and the prewar habits of shippers and travelers were broken. The Central Vermont line lasted until 1946. Eastern Steamship Lines restored summer service between Boston and Yarmouth, which it operated until 1954.[50] But World War II marked the virtual end of coastwise service in New England. The last link with the past dissolved in 1956, when the stockholders of Eastern Steamship Lines, Inc., voted to liquidate the corporation.

The effects of World War II, however, only accelerated and did not cause the demise of the coastal lines. The impossible situation they faced was vividly stated in the annual report of Eastern Steamship Lines for 1940. Since the federal government had chartered the steamers that had been employed in the New York–Portland service, the line had had to be suspended. The report saw little promise for the future: "This service has recently been enjoying the heaviest freight tonnage in its history, but with the increased volume there has been an increased loss, because of the lack of balance between low average freight rates and the highest operating costs in the history of the line."[51] Given this hopeless situation and with no way to reduce labor costs, which then represented about two-thirds of all operating expenses, the suspension or abandonment of service was the only solution for these lines. Of the companies surviving until 1946 none reestablished service on a permanent basis.

It cannot be denied that the railroad-controlled coastal steamship lines provided an essential service to New England. The Maine Central Railroad, the Central Vermont Railway, and the New Haven Railroad and its predecessors furnished a type of service that would have been difficult, if not impossible, for an independent steamship company. The need for this type of operation changed over the years, but as long as the service was economically feasible it continued.

What began in southern New England as separate extensions of local railroads to New York City evolved into a highly sophisticated rail-water system. Until at least 1880 the passenger business of the Sound lines was often more important than the freight business, but thereafter several companies built freight steamers to serve the rapidly growing industrial area of southern New England. In Maine the Maine Central Railroad recognized that easy access to the state meant more travel, and it entered the steamboat business to bring more tourist business to its rail lines.

The co-ordination between rail and water lines was excellent, particularly after 1890. Because they controlled these steamship lines, the managements of the railroads did their utmost to work closely with them. With access to larger financial resources the railroads could construct larger and safer steamers than would have been possible for most independent companies. The Sound lines under railroad control maintained modern fleets and often were in the vanguard in adopting technological and safety advances. The steamers were kept clean, and the standards of service on the Fall River Line were unexcelled anywhere in the nation. The public liked the service, and before 1900 few advocated the divorcement of the steamship lines from railroad ownership.

In the 1890s New England began to encounter economic competition from other regions, and the Sound lines aided New England industry in meeting this competition. In the 1870s the textile industry, and later other industries, looked to New York City as their principal market. New York was not only an important manufacturing center, but also the nation's principal export center. Its topography, however, made rail delivery slow and expensive; steamship service to Manhattan was faster and more dependable than rail service. Thus the unique combination of New York topography and the complementary nature of New England industry made the rail-water lines the natural routes for a large percentage of the high-grade manufactured goods produced in New England. Before the advent of the motor truck these routes were the only satisfactory ones. They also enabled the factories, wholesalers, and retailers in New York City to reduce inventories, which was important in an area where warehouse space was scarce and costly.

After 1900 New England faced increasingly severe competition from industries in other regions seeking to capture the New York market. The New Haven rail lines could not handle much additional freight because the yards and main line were already carrying close to their capacity. Passenger trains constituted a large percentage of train mileage, which made it almost impossible to add additional freight service. The Sound lines circumvented these difficulties.

In New York the New Haven Railroad modernized its freight-handling facilities and at the Sound ports provided large gangs for expeditiously loading and unloading the steamers. Shippers who testified during the investigations of the New England transportation situation were almost unanimous in asserting that both the New Haven and the Central Vermont steamship lines were well operated and vital to the New England economy. All impartial evidence supports this view.

Granting the need for good steamer service to New York, the question still remains whether the New Haven steamship monopoly was advantageous. Here too the answer, with a few qualifications, must be affirmative. Inherent in large size are savings impossible for the small corporation. The New Haven, with its large fleet, always had spare boats. A large fleet also meant better utilization and maintenance schedules. Control of all the principal Sound lines enabled the New Haven to handle emergencies by the dispatch of trains or steamers to wherever they were needed. Independent companies could never have done this.

Most of the important industries using the rail-water routes enjoyed lower commodity rates, which, combined with overnight or second-morning delivery in New York City, were a decided advantage in New England's struggle to remain competitive with other sections of the country. The reorganization of the boat train service in 1904 and later the practice of diverting trains from one Sound line to another belie the charge that the New Haven was indifferent to the needs of those using the service. Certainly many of the fervent assertions of shippers before the Interstate Commerce Commission about the desirability of railroad control were overstated. Nevertheless, in business as in other fields, attitudes are important. To have suddenly wrenched apart a long-established system in the name of competition could easily have triggered the closing of factories or their removal to another section of the country. In such circumstances New England very likely would have lost important segments of its industrial plant, especially textiles and shoes. Prolonged economic recession or depression in the region would have occurred many years earlier than it did, resulting in extensive hardship to the many people who depended for their livelihood on these industries.

What of the charges made by Louis D. Brandeis and others regarding the evils of the New Haven monopoly? Brandeis had a strong case against New Haven control of the Merchants & Miners Transportation Company and its large interest in Eastern Steamship Corporation. Given its monopoly of land transportation, the necessity of acquiring these interests is difficult to justify. The need to check Charles W. Morse was the immediate cause for the purchase of Merchants & Miners, but the New Haven could have later sold the stock at a time when prices were favorable. The New Haven acquired its interest in the Eastern Steamship Corporation long after the Morse threat had subsided and apparently only because of a desire to extend its New England monopoly.

What ultimately destroyed this combination was the indifference of its management to public sensibility and the New Haven's overburdened financial structure. This indifference explains in part the success of the attacks by Brandeis and others. Too often the management overreacted to threats of competition, as in the cases of the Joy Line and the Enterprise Line. Such unequal contests provided ammunition for those progressives who despised monopolies of any type.

Yet there were weaknesses in the argument of Brandeis and his supporters. Brandeis saw the New Haven under the control of Charles S. Mellen and J. P. Morgan as epitomizing all the evils of monopoly. The financial collapse of the railroad supported this opinion. But Brandeis never publicly considered the operational advantages of the rail-water monopoly. Like many others during the era of progressivism, he seemed convinced that competition was a sort of panacea, despite the historical evidence that competition was temporary at best and usually resulted in an agreement among the parties that fixed rates and service. In addition, Brandeis presented no alternative to railroad control of the Sound lines except independent operation, which only a diminutive minority of New England businessmen and civic leaders desired. Perhaps the fact that the Sound lines carried traffic away from Boston, thereby keeping it subordinate to New York, may have blinded Brandeis and his supporters to the economic need for the continuation of this historic combination and to the benefits it rendered New England businessmen and consumers.

In spite of all the investigations and charges of misconduct, the verdict on the railroad control of the New England coastal steamship lines must be favorable. It was a system that originated in the earliest years of New England railroading, and as long as it served a need it continued to be a profitable combination. The Maine Central Railroad, the Central Vermont Railway, and the New Haven Railroad served New England well with these lines and deserve praise for their efforts to meet the needs of shippers and travelers. This does not relieve the New Haven of the responsibility for its tactics against competitors between 1899 and 1912. But this was a relatively brief period, and these tactics did not interfere significantly with the quality of the rail-water service.

On balance, the railroad-controlled steamship lines, particularly the New Haven Sound lines to New York City, provided a vital service to an economy under siege from without. The rail-water service continued as long as it did because of the unique topography of New York City. It survived its critics because it was necessary to the industries of New England and because no equal or superior alternative was available until the advent of motorized highway transportation.

Appendixes
Notes
Sources
Index

Appendix A

Tables 1–21

TABLE I: *Annual Dividends Paid by Certain New England Coastal Steamship Companies Included in the New England Steamship Company, 1869–1905, in Percentages of Capital Stock*

Year	Bridgeport Steamboat Co.	New Haven Steamboat Co.	Norwich & New York Transportation Co.	Providence & Stonington Steamship Co.[a]	Old Colony Steamboat Co.
1869	42		10	12	
1870	9	30	15	22	
1871	0	70	10	14	
1872	70	10	10	16	
1873	12	150 (Stock)	8	16	
1874	20	5	0	17	4
1875	20	5	0	22	8
1876	20	5	0	10	8
1877	24	15	10	16	8
1878	120	10	20	12	3
1879	80	25	0	10.5	3
1880	0	10	6	5	3
1881	0	10	8	0	7
1882	0	10	0	0	8
1883	0	6	6	0	8
1884	0	7	0	0	8
1885	0	8	0	7.5	4
1886	4	10	0	10	14
1887	8	9	6	15	10
1888	0	9	0	10	10
1889	0	10	0	10	10
1890	0	2	5	10	10
1891	3	2	5	10	25

[continued]

APPENDIXES

Year	Bridgeport Steamboat Co.	New Haven Steamboat Co.	Norwich & New York Transportation Co.	Providence & Stonington Steamship Co.[a]	Old Colony Steamboat Co.
1892	3	0	2.28	10	10
1893	2	0	0	5	9
1894	2	4	4	2	5
1895	4	5.3	0	4.5	5
1896	2	8	0	7.5	30
1897	6	2	0	3	10
1898	5	2	0	5	25
1899	4	0	0	6	25
1900	0	0	0	3	25
1901	5	0	0	0	25
1902	3	0	0	0	0
1903	0	0	0	0	50
1904	0	0	0	0	25
1905					25

Source: ICC, *Docket 6469*, vol. 8, BE 43, A–22; Canal Investigation, file 4953/B–I–30–1–1, Eastern Steamship Co., Correspondence, etc.

Note: In 1904 the Bridgeport, New Haven, Norwich & New York, and Providence & Stonington companies were absorbed into the New England Navigation Co.

[a] Until 1875 the Stonington Steamboat Co. In that year this company paid 14 per cent.

TABLE 2: *Annual Dividends Paid by the Hartford & New York Transportation Company and Selected Steamship Companies in Maine, 1878–1914, in Percentages of Capital Stock*

Year	Hartford & New York Transportation Co.	Boston & Bangor Steamship Co.	Portland Steamship Co.	Kennebec Steamship Co.	International Steamship Co.
1878	10				
1879	6				
1880	10				
1881	15				
1882	0				
1883	0				
1884	20				
1885	0				
1886	0				
1887	0				
1888	0				
1889	6				
1890	3		4	6	3
1891	6	2	6	6	5
1892	6	3	6	6	6
1893	0		6	6	6
1894	4	2	6	6	6
1895	5	2	6	6	
1896	5	2.5	6	6	6
1897	6	4	6	6	6
1898	12	4	6		3
1899	12	6		8	
1900	6	6		10	
1901	6				
1902	6				
1903	6				
1904	6				
1905	8				
1906	8				
1907	0				
1908	0				
1909	8				
1910	6				
1911	4				
1912	4.5				
1913	3				
1914	1.5				

SOURCE: ICC, *Docket 6469*, vol. 8, BE 43, A–22; Canal Investigation, file 4953/B–I–30–1–1, Eastern Steamship Co., Correspondence, etc.

APPENDIXES

TABLE 3: *Freight and Passenger Earnings of the Providence &*
Stonington Steamship Company, 1876–97

Year	PROVIDENCE LINE REVENUE		STONINGTON LINE REVENUE	
	Freight	Passenger	Freight	Passenger
1876	$341,620	$ 67,932	$347,545	$183,611
1877	338,329	163,352	263,571	101,644
1878	301,676	114,324	191,518	136,579
1879	346,423	95,637	204,851	118,695
1880	338,505	150,457	200,678	103,015
1881	445,739	59,560	267,970	134,358
1882	495,683	88,214	294,682	132,391
1883	481,602	82,006	296,354	173,334
1884	443,497	94,260	278,306	156,224
1885	464,165	75,289	300,434	150,480
1886	493,402	80,056	281,744	151,886
1887	508,316	77,210	280,054	156,924
1888	510,997	133,394	268,044	122,655
1889	509,523	125,449	262,874	134,851
1890	494,670	139,877	250,754	117,556
1891	506,715	149,028	251,197	104,804
1892	552,619	178,171	274,784	127,084
1893	418,726	133,450	245,889	116,975
1894	398,256	132,146	240,250	109,530
1895	407,902	146,312	261,291	108,182
1896	400,343	142,048	208,822	106,661
1897	445,000	171,654	209,236	105,029

SOURCE: General Ledgers, Providence & Stonington Steamship Co.,
vols. 343–46 of the New York, New Haven & Hartford Railroad
Collection, Baker Library, Harvard Business School.
NOTE: Passenger revenue does not include stateroom, meal, or bar
receipts; these were separate accounts. The Providence Line passenger
service operated only about five months a year.

TABLE 4: *Freight and Passenger Earnings of the Old Colony Steamboat Company, 1878–86, 1895–1905*

| | | | REVENUE | | |
| | | Passenger | State- | | |
Fiscal Year	Freight[a]	Tickets	rooms	Meals	Bar
Ending 30 April					
1878	$ 288,245	$351,651	$ 87,631	$ 55,095	$15,375
1879	282,919	264,253	97,225	64,138	17,480
1880	377,801	349,043	189,777	107,835	31,899
1881	465,349	480,080	146,941	87,348	26,134
1882	559,284	562,119	149,560	79,646	23,649
1883	584,949	532,953	139,911	80,302	24,162
1884	585,248	562,561	154,845	87,005	25,807
1885	563,767	522,768	146,906	79,742	23,181
1886	606,229	521,344	148,700	82,647	22,221
Ending 31 May					
1895	816,833	882,874	289,405	145,061	48,795
1896	770,690	998,255	314,009	165,638	55,238
Ending 30 June					
1897	608,455	773,344	318,853	160,709	51,803
1898	765,522	884,645	250,784	128,775	41,176
1899	765,704	913,228	257,513	130,776	46,140
1900	783,965	928,483	259,453	135,908	47,751
1901	746,662	816,730	247,143	125,806	40,214
1902	843,278	748,002	240,259	131,321	41,392
1903	859,309	833,211	258,542	139,725	40,499
1904	895,518	871,826	256,123	137,556	40,444
1905	1,060,762	868,707[b]	255,083	138,709	39,551

SOURCE: Trial Balance Book No. 384½, 1874–86, and Trial Balance Book, 1894–1905, Old Colony Steamboat Co., G. W. Blunt White Library, Marine Historical Association, Mystic, Conn. Express earnings are not included: they were kept in a separate account.
[a] Probably includes earnings of the New Bedford Line.
[b] Probably includes earnings of summer service on the New Bedford Line.

APPENDIXES

TABLE 5: *Statement of the Passenger Receipts by Month on the Fall River Line for the Fiscal Year Ending 30 June 1913*

| Month | Tickets | REVENUE | | |
		Staterooms	Meals	Bar
July (1912)	$102,966	$33,586	$17,670	$4,912
August	116,044	36,925	19,443	5,125
September	98,154	30,767	14,938	3,700
October	84,595	26,115	13,551	3,884
November	49,860	18,644	10,041	3,248
December	48,789	18,201	8,702	2,889
January (1913)	33,142	14,412	6,894	2,453
February	36,450	13,240	6,950	2,310
March	52,667	20,398	11,148	3,103
April	65,705	24,495	13,036	3,594
May	90,271	26,838	14,540	4,061
June	110,234	34,192	19,786	4,695

SOURCE: ICC, *Docket 6469,* vol. 8, BE 40, Statement of Receipts by Month of New England Steamship Co.

TABLE 6: *Freight and Passenger Earnings of the Norwich &*
New York Transportation Company, 1882–1904

Fiscal Year	REVENUE	
	Freight	Passenger
Ending 30 September		
1882	$407,456	$194,409
1883	396,149	181,620
1884	354,605	163,660
1885	327,798	154,395
1886	357,162	144,676
1887	348,442	144,140
1888	332,569	137,973
1889	332,885	149,505
1890	349,672	166,523
1891	360,193	162,829
1892	350,265	169,796
1893	321,597	148,204
1894	299,605	184,690
1895	326,797	158,319
Ending 30 June		
1896	240,721[a]	69,743[a]
1897	202,651[a]	71,427[a]
1898	282,832	113,215
1899	251,532	195,349
1900	248,739	170,442
1901	247,654	162,113
1902	267,804	186,912
1903	275,498	182,975
1904	265,797	198,470

SOURCE: Ledgers, 1877–1904, Norwich & New York Transportation
Co., G. W. Blunt White Library.
[a] Revenue is only for nine months, because of the change in the
fiscal year.

TABLE 7: *Freight and Passenger Earnings of the Maine Steamship Company, 1902–3*

Month	REVENUE	
	Freight	Passengers[a]
1902		
January	$33,058	$ 622
February	30,438	357
March	33,164	598
April	36,872	1,417
May	41,112	3,868
June	36,851	11,068
July	37,913	28,011
August	35,475	37,489
September	35,834	17,782
October	40,512	3,829
November	46,052	1,511
December	37,937	974
1903		
January	45,803	1,302
February	32,045	740
March	42,429	1,695
April	34,869	1,643
May	33,474	4,191
June	33,277	12,596
July	32,794	33,775
August	29,439	46,431
September	34,309	20,051
October	41,157	3,270
November	35,462	1,360
December	38,208	1,058

SOURCE: General Ledger, 1901–4, Maine Steamship Co., vol. 331 of the New York, New Haven & Hartford Railroad Collection.
[a] Does not include revenue from staterooms, meals, and bar.

TABLE 8: *Earnings and Operating Expenses of Maine Central Boat Lines for the Fiscal Year Ending 30 June 1915*

	Penobscot Bay Line	Frenchman's Bay Line	Total
Earnings:			
Freight	$ 2,874.12	$12,652.93	$15,527.05
Passengers	8,255.27	39,794.06	48,049.33
Express	177.96	905.12	1,083.08
Mail	900.00	6,212.42	7,112.42
Other	204.98	1,493.93	1,698.91
Total earnings	$12,412.33	$61,058.46	$73,470.79
Expenses:[a]			
Maintenance of landings	$ 273.01		$ 273.01
Maintenance of equipment	11,204.30	$34,707.81	45,912.11
Operation of steamboats and landings	15,073.25	46,178.16	61,251.41
Total expenses	$26,550.56	$80,885.97	$107,436.53
Deficit	$14,138.23	$19,827.51	$33,965.74

SOURCE: ICC, *Docket 6891*, Petitioner's Exhibit 2.
[a] Maintenance expenses and operation of Bar Harbor Terminal not included with steamer accounts. They were probably included in railroad accounts.

TABLE 9: *Freight Tonnage Carried on the Lines Included in the New England Steamship Company and the Joy Steamship Company, 1903–12*

Fiscal Year (Ending 30 June)	New England Steamship Company (Tons)	Joy Steamship Company[a] (Tons)
1903	1,130,892	
1904	1,130,881	
1905	1,148,753	
1906	1,251,075	279,817
1907	1,286,464	254,074
1908	1,197,233	225,733
1909	1,482,865	317,868
1910	1,516,089	
1911	1,359,110	
1912	1,405,616	

SOURCE: ICC, *Docket 4845*, vol. 2, Brief and Argument for the New York, New Haven and Hartford Railroad Company and Boston and Maine Railroad, Respondents, pp. 154–56.
[a] Includes the Bay State Line and the Merchants Line, which were taken over by the Hartford & New York Transportation Co.

TABLE 10: *Tonnage Carried by the Central Vermont Transportation Company, 1910–16*

Fiscal Year (Ending 30 June)	From New York (Tons)	To New York (Tons)
1910	273,228	83,196
1911	244,582	88,666
1912	260,660	69,065
1913	288,214	57,375
1914	331,590	58,766
1915	332,623	47,491
1916	165,673	37,890

SOURCE: ICC, *Docket 6645*, Petitioner's Exhibit 1.

TABLE 11: *Tonnage Carried by the Metropolitan Steamship Company, 1904–5*

Direction and Commodity	1904 (Tons)	1905 (Tons)
From New York:		
Cotton	51,988	49,759
Wool	26,277	24,846
General merchandise	200,568	199,953
Total	278,833	274,558
To New York:		
Potatoes	20,001	24,179
Fish	13,689	7,884
General merchandise	102,312	119,562
Total	136,002	151,625

SOURCE: Canal Investigation, file 4953/B–I–41–1, Metropolitan Steamship Co.

TABLE 12: *Freight Tonnage and Earnings of the Lines of New England Steamship Company for the Fiscal Year Ending 30 June 1914*

Line	EASTBOUND Tons	EASTBOUND Net Earnings	WESTBOUND Tons	WESTBOUND Net Earnings
Fall River	195,277	$385,496	226,840	$490,052
New Bedford	95,474	184,976	146,383	254,024
Providence	110,643	184,295	151,601	250,021
New London (Norwich)	63,442	112,612	81,810	122,223
New Haven	98,406	146,859	92,265	126,416
Bridgeport	59,793	103,045	35,092	66,012

SOURCE: ICC, *Docket 6469*, vol. 8, BE 27.

APPENDIXES

TABLE 13: *Class Rates, 1900–1914, in Cents per 100 Pounds*

Between New York and	CLASSES					
	1	2	3	4	5	6
Bridgeport						
Water	14	11	8	7	6	5
Rail	17	15	12	9	8	8
New Haven						
Water	16	13	11	8	7	6
Rail	19	16	14	11	10	9
New London						
Water	20	17	14	12	10	9
Rail	22	19	16	13	11	10
Providence						
Water	27	23	18	16	14	12
Rail	31	27	22	18	17	15
Fall River						
Water	27	23	18	16	14	12
Rail	32	29	24	18	17	15
Newport						
Water	27	23	18	16	14	12
Rail	32	29	24	18	17	15
New Bedford						
Water	27	23	18	16	14	12
Rail	32	29	24	18	17	15
Boston						
Water	29	24	18	17	14	12
Rail	34	29	23	19	17	15
Rail and water	34	29	21	19	16	14

SOURCE: *Senate Hearings on the Panama Canal,* p. 763.

TABLE 14: *Commodity Rates, 1912, in Cents per 100 Pounds*

Between New York and	Cotton Piece Goods	Woolens	Boots and Shoes	Dry Goods
Lowell				
Rail	25	35	35	35
Rail and water	15	15	30	26
Fall River				
Rail	24	32	32	32
Rail and water	11	14	24	19
Worcester				
Rail	21	32	32	32
Rail and water	13	15	25	20
Brockton				
Rail	24	32	32	32
Rail and water	12	15	25	20
Watuppa				
Rail	24	32	32	32
Rail and water	11	14	24	19

SOURCE: *Senate Hearings on the Panama Canal,* p. 764.

TABLE 15: *Class Rates, 1914, in Cents per 100 Pounds*

Between New York and	CLASSES					
	1	2	3	4	5	6
Bridgeport						
Water	14	11	8	7	6	5
Rail	19	16	13	10	8	6
New Haven						
Water	16	13	11	8	7	6
Rail	22	19	15	12	9	7
New London						
Water	25	21	18	14	10	8
Rail	28	24	20	15	11	10
Providence						
Water	27	23	19	15	11	9
Rail	31	26	22	17	12	10
Fall River						
Water	27	23	19	15	11	9
Rail	32	27	22	18	13	11

[*continued*]

Between New York and	CLASSES					
	1	2	3	4	5	6
Newport						
Water	27	23	19	15	11	9
Rail	33	28	23	18	13	11
New Bedford						
Water	27	23	19	15	11	9
Rail	33	28	23	18	13	11

SOURCE: ICC, *Docket 6469*, vol. 7, Petitioner's Exhibit 2.

TABLE 16: *Rail-Water, Commodity Rates Compared with All-Rail, Class Rates, 1914, in Cents per 100 Pounds*

Between New York and	Cotton Piece Goods	Woolens	Boots and Shoes	Dry Goods
Bridgeport				
Water	9	14	14	14
Rail	14	19	19	19
New Haven				
Water	a	16	16	16
Rail	16	22	22	22
New London				
Water	10	13	20	25
Rail	20	28	28	28
Providence				
Water	10	13	27	27
Rail	22	31	31	31
Fall River				
Water	10	13	27	27
Rail	23	32	32	32
Newport				
Water	10	13	27	27
Rail	24	33	33	33
New Bedford				
Water	10	13	27	27
Rail	24	33	33	33

SOURCE: ICC, *Docket 6469*, vol. 7, Petitioner's Exhibit 2.
a Less-than-carload, 8; carload, 7.

TABLE 17: *Operating Expenses of the Providence & Stonington Steamship Company for Selected Years between 1876 and 1898*

Fiscal Year	Providence Line	Stonington Line
Ending 30 September		
1876	$439,043	$398,826
1877	436,287	319,964
1878	451,161	366,320
1879	452,021	332,120
1880	503,788	398,658
1881	458,674	379,840
1882	526,201	345,477
Ending 31 December		
1885	403,023	354,661
1886	479,454	402,859
1887		427,102
1888		421,749
1889	545,254	436,976
1890	527,634	421,771
Ending 30 June		
1892	749,439[a]	387,522
1898	523,698	340,241

SOURCE: Ledgers, 1875–1904, Providence & Stonington Steamship Co., vols. 343–46, New York, New Haven & Hartford Railroad Collection.
[a] The reason for the sharp increase in expenses is difficult to determine. It may have been the result of the construction of the *Maine* and the *New Hampshire*.

TABLE 18: *Cost of Operating Certain Steamers of the Old Colony Steamboat Company, 1898–1900*

Steamer	Fiscal Year (Ending 30 June)	Coal	Total Operation[a]	Repairs	Grand Total
Priscilla	1899	$41,249	$198,372	$42,185	$240,557
"	1900	49,672	231,527	35,142	266,669
Puritan	1899	41,389	196,376	59,140	255,516
"	1900	40,545	193,487	59,437	252,924

[*continued*]

APPENDIXES

Steamer	Fiscal Year (Ending 30 June)	Coal	Total Operation[a]	Repairs	Grand Total
City of Fitchburg	1899	9,297	32,349	2,739	35,088
City of Brockton	1898	16,627	58,387	11,086	69,473
" " "	1899	15,594	60,059	5,928	65,987

SOURCE: Record of Operating Expenses, 1898–1903, Old Colony
Steamboat Co., G. W. Blunt White Library.
NOTE: Steamers did not necessarily operate for the same length of
time each year, so yearly totals are not always comparable.
[a] Includes subsistence, payroll, insurance, etc.

TABLE 19: *Cost of Operating Passenger Steamers on the Metropolitan
Line of the Eastern Steamship Corporation and the Metropolitan
Steamship Company*

Steamers and Items	Cost for Month
Bunker Hill and *Massachusetts,* August 1915:	
Operating expenses, including depreciation, for 62 trips	$103,943.95
Taxes	1,030.00
Rental	4,179.59
Interest	8,382.94
Total	$117,536.48

Average for single trip, $1,895.75

Harvard and *Yale,* August 1910:	
Operating expenses, including depreciation, for 62 trips	$109,774.71
Taxes and rental	5,250.00
General administration	2,000.00
Interest ($1,600,000 @ 5%)	6,666.66
Total	$123,691.37

Average for single trip, $1,995.02

SOURCE: Memorandum for Calvin Austin, 9 December 1915, in
miscellaneous records of Eastern Steamship Corp. in possession of
A. J. McLaughlin, Lauderdale-by-the-Sea, Fla.
NOTE: Operating costs were generally higher in 1915 than in 1910.

TABLE 20: *Monthly Wages Paid by the Old Colony Steamboat
Company in 1887 and the Merchants & Miners Transportation
Company in 1900, and the Average Monthly Wages Paid at the
Ports of Boston and Portland in 1889*

Position	Old Colony (1887)	Merchants & Miners (1900)	Average in Boston, Portland (1889)
Captain	$150–225	$150–250	$106
First mate	75–80	75	56
Second mate		55	
Second, third mate			45
Clerk			64
Purser			64
First engineer	106–115	120	81
Second engineer		60	
Second, third engineer			61
Pilot			52
Seaman		25	29
Deck hand	28–29		31
Fireman	38–43	40	37
Oiler	40–55	40	40
Steward	100	55–70	

SOURCE: Payroll Book, January 1887, Old Colony Steamboat Co.,
G. W. Blunt White Library; *Report of the Industrial Commission on
Transportation* (1901), *Reports of the Industrial Commission,* 9:417;
Henry C. Adams, "Transportation by Water," in *Report on
Transportation Business in the United States at the Eleventh Census,
Part 2* (1894), *Eleventh Census of the United States, 1890,* 14:39–41.
NOTE: On the Old Colony line, crews of the passenger steamers
commanded higher wages than did crews of the freight steamers.
Higher wages were paid on the *Pilgrim* than on the smaller steamers
Bristol and *Providence.*

APPENDIXES

TABLE 21: *Breakdown of the Crew of the Fall River Line Steamer* Priscilla

Position	Number	Position	Number
Captain	1	Baker	1
First pilot	2	Butcher	1
Quartermaster	2	First messman	1
Bow watchman	2	Second messman	1
First mate	1	Kitchenman	2
Second mate	1	Pantryman (grades 1–6)	7
Third mate	1	Coffeeman	1
Watchman	2	Silverman	2
Purser	1	Head waiter	1
Freight clerk	1	Second head waiter	1
Ticket collector	1	First saloonman	1
Baggage master	1	First F. C. man	1
Coxswain	1	First S. H. man	1
Deck hand	14	Coat room man	1
Assistant freight clerk	1	Captain's waiter	1
Assistant purser	1	Porter	1
Steward	1	Waiter	68
Assistant steward	1	Emmigrant waiter	2
Night assistant steward	1	Stewardess	3
Cashier	1	Emmigrant stewardess	1
Checker	2	Chief engineer	1
Bartender	1	First assistant engineer	1
Saloon watchman	1	Second assistant engineer	1
Emmigrant night steward	1	Third assistant engineer	1
Emmigrant day steward	1	Electric engineer	1
First cook	1	Assistant electric engineer	1
Second cook	1	Watertender	3
Third cook	1	Oiler	4
Fourth cook	1	Donkeytender	3
Fifth cook	1	Fireman	20
Broiler	1	Coal passer	12
Oysterman	1	Total crew	196

SOURCE: ICC, *Docket 6469*, vol. 7, Petitioner's Exhibit 13.

Appendix B

Organizations and Business Firms Supporting the Continued Operation of the New England Steamship Company by the New York, New Haven & Hartford Railroad

SUPPORT FOR the continued operation of the Sound lines by the New York, New Haven & Hartford Railroad was widespread throughout all the New England states except Vermont, where whatever rail-water service was required was furnished by the Central Vermont Railway. The Interstate Commerce Commission received scores of letters and petitions from various trade associations, boards of trade, chambers of commerce, and business and manufacturing firms urging it to permit the New Haven to continue to operate the steamers. The pleas were especially strong regarding the lines under the control of the New England Steamship Company. Many were willing to see the Hartford & New York Transportation Company become independent because its services were primarily port-to-port operations. The commission filed all this correspondence with Docket No. 6469, Steamer Lines on Long Island Sound, but it was of no significance as evidence because it was not supported by testimony. During the hearings some groups did have representatives testify before the commission.

From every state except Vermont over seventy-five boards of trade, chambers of commerce, and commercial and trade associations wrote to the commission in favor of continued New Haven operation. Fifty of these were from Massachusetts, twelve from Connecticut, nine from Rhode Island, four from Maine, and two from New Hampshire. Below is listed a cross-section of the companies that wrote to the Interstate Commerce Commission or testified before the commission in favor of the operation of the Sound lines by the New Haven Railroad.

AMERICAN HOSIERY COMPANY, *New Britain, Conn.*
AMERICAN LOCOMOTIVE COMPANY, *New York, N.Y.*
AMERICAN PAPER TUBE COMPANY, *Woonsocket, R.I.*
AMERICAN PRINTING COMPANY, *Fall River, Mass.* (textile printing)
ARCHER RUBBER COMPANY, *Milford, Mass.*

APPENDIXES

AMERICAN SUGAR REFINING COMPANY, *New York, N.Y.*
AMERICAN TEXTILOSE COMPANY, *Newburyport, Mass.*
AMERICAN WOOLEN COMPANY, *Boston, Mass.*
ARBUCKLE BROTHERS, *New York, N.Y.* (sugar refiner and coffee miller)
BOSTON FRUIT AND PRODUCE EXCHANGE
BRIDGEPORT BRASS COMPANY, *Bridgeport, Conn.*
CAPE COD CRANBERRY GROWERS ASSOCIATION
CARROLL, HIXON, JONES COMPANY, *Milford, Mass.* (women's hats)
CHASE METAL WORKS, *Waterbury, Conn.*
COLGATE & COMPANY, *Jersey City, N.J.*
DEERFOOT FARM DAIRY, *Southboro, Mass.*
DEERING, MILLIKEN & COMPANY, *New York, N.Y.*
C. H. DEXTER & SONS, *Windsor Locks, Conn.* (paper manufacturer)
W. L. DOUGLAS SHOE COMPANY, *Brockton, Mass.*
W. H. DUVAL & COMPANY, *New York, N.Y.* (wool selling agent)
EDISON ELECTRIC ILLUMINATING COMPANY, *Brooklyn, N.Y.*
FALL RIVER IRON WORKS, *Fall River, Mass.* (cotton textiles)
FALULAH PAPER COMPANY, *Fitchburg, Mass.*
FIRST NATIONAL BANK, *Wallingford, Conn.*
FORD & KIMBALL, *Concord, N.H.* (car wheels)
GEOMETRIC TOOL COMPANY, *New Haven, Conn.*
GOODELL COMPANY, *New York, N.Y.* (cutlery)
THE GRANITE HOSIERY MILLS, *Laconia, N.H.*
LEWIS DE GROFF & SON, *New York, N.Y.* (wholesale grocer)
HUCKINS & TEMPLE COMPANY, *Milford, Mass.* (shoes)
U. T. HUNGERFORD BRASS & COPPER COMPANY, *New York, N.Y.*
J. W. LATHROP COMPANY, *Mystic, Conn.* (gasoline engines)
LIBBY, MCNEILL & LIBBY, *Brooklyn, N.Y.*
MILFORD SHOE COMPANY, *Milford, Mass.*
MYSTIC MANUFACTURING COMPANY, *Mystic, Conn.* (woolen manufacturer)
MYSTIC WOOLEN COMPANY, *Mystic, Conn.*
NASHUA GUMMED & COATED PAPER COMPANY, *Nashua, N.H.*
NEW ENGLAND FISH EXCHANGE, *Boston, Mass.*
NEW ENGLAND PAPER & PULP TRAFFIC ASSOCIATION
THE NEW HAMPSHIRE SPINNING MILLS, *Concord, N.H.*
NEW YORK INSULATED WIRE COMPANY, *New York, N.Y.*
PACIFIC MILLS, *Lawrence, Mass.* (textile manufacturer)
THE PACKER MANUFACTURING COMPANY, *Mystic, Conn.* (soap manufacturer)
PARKHILL MANUFACTURING COMPANY, *Fitchburg, Mass.* (fabrics)
PERSEVERANCE WORSTED COMPANY, *Woonsocket, R.I.*
PLYMOUTH CORDAGE COMPANY, *Plymouth, Mass.* (rope and twine manufacturer)

E. P. REED LUMBER COMPANY, *North Abington, Mass.*
W. C. RITCHIE AND COMPANY, *Brooklyn, N.Y.* (paper products)
ROYAL WORCESTER CORSET COMPANY, *Worcester, Mass.*
SARGENT & COMPANY, *New Haven, Conn.* (hardware manufacturer)
SCOTT & WILLIAMS, *Laconia, N.H.* (knitting machinery)
SHIRREFFS WORSTED COMPANY, *Fitchburg, Mass.*
SIMONDS MANUFACTURING COMPANY, *Fitchburg, Mass.* (saws, knives, etc.)
STERLING CIDER COMPANY, *Sterling, Mass.*
STERLING SALT COMPANY, *New York, N.Y.*
STEVENS MANUFACTURING COMPANY, *Fall River, Mass.* (cotton textiles)
M. T. STEVENS & SONS COMPANY, *North Adams, Mass.* (woolen manufacturer)
SULLOWAY MILLS, *Franklin, N.H.* (hosiery)
C. J. TAGLIBUE MANUFACTURING COMPANY, *Brooklyn, N.Y.* (instrument maker)
TILTON MILLS, *Tilton, N.H.* (woolens)
UNITED LACE & BRAID MANUFACTURING COMPANY, *Providence, R.I.*
U. S. RUBBER COMPANY, *New York, N.Y.*
R. WALLACE & SONS MANUFACTURING COMPANY, *Wallingford, Conn.* (silversmith)
WATERMAN WORSTED COMPANY, INC., *Putnam, Conn.*
WHITNEY REED CORPORATION, *Leominster, Mass.* (chair manufacturer)
M. J. WHITTALL, *Worcester, Mass.* (carpets)
WHOLESALE SHOE LEAGUE, *New York, N.Y.*
H. H. WOOD & COMPANY, *Lakeport, N.H.* (wool hosiery)
WORCESTER PRESSED STEEL COMPANY, *Worcester, Mass.*
WORTH & JUDD MANUFACTURING COMPANY, *New Britain, Conn.* (hardware)
WRIGHT WIRE COMPANY, *Worcester, Mass.*

Notes

Abbreviations Used in the Notes

BE	Boole Exhibit
Canal Investigation	The Canal Investigation of the Bureau of Corporations, Record Group 122, National Archives, Washington, D.C.
CFT	Interstate Commerce Commission, Cancelled Freight Tariffs, Federal Records Center, Alexandria, Va.
CPT	Interstate Commerce Commission, Cancelled Passenger Tariffs, Record Group 134, National Archives, Washington, D.C.
D&B	Dun & Bradstreet Credit Reporting Ledgers, Baker Library, Harvard Business School
Financial Transactions	Interstate Commerce Commission, *Evidence . . . Relative to the Financial Transactions of the New York, New Haven & Hartford Railroad Company, Together with the Report of the Commission Thereon*, S. Doc. 543, 63d Cong., 2d sess., 1914, 2 vols.
HCEI	*Historical Collections of the Essex Institute*
ICC, *Valuation Docket 941*	U.S., ICC, *Valuation Docket No. 941, In re Valuation of the Property of the New Bedford, Martha's Vineyard and Nantucket Steamboat Co.*, 2 vols., Record Group 134, National Archives
ICC, *Valuation Docket 1054*	U.S., ICC, *Valuation Docket No. 1054, New England Steamship Co.*, 1 vol., ICC Building, Washington, D.C.
ICC, *Docket 4845*	U.S., ICC, *Docket No. 4845, The New England Investigation in the Matter of Rates, Classifications, Regulations, and Practices of Carriers*, 21 vols., Record Group 134, National Archives
ICC, *Docket 6334*	U.S., ICC, *Docket No. 6334, New York Team Owners' Association, et al., Complainant,*

	vs. *New York Central Railroad Company et al., Defendants*, 4 vols., Record Group 134, National Archives
ICC, *Docket 6469*	U.S., ICC, *Docket No. 6469, Application of the New York, New Haven and Hartford Railroad Company for Permission to Continue Certain Service by Water after July 1, 1914: Steamer Lines on Long Island Sound*, 26 vols., Record Group 134, National Archives
ICC, *Docket 6645*	U.S., ICC, *Docket No. 6645, Application of the Central Vermont Railway, under the Provisions of Section 5 of the Interstate Commerce Act, as Amended by Section 11 of the Act of Congress of August 24, 1912,* 1 vol., Record Group 134, National Archives
ICC, *Docket 6891*	U.S., ICC, *Docket No. 6891, Application of the Maine Central Railroad under the Panama Canal Act: Operation of Boat Lines*, 1 vol., Record Group 134, National Archives
MJ	*Marine Journal*
Morse v. *Metropolitan Steamship Co.*	*In Chancery of New Jersey, between Jennie R. Morse, Complainant, and Metropolitan Steamship Co. et al., Defendants, Disposition of Calvin Austin, Boston, April 10, 1914*, copy of record in possession of Albert J. McLaughlin, Lauderdale-by-the-Sea, Fla.
NG	*The Nautical Gazette*
Senate Hearings on the Panama Canal	U.S., Congress, Senate, Committee on Interoceanic Canals, *Panama Canal: Hearings before the Committee on Interoceanic Canals on H.R. 21969*, Washington, D.C., 1912
Transportation by Water	U.S., Commissioner of Corporations, *Report of the Commissioner of Corporations on Transportation by Water in the United States*, 4 vols., Washington, D.C., 1909–13

Chapter 1

1. For more complete details of the history of steam coastal navigation in New England the following works are valuable: Edward C. Kirkland, *Men, Cities and Transportation: A Study in New England*

History, 1820–1900, 2 vols. (Cambridge, Mass., 1948); Fred Erving Dayton, *Steamboat Days* (New York, 1925); John H. Morrison, *History of American Steam Navigation* (New York, 1903); George Pierce Baker, *The Formation of the New England Railroad Systems: A Study of Railroad Combination in the Nineteenth Century* (Cambridge, Mass., 1937); Robert G. Albion, *The Rise of New York Port, 1815–1860* (New York, 1939); Alvin F. Harlow, *Steelways of New England* (New York, 1946); Charles E. Fisher, *The Story of the Old Colony Railroad* (n.p., 1919); Roger Williams McAdam, *The Old Fall River Line*, rev. and enlarged ed. (New York, 1955); Wheaton J. Lane, *Commodore Vanderbilt* (New York, 1942); Francis B. C. Bradlee, "Some Account of Steam Navigation in New England," *Historical Collections of the Essex Institute* 55 (1919):1–32, 113–28, 177–208, 257–72, and 56 (1920):113–44, 177–201.

2. Dayton, p. 108. The year 1824 is also cited by some as the date the New Haven Steamboat Co. was organized. See ICC, *Docket 6469*, 15:6048–49.

3. Dayton, p. 98.

4. See ibid., chap. 8; Lane, *Commodore Vanderbilt*, pp. 34–73.

5. See Harlow, *Steelways of New England*, pp. 219–20; Dayton, chap. 9; Baker, chaps. 1–3; ICC, *Docket 6469*, 15:6015–19.

6. Harlow, *Steelways of New England*, pp. 220–21; Dayton, pp. 187–88; Baker, pp. 41–42.

7. Dayton, pp. 176–85.

8. Ibid., p. 191.

9. Ibid., pp. 196–97; Fisher, *Old Colony Railroad*, pp. 127–28; Warren Jacobs, "The Fall River Line Boat Train," *Railway and Locomotive Historical Society Bulletin No. 2* (1921), pp. 4–5; Thomas Russell Smith, *The Cotton Textile Industry of Fall River, Massachusetts* (New York, 1944), pp. 28–29.

10. Way Bill Book, 16 November 1858–31 January 1863, Bay State Steamboat Co., FR–Ships, H–1, 31784 of Fall River Iron Works Collection, Baker Library, Harvard Business School, Boston, Mass.

11. Edward E. Chase, *Maine Railroads* (Portland, Me., 1926), pp. 7–8; Kirkland, 2:126; Dayton, pp. 258–60.

12. Kirkland, 2:125–26; Dayton, pp. 260–69.

13. Kirkland, 2:125; Dayton, pp. 271–73; Bradlee, "Steam Navigation in New England," *HCEI* 55 (July 1919):188–89.

14. Kirkland, 2:128; Dayton, pp. 283–84; Bradlee, "Steam Navigation in New England," *HCEI* 55 (July 1919):201.

15. *HCEI* 55:193–94.

16. Boston Board of Trade, *Twenty-seventh Annual Report* (1881), p. 46; Bradlee, "Steam Navigation in New England," *HCEI* 56 (July 1920):181–83.

17. Report on the Metropolitan Steamship Co., D&B, N.Y. 417:200FF.

18. Way Bill Book, Bay State Steamboat Co., Fall River Iron Works Collection.

19. Baker, p. 30; copy of authorization to sell company and its property, folder of Bay State Steamboat Co., 1849–73, marked "Dividends," in case 4 of Fall River Iron Works Collection; Old Colony & Newport Railway, *Annual Report* (1865), p. 6.

20. Charles H. Dow, *History of Steam Navigation between New York & Providence* (New York, 1877), pp. 15–27; Report on Merchants' Steamship Co., D&B, R.I. 9 : 430.

21. Dow, *Steam Navigation between New York & Providence*, pp. 15–27; Henry Whittemore, under the direction of the Providence & Stonington Steamship Co., *The Past and the Present of Steam Navigation on Long Island Sound* (n.p., 1893), pp. 56–57; Dayton, pp. 198–99. Dayton (p. 199) says the company had spent $1,500,000 on the *Bristol* and the *Providence*.

22. Whittemore, *Steam Navigation on Long Island Sound*, pp. 56–57; Report on Providence & New York Steamboat Co., D&B, R.I. 10 : 23.

23. Report on Merchants' Steamship Co., D&B, R.I. 9 : 430; Report on Narragansett Steamship Co., D&B, N.Y. 371 : 852.

24. ICC, *Docket 6469*, vol. 8, BE 43 (app. A), pp. 27–30.

25. Ibid., pp. 6–9; ibid., 15 : 6046–47, 6015–19; Dayton, pp. 163–65.

26. ICC, *Docket 6469*, vol. 8, BE 43 (app. A), pp. 17–21; Kirkland, 2 : 143.

27. Report on Narragansett Steamship Co., D&B, N.Y. 371 : 852.

28. The Dun & Bradstreet reporter claimed that the Narragansett Steamship Co. paid the Boston, Newport & New York Steamboat Co. $1 million to take over its route. This sum would have left a small surplus for distribution to the stockholders. See Report on the Boston, Newport & New York Steamboat Co., D&B, R.I. 3 : 93.

29. *The New York Boston & Providence R.R. Co., & ali.* vs. *The Old Colony Railroad Co., et al., Demurrer for the Defendants*, pp. 1–3, box 32, pamphlet 1, Rider Collection, John Hay Library, Brown University; Old Colony & Newport Railway, *Annual Report* (1869), pp. 9–10; *Fall River Line Journal*, 31 May 1909, p. 14. See Narragansett Steamship Co. stationery, boxes 4 and 6 of Old Colony Railroad Collection, Baker Library, Harvard Business School.

30. *New York Boston & Providence* vs. *Old Colony, Demurrer for Defendants*, pp. 2–5.

31. Old Colony & Newport Railway, *Annual Report* (1869), pp. 9–10.

Chapter 2

1. U.S., Congress, House, Select Committee on the Causes of the Reduction of American Tonnage, *Report and Testimony on the Causes*

of the Reduction of American Tonnage, 41st Cong., 2d sess., 1870, H. Doc. 28, pp. 64–65, 104, 115, 149, 150.

2. New York & New England Railroad, *Annual Report* (1877), pp. 5–6. For details of these consolidations see Baker, chaps. 3 and 4.

3. See Ray Morris, "A Review by Decades of American Deep-Water Steamers in the Atlantic Coastwise Service," *Railroad Gazette*, 15 August 1902, pp. 637–39.

4. ICC, *Docket 6469*, 3 : 1671–72.

5. The author listed five warnings: (1) Always have a good trunk; (2) carry thick clothing, even in the hottest weather; (3) in the hand-satchel always carry camphor, laudanum, and brandy for medicine; (4) never drink water in unaccustomed places; (5) buy through tickets, even when not going beyond a local station (Charles H. Sweetser, comp., *Book of Summer Resorts, Explaining Where to Find Them, How to Find Them and Their Especial Advantages, with Details of Time Tables and Prices* [New York, 1868], "General Introductory Chapter," p. 9).

6. Ibid., "Lakes, Rivers, and Mountains," p. 62.

7. For a description of Fisk's antics see Dayton, pp. 201–6. The effect this had can be seen in "Narragansett Steamship Co.," *NG*, 19 April 1873, p. 398.

8. Report on Narragansett Steamship Co., D&B, N.Y. 371 : 852.

9. Old Colony & Newport Railway, *Annual Report* (1871), pp. 4–5; Old Colony Railroad, *Annual Report* (1873), p. 11. In 1872 the name was changed to Old Colony Railroad. An example of some of the abuses of the Narragansett Steamship Co. is found in an editorial in the *Nautical Gazette* (27 July 1872, p. 36). The *Gazette* charged that the steamship company had given away $10,000 in free passes to journalists and reporters. The loss in revenue had been so great that the practice was halted. The occasion was the Boston Jubilee.

10. "Narragansett Steamship Co.," *NG*, 13 April 1872, p. 234; *NG*, 19 April 1873, pp. 337–38.

11. See Jules Grodinsky, *Jay Gould: His Business Career, 1867–1892* (Philadelphia, 1957).

12. ICC, *Docket 6469*, vol. 8, BE 43 (app. A), pp. 42–46; ibid. (app. A), A–12, Excerpts from Stockholders Minute Book, Old Colony Steamboat Co., in office of A. W. Adams, Treasurer, Boston Terminal Co., Boston, Mass., pp. 1–5.

13. Ibid., A–12, pp. 1–5; Old Colony Railroad, *Annual Report* (1874), p. 8; "Narragansett Steamship Co.," *NG*, 20 June 1874, p. 413; "Old Colony Steamboat Co.," *NG*, 6 June 1874, p. 395. The investment of the Old Colony Railroad in steamboat company stock dropped to $725,500 in 1877 and remained at that amount until 1887. See Old Colony Railroad annual reports for those years.

14. Report on the Old Colony Steamboat Co., D&B, Mass. 75 : 158.

15. Old Colony Railroad, *Annual Report* (1874), p. 8. The New York–Boston fare was $4.00. For details on divisions of receipts see Way Bills, 21 January 1875–20 September 1875, Old Colony Steamboat Co., vol. 282 of Old Colony Railroad Collection, in Baker Library, Harvard Business School. The keeping of separate accounts was a procedure followed by all the New England steamship companies that were controlled by railroads.

16. Old Colony Railroad, *Annual Report* (1875), p. 7, and *Annual Report* (1876), p. 9.

17. Old Colony Railroad, *Annual Report* (1874), p. 8.

18. Report on New Bedford & New York Steamship Co., D&B, Mass. 17:672.

19. "New Bedford and New York Propeller Co.," *NG*, 25 January 1873, p. 246; "New York and New Bedford S.S. Co.," *NG*, 30 May 1874, p. 387. One train alone sometimes furnished as much as twenty-six carloads of freight ("New Bedford as a Port of Entry," *NG*, 4 November 1874, p. 291). For additional details on the railroad and the steamship company see Baker, p. 36.

20. For details see Baker, pp. 32–40.

21. Report on New Bedford & New York Steamship Co., D&B, Mass. 18:380, 419.

22. Much of the information on the New Bedford & New York Steamship Co. was supplied by Martin J. Butler of New Bedford, Mass. See also ICC, *Docket 6469*, vol. 8, BE 43 (app. A), A–13, Excerpts from Directors' Minute Book, Old Colony Steamboat Co., p. 5; Report on New Bedford & New York Steamship Co., D&B, Mass. 18:419; *NG*, 16 August 1879, p. 139. A note was authorized by the Old Colony directors for $47,500 to pay for the *City of New Bedford*. See ICC, *Docket 6469*, BE 43 (app. A), A–13. The increased traffic resulting from the acquisition of the New Bedford Line forced the Old Colony Steamboat Co. to enlarge its facilities in New York City (*NG*, 9 August 1879, p. 130).

23. There is some difficulty in determining just when through service began again after the Civil War. The advertisement of the Providence & Stonington Steamship Co. stated that the first-class line that resumed operation in May 1877 had not operated since 1847. Yet an advertisement in the *Nautical Gazette* in 1873 stated that through tickets were sold to Boston. See advertisement of the Sprague family's Neptune Line in the *Nautical Gazette* (October and November 1873); Charles H. Dow, *History of Steam Navigation between New York & Providence*, pp. 25–27; *NG*, 5 June 1880, p. 58.

24. Dayton, pp. 197–98; Report on Providence & New York Steamboat Co., D&B, R.I. 10:23.

25. D&B, R.I. 10:355.

26. Ibid.; *NG*, 28 April 1875, p. 279; New York, Providence & Boston Railroad, *Annual Report* (1879), p. 5.

27. Compare Edward S. Sears, *Faxon's Illustrated Hand-Book of Summer Travel* (Boston, 1875), pp. 9–10; "The Old Massachusetts," *MJ*, 23 April 1904, p. 8; William K. Covell, "Steamboats on Narragansett Bay," *Bulletin No. 99 of the Newport Historical Society* (January 1934), p. 47. Covell claims that the *Massachusetts* was the first Sound steamer with the dining saloon on the main deck.

28. ICC, *Docket 6469*, vol. 8, BE 43 (app. A), A–8, Directors' Minutes of the Providence & Stonington Steamship Co., 12 December 1876.

29. General Ledger A of the Providence Line, 1876–82, Providence & Stonington Steamship Co., vol. 344 of New York, New Haven & Hartford Railroad Collection, Baker Library, Harvard Business School; New York, Providence & Boston Railroad, *Annual Report* (1877), p. 8. The new route also connected at the wharf with trains directly to the White Mountains (Dow, *Steam Navigation between New York & Providence*, pp. 26–27).

30. See Appendix A, table 1.

31. "Norwich Line," *NG*, 19 April 1873, p. 342; *NG*, 9 August 1873, p. 54. When the trackage rights agreement expired in December 1873, the Norwich Line terminal again was Allyn's Point. A new agreement between the Norwich & Worcester Railroad and the Vermont Central was signed, and service via New London was re-established on 20 July 1874. The New London Northern wharf remained the terminus until 1899 (ICC, *Docket 6469*, 15:6015–19, 6041). Allyn's Point was used occasionally by freight steamers until 1896.

32. ICC, *Docket 6645*, pp. 470–73.

33. See Appendix A, table 1.

34. Report on New Haven Steamboat Co., D&B, Conn. 40:814; *NG*, 22 November 1873, p. 176.

35. These railroads were the Fitchburg Railroad, Boston & Lowell Railroad, Boston & Maine Railroad, and Eastern Railroad ("Metropolitan Line," *NG*, 19 April 1873, p. 342).

36. Reports on Metropolitan Steamship Co., D&B, N.Y. 417:200FF; ibid., Mass. 82:106.

37. D&B, Mass. 82:106; "Launch of the 'Gen. Whitney,'" *NG*, 26 July 1873, p. 34; "Two New Steamships," *Scientific American*, 29 November 1873, p. 341; Dayton, p. 256.

38. Boston Board of Trade, *Twenty-seventh Annual Report* (1881), p. 46.

39. Report on Maine Steamship Co., D&B, Maine 14:75. The Packet Company was sold at auction for $157,000 (ibid., p. 341).

40. Ibid., p. 75; *NG*, 3 April 1880, p. 403; "Maine Steamship Co.," *NG*, 13 December 1873, p. 198; *NG*, 7 October 1874, p. 230.

41. Maine Central Railroad, *Annual Report* (1870), p. 3.

42. Maine Central Railroad, *Annual Report* (1876), pp. 6–8, and *Annual Report* (1877), p. 6.

260

43. Report on International Steamship Co., D&B, Maine 20 : 106.
44. Canal Investigation, file 4953/B–VII–29, Portland, Mt. Desert & Machias Steamboat Co., history of the company.
45. See Boston & Maine Railroad passenger timetable (17 February 1879), Collection of Employees' Timetables, Division of Transportation, Smithsonian Institution, Washington, D.C.
46. Report on Portland, Bangor & Machias Steamboat Co., D&B, Maine 20 : 146; *NG*, 26 June 1880, p. 87; ICC, *Docket 6891*, Petitioner's Exhibit 16, pp. 1–2; "Portland and the Coast Trade," *Portland* (Me.) *Board of Trade Journal* 9 (April 1897):361.
47. Kirkland, 2 : 128–29; Report on Portland Steam Packet Co., D&B, Maine 20 : 72.
48. *The New York Boston & Providence R.R. Co., & ali.* vs. *The Old Colony Railroad Co., et al., Demurrer for the Defendants*, pp. 1–7, box 32, pamphlet 1, Rider Collection, John Hay Library, Brown University.
49. "A New Freight Combination," *NG*, 5 May 1875, p. 295.
50. New York, Providence & Boston Railroad, *Annual Report* (1877), p. 8; copy of Onslow Stearns to William T. Hart, June [n.d.], 1877, folder marked "Webster, Daniel, Letter to I. Hedge, 1851," box 4, Old Colony Railroad Collection.
51. Stearns to Hart, June 1877; New York, Providence & Boston Railroad, *Annual Report* (1877), p. 8; Boston & Providence Railroad, *Annual Report* (1877), pp. 7–8.
52. New York, Providence & Boston Railroad, *Annual Report* (1877), p. 8.
53. Stearns to Hart, June 1877; Old Colony Railroad, *Annual Report* (1878), pp. 11–12.
54. Old Colony Railroad, *Annual Report* (1878), pp. 11–12; New York & New England Railroad, *Annual Report* (1877), pp. 5–6; New York, Providence & Boston Railroad, *Annual Report* (1879), p. 8. During the fiscal year of 1877–78 the Stonington Line receipts were down $84,853.53 from the preceding year, and the Providence Line receipts were down $132,075.95 (ICC, *Docket 6469*, vol. 8, BE 43 (app. A), A–7, Directors' Minutes of the Providence and Stonington Steamboat [*sic*] Co., 11 December 1878).
55. ICC, *Docket 6469*, vol. 8, BE 43 (app. A), A–7; ibid., A–6, Excerpt from President's Report to the Directors of the Providence & Stonington Steamship Co., 10 December 1879; *NG*, 19 April 1879, p. 3; "New Boston Steamers' Program," *NG*, 14 June 1879, p. 65. The Old Colony suffered additional losses when in 1880 the Maine Steamship Co. began stopping at Martha's Vineyard on its semiweekly trips between New York and Portland; the fare between Martha's Vineyard and New York was $3.00 (ibid., 26 June 1880, p. 83).
56. ICC, *Docket 6469*, vol. 8, BE 43 (app. A), A–5, Directors' Min-

utes, Stonington Steamboat Co.; ibid., A–6, p. 2. In the period from 1869 to 1872 the average number of passengers carried was about 70,000 per year; in 1878 and 1879 the Stonington Line carried 142,970 and 196,771 respectively (ibid.). Old Colony Railroad, *Annual Report* (1879), p. 11, and *Annual Report* (1880), p. 8; *NG*, 22 November 1879, p. 251. Despite the fact that the Old Colony failed to pay any dividend, it was able to retire $56,500 of its bonded debt and to purchase an additional steamer for $47,500 (Old Colony Railroad, *Annual Report* [1879], p. 11).

57. *NG*, 19 April 1879, p. 3; *NG*, 21 June 1879, p. 75; *NG*, 6 December 1879, p. 267.

58. *NG*, 19 July 1879, p. 107; see also Report on Metropolitan Steamship Co., D&B, Mass. 82:106; U.S., Congress, Senate, Select Committee on Interstate Commerce, *Report of the Senate Select Committee on Interstate Commerce*, 49th Cong., 1st sess., 1886, S. Rept. 46, pt. 2, 2 vols., 2:429.

59. *NG*, 24 May 1879, p. 46; *NG*, 19 July 1879, p. 118; *NG*, 3 April 1880, pp. 403–4.

60. *NG*, 21 June 1879, p. 75; *NG*, 5 June 1880, p. 58.

61. The signatories were: The New York, New Haven & Hartford Railroad; the Boston & Providence Railroad; the New York, Providence & Boston Railroad; the Providence & Stonington Steamship Co.; the Old Colony Railroad; the Old Colony Steamboat Co.; the New York & New England Railroad; and the Metropolitan Steamship Co.

62. *Report of the Senate Select Committee on Interstate Commerce* (1886), 2: 425–29; New York, Providence & Boston Railroad, *Annual Report* (1881), p. 10.

63. Old Colony Railroad, *Annual Report* (1881), p. 8.

64. Thomas C. Cochran, *Railroad Leaders, 1845–1890: The Business Mind in Action* (Cambridge, Mass., 1953), p. 496.

65. For details see Dayton, pp. 207–8.

66. "The Narragansett-Stonington Disaster," *NG*, 19 June 1880, p. 72. The testimony at the investigation brought out that many passengers had difficulty locating a life preserver "which was even in fair condition" (*NG*, 14 August 1880, p. 140).

67. "The Stonington Line Management," *NG*, 26 June 1880, p. 84; *NG*, 5 June 1880, p. 58; "Tempting Providence," *NG*, 28 August 1879, p. 149. The reporter for Dun & Bradstreet believed that the company was well managed despite all the adverse publicity in the press. See Report on Providence & Stonington Steamship Co., D&B, R.I. 10:428.

68. An example of the hostility of the *Nautical Gazette* is found in the following comment: "It is muttered around that the Stonington Line want to build a new iron steamer for their route. She ought to be fire and collision proof, and be commanded and piloted by men who

thoroughly understand their business and the whole concern managed by a gentleman who knows something about practical steamboating and civility" (*NG*, 24 July 1880, p. 115).

69. "The Narragansett-Stonington Collision," *NG*, 2 October 1880, p. 195.

70. *NG*, 9 April 1881, p. 203; Dayton, pp. 208–9; Report on Providence & Stonington Steamship Co., D&B, R.I. 10:428. The company did about 25 per cent of the through business between New York and Boston (ibid.).

71. *New York Times*, 24 November 1882; "The *N.Y. Times* and the Sound Steamers," *NG*, 7 December 1882, p. 68; "The *City of Worcester–Saginaw* Collision," *NG*, 14 December 1882, p. 73.

Chapter 3

1. Dayton, pp. 102–3; ICC, *Docket 6469*, vol. 8, BE 43 (app. A), pp. 17–21; ibid. (app. A), A–22; Report on Bridgeport Steamboat Co., D&B, Conn. 4:156.

2. Old Colony Railroad, *Annual Report* (1884), p. 8, and *Annual Report* (1885), p. 7; Providence & Stonington Steamship Co., *Annual Report* (1886), p. 11. For dividends paid see Appendix A, table 1.

3. Kirkland, 2:125–26; Dayton, pp. 268–69.

4. Report on Portland, Bangor & Machias Steamboat Co., D&B, Maine 20:146; ICC, *Docket 6891*, Petitioner's Exhibit 16, pp. 2–6.

5. Report on Portland, Bangor & Machias Steamboat Co., D&B, Maine 17:7. The two steamers acquired were the *City of Richmond* and the *Lewiston*.

6. Ibid.; ICC, *Docket 6891*, Petitioner's Exhibit 16, pp. 2–6; ibid., Testimony, pp. 74–77.

7. ICC, *Docket 6891*, Petitioner's Exhibit 16, pp. 2–6; "New England News," *Seaboard*, 14 June 1894.

8. See Report on Maine Steamship Co., D&B, Maine 20:350; Report on Portland Steam Packet Co., D&B, Maine 17:66, and D&B, Maine 20:72; Report on International Steamship Co., D&B, Maine 20:106, 367; *Portland* (Me.) *Board of Trade Journal* 1 (September 1888):159. By 1896 J. B. Coyle was general manager of the International Steamship Co., the Portland Steamship Co. (formerly Portland Steam Packet Co.), and the Maine Steamship Co. ("Our Splendid Steamship Lines," ibid. 8 [February 1896]:296).

9. Kirkland, 2:128–29.

10. For the history of the difficulties leading to the establishment of the Interstate Commerce Commission see Lee Benson, *Merchants, Farmers & Railroads: Railroad Regulation and New York Politics, 1850–1887* (Cambridge, Mass., 1955); Gabriel Kolko, *Railroads and Regulation, 1877–1916* (Princeton, N.J., 1965); I. L. Sharfman, *The*

Interstate Commerce Commission: A Study in Administrative Law and Procedure, 5 vols. (New York, 1931–37).

11. Maine Board of Railroad Commissioners, *Annual Report of the Railroad Commissioners of the State of Maine* (1891), p. 10; "The Railroad War on Steamboats," *MJ*, 5 January 1889, p. 9; "The Inter-State Law," *NG*, 6 April 1888, p. 2. In its first annual report the Interstate Commerce Commission stated the reason why water lines were not included in the commission's jurisdiction: "For the omission to include them [carriers by water] many reasons may be suggested, but perhaps the most influential were the evils of corporate management had not been so obvious in the case of carriers by water as in that of carriers by land, and moreover the rates of transportaton by water were so extremely low that they were seldom complained of as a grievance even when they were unequal and unjustly discriminating. In their competition with the carriers by land the carriers by water were sometimes at a disadvantage and compelled to accept lower rates, and this also had some influence in propitiating public favor, inasmuch as they appeared to operate as obstacles to monopoly and as checks upon extortion" (ICC, *First Annual Report* [1887], p. 272).

12. Report on International Steamship Co., D&B, Maine 20:367; Maine Central Railroad, *Annual Report* (1887), p. 6.

13. U.S., Department of Commerce, *Historical Statistics of the United States, Colonial Times to 1957* (Washington, D.C., 1960), pp. 12–13. Only Vermont failed to show any substantial gain in population between 1870 and 1890 (ibid.).

14. Charles A. Sweetser, *Book of Summer Resorts*, "Lakes, Rivers, and Mountains," p. 163; ibid., "Seaside Resorts," p. 56. To reach Moosehead Lake required a sixty-mile stage ride from the nearest railheads at Newport and Bangor; there was, however, a steamer on the lake (ibid., "Lakes, Rivers, and Mountains," p. 163).

15. Maine Central Railroad, *Annual Report* (1882), p. 6; Maine Central Railroad, *Maine: Present Condition of the State* (Augusta, Me., 1885), pp. 23–24; ICC, *Docket 6891*, pp. 29–33.

16. Maine Central Railroad, *Maine*, pp. 29–33; Maine Central Railroad, *Annual Report* (1886), p. 7.

17. [Maine] Secretary of State, *Statistics of Industries and Finances of Maine, 1886*, p. 156; [Maine] Commissioner of Industrial and Labor Statistics, *First Annual Report of the Bureau of Industrial and Labor Statistics of the State of Maine* (1887), p. 239; ICC, *Docket 6891*, pp. 32–33. It was estimated that 100,000 persons visited Maine during the summer months; their total expenditures were around $10 million (*First Annual Report, Industrial and Labor Statistics*, p. 239).

18. *Statistics of Industries and Finances of Maine, 1886*, pp. 160–61; Harold Fisher Wilson, *The Hill Country of Northern New England: Its Social and Economic History, 1790–1930* (New York, 1936), pp.

287–90. In 1873 the New Hampshire Board of Agriculture estimated that the state was receiving nearly $3 million annually from summer visitors; in 1891 the estimate was $5 million; by 1900 it was up to $6.6 million per year (ibid., p. 287). Vermont did not share in the resort boom as did Maine and New Hampshire; in 1894 a cursory investigation was made by the state, which concluded that during the preceding summer visitors left nearly $394,000 in Vermont (ibid., p. 289).

19. ICC, "Report of the Commission on New England Steamship Company et al.," *Interstate Commerce Commission Reports: Valuation Reports* 36 (1932):799–809; "Good News for Travelers to and from New England," *NG*, 30 June 1886, p. 5. By 1889 the Old Colony Railroad owned $40,000 worth of stock in the New Bedford, Martha's Vineyard & Nantucket Steamboat Co. (Old Colony Railroad, *Annual Report* [1886], p. 14, and *Annual Report* [1889]).

20. "Good News for Travelers," *NG*, 30 June 1886, p. 5. Each steamer carried a band.

21. "Norwich Line Steamer City of Worcester," *NG*, 5 November 1881, p. 25; "The City of Worcester," *Scientific American*, 11 February 1882, pp. 79, 84. The steamer cost $408,000.

22. "The Pilgrim," *NG*, 31 May 1883, pp. 57–59.

23. For an example, see article on a ship of the Portland Steam Packet Co. ("The Tremont," *NG*, 21 June 1883); Report on Portland Steam Packet Co., D&B, Maine 17:66; Report on Maine Steamship Co., D&B, Maine 20:350.

24. Old Colony Railroad, *Annual Report* (1889), p. 8.

25. The tonnage and revenue of the Old Colony Steamboat Co. on eastbound shipments from New York City to Fall River are shown in copies of Way Bills of Merchandise from New York to Fall River, 1887–88, Old Colony Steamboat Co., vols. 310–12 of Old Colony Railroad Collection, Baker Library, Harvard Business School. For example: on 6 October 1887 the *City of Fall River* carried 1,452 bales of cotton (830,330 lbs.), for which the freight charges totaled $7,926; on 31 December 1887 the *City of Brockton* carried 2,476 bales (1,251,244 lbs.), for which the freight charges totaled $10,121. To be sure, these were unusually large shipments of one commodity, but they illustrate the tremendous tonnage moving on the steamship lines. For the freight revenue of the Providence & Stonington Steamship Co. and the Old Colony Steamboat Co. see Appendix A, tables 3 and 4.

26. *NG*, 22 February 1883, p. 155. The distance between Fall River and New York is 181 miles. The *City of Fall River* cost $225,552 (Ledgerbook, 1874–1884, Old Colony Steamboat Co., vol. 335 of New York, New Haven & Hartford Railroad Collection, Baker Library, Harvard Business School).

27. *NG*, 23 May 1887, p. 5.

28. Kirkland, 2:129; Report on Maine Steamship Co., D&B, Maine

20 : 350; Report on Portland Steam Packet Co., D&B, Maine 17 : 66; Report on International Steamship Co., D&B, Maine 20 : 106. See Appendix A, table 7 for revenue of Maine Steamship Co. in 1902–3.

29. See copies of Way Bills of Merchandise from New York to Fall River, 1887–88, Old Colony Steamboat Co., vols. 310–12 of Old Colony Railroad Collection. See also list of firms shipping over the Sound lines in Appendix B.

30. See statistics on passenger and freight earnings in Appendix A.

31. See Appendix A, tables 1 and 2.

32. For details of these events see Baker, pp. 80–85; Kirkland, 2 : 72–90.

33. See Kirkland, 2 : 86–90; Baker, pp. 85–87.

34. Massachusetts General Court, Joint Standing Committee on Railroads, *Report of Hearings before the Joint Standing Committee on Railroads; under the Order for Said Committee to Investigate the Conduct of the New York, New Haven and Hartford Railroad Company* (n.p., [1893]), pp. 93–95; Kirkland, 2 : 50–51.

35. Kirkland, 2 : 53–63; Baker, pp. 57–59.

36. Baker, pp. 57–59; Kirkland, 2 : 53–64.

37. Clarence W. Barron, *More They Told Barron: Conversations and Revelations of an American Pepys in Wall Street*, ed. Arthur Pound and Samuel Taylor Moore (New York, 1931), pp. 136–37; Baker, pp. 59–60, 89–92; Kirkland, 2 : 64–68, 90–95.

38. Kirkland, 2 : 92–95.

39. See *Massachusetts Hearings to Investigate the New Haven Railroad*, pp. 240–45; Barron, *More They Told Barron*, p. 123. The New Haven Railroad paid the New York Central Railroad $800,000 a year for the use of Grand Central Station and trackage rights into the station, which made it awkward for the New York Central to co-operate with the New York & New England Railroad even if it desired to do so. The New York Central was forbidden by law to discriminate, but the law had no penalties attached (ibid.).

40. Barron, *More They Told Barron*, p. 128; *Massachusetts Hearings to Investigate the New Haven Railroad*, pp. 10–32, 46–89, 180–95. Clark defended the actions of the New Haven in a conversation he had with Clarence W. Barron, saying that "the newspapers had been going all wrong on New York, New Haven & Hartford. It was the duty of that Company to run its road for its stockholders, and when business fell off it must consolidate trains. That noon a New York & New England train came down with two Boston passengers" (Barron, *More They Told Barron*, p. 128).

41. Kirkland, 2 : 99–100; ICC, *Docket 6469*, vol. 8, BE 43 (app. A), A–22; New York & New England Railroad, *Annual Report for 1892* (1893), pp. 16–17.

42. *Financial Transactions*, 2 : 2336–37.

43. For details see Baker, pp. 65–66; Kirkland, 2 : 68–71.

44. See Kirkland, 2 : 70; Frederick Lewis Allen, *The Great Pierpont Morgan* (New York, 1949), passim.

45. Norwich Line passengers could get only one through train to Boston. It left New London at 3:00 A.M., taking four hours to make the run. In contrast, the Fall River Line and Providence Line had express trains leaving at 6:00 A.M. for the one hour and twenty minute ride to Boston. In addition, the New York & New England was refused by other parties to the Sound lines' agreement a differential on its business via the Norwich Line (New York & New England Railroad, *Annual Report for 1892* [1893], pp. 16–17).

46. See Baker, p. 173; Kirkland, 2 : 31. J. P. Morgan was instrumental in getting the warring parties together (ibid.).

47. Kirkland, 2 : 70; Baker, p. 67; U.S., Industrial Commission, *Report of the Industrial Commission on Transportation* (Washington, D.C., 1901), *Reports of the Industrial Commission*, 9 : 456.

48. The whole transcript of the testimony is full of details regarding the handling of freight and passenger traffic into Boston. See *Massachusetts Hearings to Investigate the New Haven Railroad*, passim.

49. See Kirkland, 2 : 100–101.

50. New York, New Haven & Hartford Railroad, *Annual Report* (1895), pp. 4–5.

51. *Financial Transactions*, 2 : 2335. The stock was carried on the books of the New York, Providence & Boston Railroad at $1,437,300 (ibid.).

52. ICC, *Docket 6469*, vol. 8, BE 43 (app. A), A–8½; ibid. (app. A), pp. 35–42. C. P. Clark, president of the New Haven, at a joint meeting of the directors of the railroad and those of the Providence & Stonington Steamship Co. on 20 May 1893, was strongly opposed to any idea of valuating the steamship property on the basis of the fact that it had been paying a 10 per cent dividend; he doubted that it could earn 8 per cent and said that there was not enough rail traffic to fill the Providence steamers unless trains were run from other areas to the Fox Point terminal (ibid. [app. A], A–8½).

53. Ibid. (app. A), pp. 37–41; ibid. (app. A), A–10.

54. *Financial Transactions*, 2 : 2336–37. The total 12,000 shares were carried on the books at a value of $1,277,500; the agreed value of the steamboat company was $3,600,000, an amount in excess of the combined capital and surplus by $1,691,478.61 (ibid., p. 2337).

55. ICC, *Docket 6469*, vol. 8, BE 43 (app. A), pp. 46–49.

56. For details see Baker, pp. 67–69.

57. ICC, *Docket 6469*, 6 : 5122–25.

58. *Financial Transactions*, 2 : 2334–35.

59. *Providence Daily Journal*, 9 February 1893; "The Consolidated Line to Boston," *Commercial and Financial Chronicle*, 11 February

1893, pp. 226–27; "The Extension of the New Haven Road to Boston," *Railroad Gazette*, 10 February 1893, p. 114. It is interesting that the Providence Board of Trade and the Boston Chamber of Commerce made no extensive comment on these acquisitions in their official publications. The *Nautical Gazette* reacted in a similar way to the three publications above when the Old Colony Railroad leased the Boston & Providence Railroad ("The Old Colony Railroad," *NG*, 12 November 1887, p. 7).

60. U.S., Industrial Commission, *Report of the Industrial Commission on Transportation* (Washington, D.C., 1900), *Reports of the Industrial Commission*, 4:153.

61. Knapp believed it was unwise to foster competition between railroads or to treat them as purely private businesses were treated (ibid., p. 93).

62. ICC, *Twelfth Annual Report, January 11, 1899* (Washington, D.C., 1899), p. 16.

63. "Resumption of Passenger Service to New York by the Providence Line," *Providence Journal of Commerce* 3 (June 1895):24; "The New Steamer of the Merchants and Miners Transportation Company," ibid., p. 10.

64. "A New Sound Line between New York and Providence," *Seaboard*, 25 July 1895, p. 639; ibid., 30 July 1896, p. 654; *Marine Journal*, 23 October 1897, p. 4. The May 1896 *Providence Journal of Commerce* (p. 22, "A New Steamship Line between Providence and New York") reported that a company called the Commercial Steamship Co. had been organized with F. M. Mathewson as president. He headed a butterine manufacturing firm in Providence. Others in the group were heads of a grocery house, a dyeing and printing company, and a drug wholesale house. Two propeller steamers of about 400–500 tons each were to be purchased. The company was expected to be in operation in two or three months. Tonnage was at first expected to total around 200 tons outbound a day. Later, inbound tonnage was expected to exceed this.

65. See New York, New Haven & Hartford Railroad, *Annual Report* (1893) and *Annual Report* (1894).

Chapter 4

1. See Samuel Ward Stanton, *American Steam Vessels* (New York, 1895) and John H. Morrison, *History of American Steam Navigation* (New York, 1903) for dimensions and details on the early steamers. The registered dimensions listed in the notes below are from U.S., Department of Commerce, Bureau of Navigation, *Forty-fifth Annual List of Merchant Vessels of the United States* (1913).

2. *City of Lawrence* measured 243′ x 40′ x 11′9″; she was powered

by a beam engine with a 65″ cylinder and an 11′ stroke (Morrison, p. 337). She cost $230,793 (ICC, *Docket 6469*, vol. 8, BE 43 [app. A], A–14, H. M. Kochersperger to John M. Hall, 6 June 1899). The *General Whitney* had hull dimensions of 240′ x 40′ x 30′ depth of hold; her engines had cylinders of 36″ and 60″ ("Launch of the 'Gen. Whitney,'" *NG*, 26 July 1873, p. 34).

3. See Kirkland, 2 : 198.

4. *Rhode Island* had dimensions of 325′ x 45′ x 15′; her beam engine had a 90″ cylinder and a 14′ stroke (*NG*, 1 June 1905, p. 413). The *Massachusetts* measured 323′ x 42′ x 15′; her beam engine was the same size as the one on the *Rhode Island* (ibid.). The construction account for the *Massachusetts* totaled $419,026.95 (General Ledger A, Stonington Line, 1875–82, Providence & Stonington Steamship Co., vol. 343 of the New York, New Haven & Hartford Railroad Collection, Baker Library, Harvard Business School).

5. *City of Worcester* had dimensions of 340′ x 46′ x 16′; her beam engine had a 90″ cylinder and a 12′ stroke (*NG*, 1 June 1905, p. 413). For additional information see "Norwich Line Steamer City of Worcester," *NG*, 5 November 1881, p. 25; "The City of Worcester," *Scientific American*, 11 February 1882, pp. 79, 84.

6. Old Colony Railroad, *Annual Report* (1882), p. 8; "The 'Pilgrim,'" *NG*, 31 May 1883, pp. 57–59; "The Fall River Line," *Engineering* (London), 16 January 1891, p. 64; *NG*, 27 December 1883, p. 90; "The Great Fall River Line," *NG*, 23 January 1886, p. 121; ICC, *Docket 6469*, vol. 8, BE 43 (app. A), A–14, Kochersperger to Hall, 6 June 1899. An interesting side light to the construction of the *Pilgrim* is the fact that she drew about a foot more than was anticipated. This was apparently the result of a lack of experience in construction with iron and the effect iron has on buoyancy. It in no way affected the ability of the *Pilgrim* in heavy weather, but she did take seas harder due to this lower freeboard. George Pierce had never before been connected with designing a steamer with an iron hull. Stevenson Taylor, of W. & A. Fletcher Co., gave the above information.

7. *NG*, 22 February 1883, p. 155. The *City of Fall River* measured 260′ on the water line, 41′ beam, 17′ depth of hold; her engine had one high-pressure cylinder of 44″ with an 8′ stroke and one low-pressure cylinder of 68″ with a 12′ stroke (ibid.). She cost $234,102 (ICC, *Docket 6469*, vol. 8, BE 43 [app. A], A–14, Kochersperger to Hall, 6 June 1899). The *City of Brockton* cost about $225,000 (Old Colony Railroad, *Annual Report* [1886], p. 7).

8. "Steamer Notes," *NG*, 10 December 1885, p. 75. The *Nashua* cost $226,659.15. See construction account for *Nashua* in General Ledger 1, 1883–91, Providence & Stonington Steamship Co., vol. 345 of the New York, New Haven & Hartford Railroad Collection.

9. "The 'H. F. Dimock,' of the Metropolitan S.S. Company," *NG*, 26

June 1884, p. 89; *NG*, 9 October 1884, p. 2. Her speed was 14.8 miles per hour, and her dimensions, 278.6' over-all length, 41.6' beam, 29' depth of hold; her compound engine had a 36" cylinder and a 68" cylinder with a 54" stroke (*NG*, 26 June 1884, p. 89). She cost $279,569.80 (Property Account of Metropolitan Steamship Co., February 1910, in miscellaneous records of Eastern Steamship Lines, Inc., in possession of Albert J. McLaughlin, Lauderdale-by-the-Sea, Fla.).

10. "The Tremont," *NG*, 21 June 1883. The *Tremont* had dimensions of 260' x 36' x 9.6'; her beam engine had a 56" cylinder and an 11' stroke; her average speed was 16 miles per hour (ibid.). The *Penobscot* measured 249' over-all x 38' x 13' depth of hold; her vertical beam engine had a 58" cylinder and a 12' stroke; her speed was 16.1 miles per hour (Stanton, p. 285).

11. "The Engines of the Steamer Connecticut," *Scientific American*, 26 January 1889, pp. 47, 56; General Ledger 1, 1883–91, Providence & Stonington Steamship Co., vol. 345 of the New York, New Haven & Hartford Railroad Collection. The dimensions of the *Connecticut* were 358' over-all x 48' x 18' depth of hold; her engine had a 56" and a 104" cylinder with an 11' stroke (Stanton, p. 356). She cost $673,125. For references to her breakdowns see *MJ*, 26 June 1897, p. 2; ibid., 1 January 1898, p. 2; ibid., 10 December 1898, p. 2; ibid., 12 August 1899, p. 2. *Seaboard* reported similar occurrences.

12. "The Fall River Line," *Engineering* (London), 16 January 1891, pp. 64–68; Old Colony Railroad, *Annual Report* (1889), p. 8. The registered dimensions of the *Puritan* were 403.5' x 52.5' x 18.1'. Her engine had a high-pressure cylinder of 75" with a 9' stroke and a low-pressure cylinder of 110" with a 14' stroke (Stanton, p. 353).

13. Old Colony Railroad, *Annual Report* (1889), p. 8; *Annual Report* (1891), pp. 8–9. The registered dimensions of the *Plymouth* were 352' x 50.4' x 18.8'. Her engine had four cylinders, measuring 50", 75", and two of 81.5", with a stroke of 99"; the total original cost was $1,112,000, of which $750,000 was paid to the builder (ICC, *Valuation Docket 941*, vol. 2; ICC, *Valuation Docket 1054*, Engineering Report, p. 29).

14. Old Colony Railroad, *Annual Report* (1891), pp. 8–9; "The New Freight Steamer City of Taunton," *Fall River Line Journal*, 31 October 1892, p. 5. The registered dimensions of the *City of Taunton* were 283' x 43' x 18.2'. She was almost 12' longer than the *City of Brockton*. Her compound beam engine had 47" and 71" cylinders with 8' and 12' strokes (ICC, *Valuation Docket 941*, vol. 2). She cost $275,540 (ICC, *Docket 6469*, vol. 8, BE 43 [app. A], A–14, Kochersperger to Hall, 6 June 1899).

15. "The Fall River Steamer 'Priscilla,'" *Engineering* (London), 13 July 1894, pp. 38–41; ICC, *Valuation Docket 1054*, Engineering Report, p. 29. The registered dimensions of the *Priscilla* were 425.8' x

52.3′ x 18.3′. Her engine had two 51″ cylinders and two 95″ cylinders with an 11′ stroke (ICC, *Valuation Docket 941*, vol. 2).

16. Ibid. Registered dimensions of the *New Hampshire* were 302.7′ x 44′ x 17.5′. Her triple expansion engine had four cylinders, of 28″, 45″, and two of 51″, with a 42″ stroke; the amount paid to the builder was $409,984.13, which included a bonus of $15,000 for an additional ¾ knot speed (ICC, *Valuation Docket 941*, vol. 2).

17. "How a Noted Yacht Designer Became a Designer of Steamships," *NG*, 12 November 1908, pp. 250–51.

18. Ibid. The *Richard Peck* cost $456,069.31 (Ledger, 1894–1901, New Haven Steamboat Co., G. W. Blunt White Library, Marine Historical Association, Inc., Mystic, Conn.). The registered dimensions of the *Richard Peck* were 303.3′ x 48′ x 17.8′; her two triple expansion engines each had three cylinders, of 24″, 38″, and 60″, with a 30″ stroke (ICC, *Valuation Docket 941*, vol. 2). An indication of the durability of this steamer is that she was in active service until 1953.

19. "How a Noted Yacht Designer Became a Designer of Steamships," *NG*, 12 November 1908, p. 251. The *City of Lowell* had registered dimensions of 322.3′ x 49.7′ x 17.7′. She was powered by two triple expansion engines with cylinders of 26″, 40″, and 64″, with a 36″ stroke (ICC, *Valuation Docket 941*, vol. 2). She cost $478,600 (ICC, *Valuation Docket 1054*, Engineering Report, p. 29). The *Chester W. Chapin* had registered dimensions of 312′ x 48′ x 16.9′. She was powered by two triple expansion engines with cylinders of 24″, 38″, and 60″, with a 30″ stroke (ICC, *Valuation Docket 941*, vol. 2). She cost $485,676.03 (Ledger, 1894–1901, New Haven Steamboat Co., G. W. Blunt White Library).

20. "Disaster to Shipping," *Seaboard*, 1 December 1898, p. 101. The dimensions of the *Portland* were 291′ over-all x 42′ x 15.5′; she was powered by a beam engine with a 62″ cylinder and a 12′ stroke, and cost $250,000 (Stanton, pp. 386–87).

21. "Magnificent Coastwise Steamer," *NG*, 31 May 1900, p. 3. The registered dimensions of the *Governor Dingley* were 298.9′ x 60.8′ x 17.8′. She was powered by a triple expansion engine with cylinders of 27.5″, 44.5″, and 70″ and a stroke of 36″ (Dayton, p. 275).

22. Dayton, p. 278; Stanton, pp. 396–97. The dimensions of the *Cottage City* were 250′ x 40′ x 23′; she had one triple expansion engine with cylinders of 22″, 34″, and 55″, and a stroke of 36″; she cost $150,000 (ibid., p. 397).

23. "Arrival of the John Englis," *Seaboard*, 31 December 1896, p. 179; "The New Steamship Horatio Hall," ibid., 31 March 1898, p. 379. In the 1870s and 1880s the schedule had been 35 hours between New York and Portland. The dimensions of the *John Englis* were 313.3′ x 46′ x 17.5′; she had a double bottom and a triple expansion engine, and cost $350,000 ("Arrival of the John Englis," ibid., 31 December 1896, p. 179).

24. "The New Steamship Horatio Hall," p. 379; "Magnificent Coastwise Steamer," *NG*, 31 May 1900, p. 3. The dimensions of the *North Star* were 325' over-all, 46' beam, 19'10" depth of hold; her triple expansion engine had cylinders of 28", 48", and 75", and a 54" stroke ("Elegant Passenger Steamship Launched," *NG*, 9 May 1901, p. 8). She cost $370,071.62 (Memorandum regarding *North Star*, dated 1/18/18, initialed R. T. B., in miscellaneous records of Eastern Steamship Lines in possession of A. J. McLaughlin).

25. "New American Steamers—XV," *Seaboard*, 28 May 1896, p. 504. See also "New Long Island Sound Freight Steamer Pequonnock," *NG*, 10 May 1906. One of the Central Vermont–leased freighters was the *Mohawk*, with registered dimensions of 265' x 43' x 16.8'. She was powered by a triple expansion engine with cylinders of 21", 34", and 56", and a 42" stroke (ICC, *Valuation Docket 941*, vol. 2). On one of her best runs from New London to New York the *Mohawk*, loaded with freight, averaged 18 miles per hour ("New American Steamers—XV").

26. "Long Island Sound Steamboats," *NG*, 1 June 1905, pp. 403–9; "The Steamer Commonwealth," *NG*, 26 November 1908, pp. 273–77. The *Providence* was the last steamer designed by George Pierce. Her registered dimensions were 379.4' x 50' x 18.6'. Her engine had two 44" cylinders and two 83" cylinders, with a 9' stroke (ICC, *Valuation Docket 941*, vol. 2). The registered dimensions of the *Commonwealth* were 437.9' x 55' x 19.3'. Her engine had two 50" cylinders and two 96" cylinders, with a 114" stroke (ibid.). The *Providence* cost $1,110,000, and the *Commonwealth* $1,783,000 (ICC, *Valuation Docket 1054*, Engineering Report, p. 29). On her trials the *Commonwealth* averaged 23.09 miles per hour ("Progressive Speed Trials of Fall River Line Steamboat Commonwealth," *NG*, 17 December 1908, p. 312).

27. "The First American-Built Turbine-Propelled Steamship," *NG*, 1 November 1906, pp. 305–11, 320. The registered dimensions of the *Governor Cobb* were 289.1' x 54' x 18'. She had three Parsons turbines fitted to three shafts, with the high-pressure turbine in the center, the standard arrangement; she attained a speed of 21.66 miles per hour on her trials and had a double hull (ibid.).

28. "Launch of the American Turbine Steamship Yale," *NG*, 29 December 1906, pp. 385–89; "New American Turbine Steamers Yale and Harvard," *NG*, 8 August 1907, pp. 79–87; *Morse v. Metropolitan Steamship Co.*, pp. 530–36. The dimensions of the *Harvard* and the *Yale* were 386.5' x 50.5' x 22'; they had double hulls (*NG*, 8 August 1907, pp. 79–87).

29. "Details of the Three New Steamers Which Will Be Placed on the New York and Boston 'Outside' Route by the New England Navigation Company," *NG*, 4 April 1907, pp. 297–99. The *Massachusetts* cost $671,192.78; the *Bunker Hill* $665,543.07; the *Old Colony*

$665,281.09 (Memorandum on the *Massachusetts, Old Colony*, and *Bunker Hill*, dated 1/8/18, initialed R. T. B., in miscellaneous records of Eastern Steamship Lines in possession of A. J. McLaughlin). The reason the *Massachusetts* cost more is probably that she was the first one built. Her dimensions were 375′ over-all x 52′ breadth molded x 22′ depth molded; she was powered by two four-cylinder triple expansion engines with cylinders of 26″, 43″, and two of 51″, and a 42″ stroke (*NG*, 4 April 1907, pp. 297–99).

30. See Henry Hall, *Report on the Shipbuilding Industry* (Washington, D.C., 1882), *Tenth Census of the United States, 1880*, 10 : 153–54.

31. For details on steamers mentioned in the text see "The 'Pilgrim,'" *NG*, 31 May 1883, pp. 57–59; ICC, *Valuation Docket 941*, vol. 2.

32. *Seaboard*, 8 December 1892, p. 125; "Hyde Propeller Wheels," *NG*, 22 November 1906, p. 366. The *City of Lowell* was the first vessel in Sound service to be equipped with bronze wheels, which cost about $4,000 apiece, compared to $500 for her original, cast iron wheels. According to George W. Brady, the superintendent of the Norwich Line, the new wheels had *"increased her speed considerably"* ("The *Lowell's* New Bronze Wheels," *MJ*, 9 March 1895, p. 6). The 78.3 per cent efficiency of the *Lowell's* wheels compared quite favorably with the 50 per cent efficiency of the feathering wheels of the *Commonwealth* ("Progressive Speed Trials of the Fall River Line Steamboat Commonwealth," *NG*, 17 December 1908, p. 312).

33. Stanton, pp. 287, 497; ICC, *Valuation Docket 941*, vol. 2; *Seaboard*, 22 December 1892, p. 168. Roger Williams McAdam says that some consideration was given to constructing a large propeller-driven steamer at the time designs were being considered for what was to be the *Commonwealth*; it was finally decided that the side-wheel type was best adapted for the conditions encountered on the Fall River route (*The Old Fall River Line* [Brattleboro, Vt., 1937], p. 78).

34. "The First American-Built Turbine-Propelled Steamship," *NG*, 1 November 1906, pp. 305–11, 320; "New American Turbine Steamers Yale and Harvard," *NG*, 8 August 1907, pp. 79–87; "New Turbine Steamer Camden," *NG*, 7 March 1907, p. 236.

35. *NG*, 14 December 1905, p. 430; *NG*, 18 January 1906, p. 52; "New Down-East Sternwheeler that Didn't Steer," *NG*, 3 May 1906, pp. 330–31.

36. Morrison, pp. 319–20; *NG*, 27 July 1899, p. 5. For comparison, the *City of Worcester* on her shorter run to New London burned an average of 32 tons per trip (Morrison, p. 337).

37. "The Fall River Steamer 'Priscilla,'" *Engineering* (London), 13 July 1894, p. 39. This is about 1.18 pounds per horsepower per hour and compares with efficiencies of about 4 pounds per horsepower per hour in 1860 (Kirkland, 2 : 213–14).

38. Boats Running Expenses, Stonington Line, 1887–95, Providence & Stonington Steamship Co., G. W. Blunt White Library.

39. ICC, *Docket 6469*, 4:2599–2601. Similar savings were made with the *Richard Peck*, which burned only 19 tons of coal on the New Haven–New York run compared to about 40 tons for the side-wheeler *C. H. Northam* ("How a Noted Yacht Designer Became a Designer of Steamships," *NG*, 12 November 1908, p. 251).

40. Detail Ledger A, 1883–98, Providence and Stonington Steamship Co., vol. 347 of New York, New Haven & Hartford Railroad Collection.

41. Record of Operation Expenses, 1898–1903, Old Colony Steamboat Co., G. W. Blunt White Library. There was a considerable rise in the price of coal. In the period around 1905 it was about $2.00 a ton; by 1914 the price was $3.25 a ton (*Morse* v. *Metropolitan Steamship Co.*, p. 673). See also Appendix A, table 18.

42. T. C. Purdy, "Report on Steam Navigation in the United States," in *Report of the Agencies of Transportation in the United States* (Washington, D.C., 1883), *Tenth Census of the United States, 1880*, 4:34; *NG*, 14 August 1902, p. 10; ICC, *Docket 6891*, pp. 33–38; Stanton, p. 397.

43. *Morse* v. *Metropolitan Steamship Co.*, pp. 591–94, 668. The *Harvard* and the *Yale* each burned about 52,000 gallons of oil on the New York–Boston run; the *Massachusetts* and the *Bunker Hill* each burned about 42,000 gallons (ibid., pp. 591–94). In October 1919 the directors of Eastern Steamship Lines voted to convert the *Belfast*, *Camden*, *Calvin Austin*, *Governor Cobb*, *Governor Dingley*, and *North Land* to oil (Minutes of special directors' meeting, Boston, 20 October 1919, Minute Book of Directors Meetings (1917–21), Eastern Steamship Lines, Inc., in office of Pierce, Atwood, Scribner, Allen & McKusick, Portland, Me.).

44. "From New York to Fall River," *MJ*, 29 June 1907, p. 8. For representative running times of steamers on the Sound lines see Morrison, pp. 265–354.

45. *Seaboard*, 1 July 1897, p. 598; "The Steamship John Englis," ibid., 22 July 1897, p. 641; Dayton, p. 280.

46. The *Chester W. Chapin* did 21 m.p.h. on her trials ("The Providence Line's New Steamer," *MJ*, 6 January 1900, p. 5). The *Providence* made 23 m.p.h. on her trial trip, which lasted four hours (ibid., 15 April 1905, p. 7). The *Calvin Austin*, of the Eastern Steamship Co., averaged 17.2 m.p.h. between Eastport, Maine, and St. John, New Brunswick (*NG*, 22 June 1905, p. 472). The *Governor Cobb* averaged 22.16 m.p.h. between Execution Light and Boston Harbor (ibid., 1 November 1906, p. 318). The *Camden* made 21.475 m.p.h. on her speed trials ("Speedy New Turbine Steamer Camden," ibid., 30 May 1907, p. 429).

47. William K. Covell says that the *Boston* was not a success because it was soon found that there was not sufficient demand to justify running a separate express freight steamer. The *Boston* could carry only slightly more freight than the company's other freighters while burning substantially more fuel to attain her higher speed. After World War I the *Boston* was laid up more often than she was in service ("Steamboats on Narragansett Bay," *Bulletin No. 99 of the Newport Historical Society*, pp. 48–49).

48. "The 'Pilgrim,'" *NG*, 31 May 1883, pp. 57–59; *NG*, 29 May 1884, p. 61. A similar incident happened to the *Puritan* in the autumn of 1895. She was grounded on a ledge for four days, but after being floated she returned to New London under her own steam with her inside hull intact. The *Marine Journal* (16 November 1895, p. 9) commented: "The incident showed that the management of this line do nothing by halves and that the steamers are just as stanch and safe as they are elegant and comfortable."

49. Old Colony Railroad, *Annual Report* (1884), p. 8; "Electric Lights on Steamers," *NG*, 19 July 1883, p. 116.

50. "Steamer Notes," *NG*, 10 December 1885, p. 75.

51. "The 'Pilgrim,'" *NG*, 31 May 1883, p. 58.

52. "The Fall River Line," *Engineering* (London), 16 January 1891, pp. 64–65.

53. "Long Island Sound Steamboats," *NG*, 1 June 1905, pp. 404–6; "The Steamer Commonwealth," *NG*, 26 November 1908, 275–76; "The Commonwealth," *MJ*, 12 October 1907, p. 7; ICC, *Docket No. 5733, Colonial Navigation Co., Complainant, v. the New York, New Haven & Hartford Railroad Company, Defendant*, 1 vol., R.G. 134, National Archives, pp. 146–49, 152. J. Howland Gardner, of the New England Steamship Co., stated that the fire pumps on the *Commonwealth* were 5½ times what the law required; on the *Priscilla* and *Providence* they were 4 times the requirements; on the *Plymouth* 4¾ times; on the *City of Lowell* 1⅓ times; on the *Richard Peck, Chester W. Chapin, Maine,* and *New Hampshire* 1½ times (ICC, *Docket 6469*, 2 : 175–77).

54. *NG*, 16 October 1880, p. 4; "The Fall River Line," *Engineering* (London), 16 January 1891, p. 64; *MJ*, 13 May 1893, p. 9; "The Great Fall River Line," *NG*, 23 January 1886, p. 121. Typical of the comments is this one: "There are no steamers in the United States kept in better order and more liberally managed and carefully run than those belonging to the Old Colony system, and we guarantee that very few of our readers were aware that their fleet comprised fourteen steamboats" (*MJ*, 13 May 1893, p. 9).

55. *NG*, 21 July 1904, p. 46; *NG*, 20 April 1905, p. 309; *NG*, 8 August 1907, p. 83. For an example of the care with which the steamers were operated see Captain's Log of Steamer *Providence*, 1 March 1892–9 August 1894, vol. 173 of Old Colony Railroad Collection, Baker Library, Harvard Business School.

56. ICC, *Docket 6469*, 2:50–53, 4:2404–5, 4:2555–56.

57. "Narragansett Steamship Co.," *NG*, 15 June 1872, p. 406; *NG*, 11 October 1873, p. 126. The shops in Fall River were used as late as the latter part of the 1880s.

58. "Steamer Notes," *NG*, 10 December 1885, p. 75.

59. Rhode Island Railroad Commissioner, *Annual Report*, 1900 (1901), pp. 42–43; New York, New Haven & Hartford Railroad, *Annual Report* (1902), p. 5; ICC, *Docket 6469*, 4:2881–84; ibid., vol. 17, Brief of Petitioner, p. 17; ibid., vol. 11, blueprint Map of Newport Shop Facilities.

60. *NG*, 7 December 1882, p. 67; ICC, *Valuation Docket 941*, 2:474–83. All work on cabins, joinery, and machinery above the main deck on the *City of Brockton* and *City of Taunton* was done at Newport; on the *Providence* the work totaled $100,000 (ibid.).

61. ICC, *Docket 6469*, vol. 17, Brief of Petitioner, p. 17. At any time from two to eight steamers were undergoing repairs or annual overhauling (ibid.). The Newport shops did much of the work installing the electric lighting systems on the older steamers.

62. Edward S. Sears, *Faxon's Illustrated Hand-Book of Summer Travel*, pp. 9–10; *NG*, 9 June 1886, p. 7; "The Fall River Line," *Engineering* (London), 23 January 1891, pp. 94–95; "The Fall River Steamer 'Priscilla,'" ibid., 13 July 1894, p. 39; "New Sound Flyer," *NG*, 11 January 1900, p. 3; "Long Island Sound Steamboats," *NG*, 1 June 1905, p. 404.

63. "The Steamer Commonwealth," *NG*, 26 November 1908, p. 277. For the arrangement of the interior see the plans of the *Commonwealth* in Steamship Plans, Division of Transportation, Museum of History and Technology, Smithsonian Institution, Washington, D.C.

64. "Launch of the American Turbine Steamship Yale," *NG*, 29 December 1906, p. 389.

65. See deck plan of the *Puritan* in "The Fall River Line," *Engineering* (London), 16 January 1891, p. 65. See also plans of the *Providence* and the *Commonwealth* in Steamship Plans, Division of Transportation, Museum of History and Technology, Smithsonian Institution.

66. "New American Steamers Yale and Harvard," *NG*, 8 August 1894, pp. 933–36).

67. "Steamer Notes," *NG*, 2 February 1887, p. 11.

68. See Sears, *Faxon's Illustrated Hand-Book of Summer Travel*, pp. 9–10. William K. Covell states that the *Massachusetts* was the first Sound steamer to have the dining saloon on the main deck and that the trend started on the Hudson River steamers ("Steamboats on Narragansett Bay," *Bulletin No. 99 of the Newport Historical Society*, p. 47).

69. "New Sound Boats," *Seaboard*, 23 January 1892, p. 217. The *City of Lowell* continued the trend, with her dining saloon and kitchen

on the upper deck ("A Long Island Sound Palace," *NG,* 4 October 1894, pp. 933–36).

70. "The 'Pilgrim,'" *NG,* 31 May 1883, p. 58; "The Steamer Commonwealth," *NG,* 26 November 1908, p. 277.

71. "The 'Pilgrim,'" pp. 58–59.

72. ICC, *Docket 6469,* vol. 17, Brief of Petitioner, p. 17.

73. "The Narragansett Steamship Co.," *NG,* 7 June 1873, p. 398; "Sixty Years of the Fall River Line," *Fall River Line Journal,* 31 May 1909, p. 4. For the type of music played at these concerts see programs in the *Fall River Line Journal.* On Sunday evening the concerts featured sacred music (*MJ,* 30 March 1889, p. 7).

74. The Providence & Stonington Steamship Co. began publishing its *Bulletin* in 1878 (*MJ,* 21 January 1893, p. 3). The Norwich Line did not establish its *Norwich Line News* until around 1895 ("Norwich Line 'News,'" *MJ,* 27 July 1895, p. 5). The Metropolitan Steamship Co. issued the *Aerogram* nightly on the *Harvard* and the *Yale;* it was printed on the steamers and carried the latest sports news, racing results, and other late items (*NG,* 28 July 1908, p. 46). The *Fall River Line Journal* appeared every two weeks in the summer and once a month, when published, during the winter. Later it appeared once a month throughout the year. Another innovation on the *Harvard* and the *Yale* was the filtering of all the fresh water through charcoal (*NG,* 3 September 1908, p. 119). These are examples of what was required to remain competitive.

75. Report on Old Colony Steamboat Co., D&B, Mass. 75:158. ICC, *Docket 6469,* 2:210–11. J. Howland Gardner, vice-president of New England Steamship Co., stated that the difficulty in determining the profitability of individual lines was caused by the constant shifting of equipment (ibid.). During the New England Investigation in 1913 David E. Brown, one of the ICC accountants examining the New Haven books, said that "the system of bookkeeping on the New Haven is a rather complicated one; it is one that on the face of the accounts they do not explain the transactions; and secondly, the documents which should support the entries in the books are not properly supported." Another problem he stated this way: "The New Haven's dealings with their allied and subsidiary companies are great; the methods employed in transferring items from one company to another appear through the cash records when in reality they are not cash transactions. The result of that is that such items as should appear in the cash as being cash receipts or disbursements are omitted from that record" (ICC, *Docket 4845,* 10:3938–39).

76. *Transportation by Water,* 1:182–83; U.S., Industrial Commission, *Report of the Industrial Commission on Transportation* (Washington, D.C., 1900), *Reports of the Industrial Commission,* 4:63.

77. *Transportation by Water,* 1:183. For the fiscal year ending 30 June 1907 the New England Navigation Co. had an operating ratio of

almost 89 per cent (New York, New Haven & Hartford Railroad, *Annual Report* [1907], p. 15); for fiscal year 1912 the ratio was 83.19 per cent (*Annual Report* [1912], p. 60); in 1913 the ratio was 89.36 per cent (*Annual Report* [1913], p. 72).

78. See Appendix A, tables 17–19; Ledger with Monthly Trial Balances, 1889–93, Old Colony Steamboat Co., vol. 341A of New York, New Haven & Hartford Railroad Collection.

79. Memorandum for Calvin Austin, 9 December 1915, in miscellaneous records of Eastern Steamship Lines in possession of A. J. McLaughlin; Statement of Expenses, 4/4/14, file 374, ibid. See also Appendix A, table 19.

80. *Morse* v. *Metropolitan Steamship Co.*, pp. 678–80; ICC, *Docket 6469*, 6:2589–91, 2602–3; General Ledger, 1901–4, Maine Steamship Co., vol. 331 of New York, New Haven & Hartford Railroad Collection. During 1902 and 1903 the payroll of steamer *Horatio Hall* ranged from around $2,000 in the colder months to $3,100 in the summer (ibid.). For the size and make-up of the crew on the *Priscilla* see Appendix A, table 21.

81. Industrial Commission, *Report on Transportation* (1900), p. 689. In February 1900 the wages in the coastwise service were at least $7.00 more than in deep-sea service (ibid., pp. 688–89). This refers to the port of New York.

82. Ibid. On the steamers of the Merchants & Miners Transportation Co. 75 per cent of the crews were American (U.S., Industrial Commission, *Report of the Industrial Commission on Transportation* [Washington, D.C., 1901], *Reports of the Industrial Commission*, 9:417). See also ibid., pp. 413–15.

83. Henry C. Adams, "Transportation by Water," in *Report on Transportation Business in the United States at the Eleventh Census, Part 2* (Washington, D.C., 1894), *Eleventh Census of the United States, 1890*, 14:39–42; Payroll Book, January 1887, Old Colony Steamboat Co., G. W. Blunt White Library; "Steamer Notes," *NG*, 6 April 1887, p. 7; Industrial Commission, *Report on Transportation* (1901), p. 417. For a comparison of wages see Appendix A, table 20.

84. Dayton, p. 172; H. A. Kimball, 7 June 1875, in Press Copies of Letters of H. A. Kimball, July 1874–March 1877, vol. 303 of Old Colony Railroad Collection, pp. 444–45. Kimball suggested that perhaps the caps should have the word *band* on them or a distinctive color like red should be used. The Providence & Stonington Steamship Co. spent $1,383.35 on uniforms in August 1886; between 31 May and 29 September 1888, the company spent $1,597.25 (General Ledger 1, 1883–91, Providence & Stonington Steamship Co., vol. 345 of New York, New Haven & Hartford Railroad Collection).

85. "The Sound Steamer Monopoly," *MJ*, 12 August 1899, p. 9; "New Wage Scale," *NG*, 16 April 1903, p. 7.

86. *NG*, 7 February 1907, p. 180. The increase to pilots and most

mates averaged about $10 a month. That to captains affected only those who were receiving less than $200 a month, the men in charge of the freight steamers. First mates on the passenger boats had been receiving $90, second mates $60, and third mates $50 a month; they each received a $10 raise. The first and third mates on the freight boats, who had received $80 and $40 respectively, got a $5 increase; second mates, who had received $50, were advanced to $60. Pilots on the passenger steamers who had received $125 a month were advanced to $135; second pilots who had been at $110 were advanced to $120 (ibid.). These wages were much higher than on the Chesapeake Bay steamers between Baltimore and ports on the bay (information from William E. Geoghegan, Arlington, Va.). See also Appendix A, table 20.

87. *NG*, 19 September 1907, p. 200; *Morse v. Metropolitan Steamship Co.*, p. 673.

88. *Morse v. Metropolitan Steamship Co.*, pp. 593–94.

89. See *MJ*, 13 May 1893, p. 9; "The Fire on the Steamer Providence," ibid., 21 March 1908, p. 3.

Chapter 5

1. *NG*, vol. 11 (1878–79), passim; *NG*, 6 December 1879, p. 267; ibid., 3 January 1880, p. 301; "Steamer Notes," ibid., 12 April 1883, p. 5. After 1900 the Providence Line steamer stopped at Newport on Sunday nights to aid the regular Fall River Line steamer in handling the heavy load usually traveling to New York City at that time (ICC, *Docket 6469*, 2:57).

2. "Portland's Summer Steamers," *Portland* (Me.) *Board of Trade Journal* 10 (May 1897):6; ICC, *Docket 6891*, Petitioner's Exhibit 16, pp. 1–6.

3. ICC, *Docket No. 5733, Colonial Navigation Co. v. N.Y., N.H. & H. R.R. Co.*, R.G. 134, National Archives, Washington, D.C., pp. 92–94; "Great Importance to Maine," *Portland* (Me.) *Board of Trade Journal* 14 (May 1901):13–15; "Through Trains from New York," ibid. 15 (May 1902):6.

4. *Seaboard*, 11 June 1896, p. 542; *NG*, 6 August 1908, p. 126; ibid., 1 October 1903, p. 240; ibid., 14 July 1904, p. 32; ibid., 1 June 1905, p. 416; ibid., 30 June 1910, p. 428.

5. The *Fall River Line Tours* for the summer season of 1893 listed five routes from New York City to Gorham, N.H. Two of these were: (1) Fall River Line to Concord Junction, Concord & Montreal Railroad to Gorham; (2) Fall River Line to Boston, Portland Steam Packet Co. to Portland, Grand Trunk Railway to Gorham. The excursion fare was $8.60 one way and $15.00 round trip. Other trips had similar choices

and low round-trip excursion fares. See *Fall River Line Tours*, Summer 1893, ICC No. 406, box 608, CPT.

6. *First Annual Report of the Bureau of Industrial and Labor Statistics of the State of Maine* (1887), p. 239; "Summer Travel to Maine," Portland (Me.) *Board of Trade Journal* 3 (October 1890):167, 177; "Portland, Maine," ibid. 13 (August 1900):106; "What Tourist Business Means to Maine," ibid. 21 (October 1908):282.

7. *Eleventh Annual Report of the Bureau of Industrial and Labor Statistics of the State of Maine* (1897), pp. 113–23; "What Tourist Business Means to Maine," p. 282. In 1878 less than $500,000 was invested in resort property (ibid.).

8. "What Tourist Business Means to Maine," p. 282. See "A Twenty-five Million Dollar Industry," *Advance New England* 2 (October 1910):13–16; *Eleventh Annual Report, Industrial and Labor Statistics*, pp. 113–23. The hunting, fishing, and camping business supported 1,300 guides in 1897 (ibid.). In 1900 an estimated 250,000 visitors came to Maine during the summer ("Portland, Maine," p. 106).

9. The Maine Bureau of Industrial and Labor Statistics commented on the importance of a good transportation system: "While Maine has long been known as a resort par excellence in the summer months, yet it is only within recent years that the tourist business has assumed anything like its present immense proportions. Maine's attractions have only to be heralded abroad in order to draw people hither, and the limited advertising already done has resulted in benefiting the State and its people a thousand fold. With the growth and development of railroad and steamship lines, localities heretofore inaccessible have been brought into easy reach from the outside world, and resorts have sprung up all over the State. The great transportation lines have labored earnestly in spreading abroad information as to Maine's resort advantages and they have reaped substantial benefits in the rapidly expanding travel" (*Ninth Annual Report* [1895], pp. 114–15).

10. Maine Central Railroad, *Annual Report* (1902), pp. 8–9, and *Annual Report* (1903), p. 9; Portland (Me.) *Board of Trade Journal* 14 (July 1901):84; ICC, *Docket 6891*, Commission's Exhibit 5. For the fiscal year ending in June 1915 the deficit was $33,965.74 for both lines (ibid., pp. 21–22).

11. "Steamer Notes," *NG*, 27 December 1883, p. 93; Stanton, p. 360; ICC, *Docket 5733, Colonial Navigation Co. v. N.Y., N.H. & H. R.R. Co.*, pp. 143–45.

12. "The Tremont," *NG*, 21 June 1883, p. 75; "Disaster to Shipping," *Seaboard*, 1 December 1898, p. 101; "City of Bangor," ibid., 26 July 1894, p. 773; "Magnificent Coastwise Steamer," *NG*, 31 May 1900, p. 3. The *Calvin Austin* had 260 two-berth rooms ("Handsome Coasting Steamer," ibid., 6 August 1903, p. 114). The *Camden* had

over 400 of her 600 berths in staterooms ("New Turbine Steamer Camden," ibid., 7 March 1907, p. 236). The *Horatio Hall* had 130 staterooms for 500 passengers ("The New Steamship Horatio Hall," *Seaboard*, 31 March 1898, p. 379).

13. Way Bills, 21 January–20 September 1875, Old Colony Steamboat Co., vol. 282 of Old Colony Railroad Collection, Baker Library, Harvard Business School; ICC, *Docket 6469*, vol. 8, BE 40, Statement of Passengers and Gross Passenger Receipts by Lines. See also Appendix A, tables 4 and 5.

14. ICC, *Docket 6469*, BE 43 (app. A), A–6, p. 2; ICC, "Report of the Commission on Further Hearing of Steamer Lines on Long Island Sound," *ICC Reports* 183 (1932):353; "Steamer Notes," NG, 17 December 1885, p. 83. Bay State Line out of Providence carried 75,308 passengers in 1912 (ICC, "Further Hearing of Steamer Lines," p. 353). See also Appendix A, tables 3 and 6.

15. ICC, *Docket 6469*, vol. 8, BE 43 (app. A), A–6, p. 2; ICC, "Further Hearing of Steamer Lines," p. 353. The *Marine Journal* (11 July 1903, p. 4) reported that passenger traffic on the Sound lines making rail connections for Boston was increasing at the rate of 20 per cent a year. This estimate seems much too high considering other available data. See also Appendix A, table 3.

16. "Summer Travel to Bar Harbor," *Portland* (Me.) *Board of Trade Journal* 9 (December 1896): 234; ICC, *Docket 6891*, Petitioner's Exhibit 5; U.S. Chief of Engineers, *Water Terminal and Transfer Facilities*, 62d Cong., 1st sess., 1913, Doc. 226, pp. 33, 61; T. C. Purdy, "Report on Steam Navigation in the United States," in *Report on the Agencies of Transportation in the United States* (Washington, D.C., 1883), *Tenth Census of the United States, 1880*, 4 :34. See also Appendix A, table 8.

17. ICC, *Docket 6469*, 6:5007. See also Appendix A, tables 5 and 7.

18. New York, New Haven & Hartford Railroad, ICC No. A–418, effective 1 May 1908, box 653, CPT.

19. All fares taken from tariffs of the New York, New Haven & Hartford Railroad, Old Colony Railroad, New York & New England Railroad, Maine Central Railroad, 1888–1916, ibid.; steamship schedules in Robert McRoberts Memorial Collection of Steamship Line Schedules, Peabody Museum, Salem, Mass.

20. John Moody, *How to Analyze Railroad Reports*, 2d ed. (New York, 1912), p. 130. Railroads did sell so-called mileage tickets, which were usually sold in 500-mile and 1,000-mile books. They were honored until used and cost $10.00 and $20.00 respectively. They were not good on limited trains. See New York, New Haven & Hartford Railroad, ICC No. 405, effective 25 March 1908, box 653, CPT.

21. Data taken from CPT. See also New York, New Haven & Hartford Railroad, *Annual Report* (1910), p. 10.

22. Data taken from CPT; steamship schedules in Robert McRoberts Memorial Collection; ICC, *Docket 5733, Colonial Navigation Co. v. N.Y., N.H. & H. R.R. Co.*, pp. 102–4.

23. Maine Central Railroad, ICC No. 48, effective 1 May 1892, box 535, CPT.

24. Way Bills, 21 January–20 September 1875, Old Colony Steamboat Co., vol. 282 of Old Colony Railroad Collection; ICC, *Docket 6469*, vol. 8, BE 43 (app. A), pp. 30–35, 6–9; ICC, *Docket 6891*, p. 8.

25. ICC, *Docket 6469*, vol. 17, Brief of Petitioner, pp. 22–23; ibid., 2 : 381–82, 389–91; ICC, *Docket 6891*, pp. 21–22; D. A. Ham, "Old Steamboat Days," *Bar Harbor* (Me.) *Times*, 18 November 1937. For additional information on the Fall River Line boat train see Charles E. Fisher, *The Story of the Old Colony Railroad* (n.p., 1919), p. 115.

26. Fisher, *The Old Colony Railroad*, p. 106; Warren Jacobs, "The Fall River Line Boat Train," *Railway and Locomotive Historical Society Bulletin No.* 2 (1921), pp. 4–11; ICC, *Docket 6469*, 2 : 377. For additional information about the crew of the boat train and its reputation see Alvin F. Harlow, *Steelways of New England* (New York, 1946), p. 231.

27. Charles H. Dow, *History of Steam Navigation Between New York & Providence* (New York, 1877), pp. 26–27; "Providence Line," *Seaboard*, 15 June 1892, p. 673; Providence & Stonington Steamship Co. schedules in Robert McRoberts Memorial Collection; *NG*, 10 May 1879, p. 30. By 1916 the Norwich Line no longer had through connections to Boston; it had connections only from Providence and Worcester (ICC, *Docket 6469*, vol. 17, Brief of Petitioner, pp. 22–23). For New Haven and Bridgeport connecting train service see ibid.

28. ICC, *Docket 6469*, 15 : 6267–78.

29. ICC, *Docket 6891*, pp. 29–52.

30. *MJ*, 8 August 1896, p. 6; "Stenographic Service on the Commonwealth," *Fall River Line Journal*, 27 July 1908, p. 23; Storeroom Accounts, Old Colony Steamboat Co., vols. 303 and 305 of Old Colony Railroad Collection; *MJ*, 9 April 1904, p. 7; New York, New Haven & Hartford Railroad, *Combination Folder, Boston and New England Points from New York* (3 October 1909), pp. 15–20. See also ICC, *Docket 6469*, 5 : 4018.

31. "Narragansett Steamship Co.," *NG*, 13 April 1872, p. 234; "A Popular Institution," *Seaboard*, 2 July 1896, p. 591; *MJ*, 27 February 1897, p. 2.

32. ICC, *Docket 6469*, 5 : 3936, 3 : 1207–8.

33. ICC, *Docket 6891*, pp. 52–56; ibid., Correspondence, Arthur T. Richardson to Commissioner James S. Harlan, 21 February 1916, ICC No. 29770; ibid., Seth M. Carter to James S. Harlan, 27 March 1916, ICC No. 38476.

34. ICC, *Docket 6469*, 4 : 2541–42, 5 : 3904–5, 2 : 63; "A Great Ob-

282

NOTES TO PAGES III–14

ject Lesson," *MJ*, 23 June 1894, p. 11; "A Slight Accident Off Point Judith," ibid., 12 March 1904, p. 8. Another extra allowed passengers on the Fall River Line to remain on the boat into Fall River and then return to Newport at no extra fare, thus avoiding the very early disembarkation at Newport (ICC, *Docket 6469*, 4:2916).

35. On the *Priscilla* over 100 of the 196-man crew were concerned only with duties involving the passengers, such as cooking, waiting on table (68 waiters), and serving as steward or stewardess. See Appendix A, table 21.

36. The Hartford & New York Transportation Co., wholly owned by the New Haven Railroad, operated the Bay State Line from Providence to New York. Charles C. Goodrich described the service of the line: During the winter "we continue to carry that travel from poor people and those classes who must save a dollar and make it go as far as they can, as long as the boats run." He thought that 80 per cent of the business of the Hartford Line disappeared in the colder months and between 30 and 50 per cent of the passenger business of the Bay State Line (ICC, *Docket 6469*, 15:5553–54).

37. For the public attitude toward the ownership of steamship lines by the New England railroads see ICC, *Docket 6469*, vol. 15, Testimony and Correspondence; ICC, *Docket 4845*, Testimony and Correspondence; ICC, *Docket 6891*.

38. *NG*, 25 April 1911, p. 8.

39. E. O. Merchant, "Rate Making in Domestic Water Transportation," *Annals*, American Academy of Political and Social Science, 55 (September 1914):205–6; ICC, *Docket 6469*, 4:2647. See also Emory R. Johnson, Grover G. Huebner, and Arnold K. Henry, *Transportation by Water* (New York, 1935), p. 406; ICC, *Sixteenth Annual Report of the Interstate Commerce Commission, December 15, 1902*, app. G, pt. 2 (published as 58th Cong., 2d sess., 1904, H. Doc. 253, pt. 3), pp. 13–14; Thomas Thorburn, *Supply and Demand of Water Transport: Studies in Cost and Revenue Structures of Ships, Ports and Transport Buyers with Respect to Their Effects on Supply and Demand of Water Transport of Goods* (Stockholm, 1960), pp. 171–72. For a list of rules in establishing water rates see Merchant, "Rate Making," pp. 224–25.

40. Merchant, "Rate Making," p. 206.

41. Detail Ledger A, 1883–98, Providence & Stonington Steamship Co., vol. 347 of New York, New Haven & Hartford Railroad Collection, Baker Library, Harvard Business School; Canal Investigation, file 4953/B–I–30–1–2, Eastern Steamship Corp., Correspondence, etc. The cost of marine insurance was fairly high. For the year ending June 1893 the Providence & Stonington Steamship Co. paid $49,000 for marine insurance on the Providence Line and the same amount for the Stonington Line (General Ledger B, 1891–1904, Providence & Stonington Steamship Co., vol. 346 of New York, New Haven & Hart-

ford Railroad Collection). For a copy of a typical waybill see U.S., Congress, Senate, Committee on Interoceanic Canals, *Panama Canal: Hearings before the Committee on Interoceanic Canals on H.R. 21969* (Washington, D.C., 1912), p. 431.

42. For additional details see John L. Hazard, *Crisis in Coastal Shipping: The Atlantic-Gulf Case* (Austin, Texas, 1955), p. 76.

43. See ICC, *Docket 6469*, 2:481–82; *Financial Transactions*, 1: 947. For information on the effect of tramp competition see Merchant, "Rate Making," p. 212.

44. The differential of the Colonial Navigation Co. was two cents for each 100 pounds on all six classes (Merchant, "Rate Making," pp. 212–13). For details of the Central Vermont Railway differential see ICC, *Docket 6645*, pp. 141–44, 148.

45. As late as 1890 the Old Colony Steamboat Co. quoted a rate on boots and shoes at 3 cents a cubic foot (Old Colony Railroad, ICC No. 890, effective 15 May 1890, box 126, CFT). See also ICC, *Docket 6469*, 4:3038–39.

46. Canal Investigation, file 4953/B–I–30–1–2, Eastern Steamship Corp., Correspondence, etc.

47. ICC, *Docket 6469*, 4:2282, 2307, 2379; Industrial Commission, *Report on Transportation* (1901), p. 132; Thomas C. Cochran, *Railroad Leaders, 1845–1890*, pp. 199–200.

48. See CFT; William Z. Ripley, *Railroads: Rates and Regulation*, new ed. (New York, 1913), p. 323; U.S. Industrial Commission, *Final Report of the Industrial Commission* (Washington, D.C., 1902), *Reports of the Industrial Commission*, 19:387; Industrial Commission, *Report on Transportation* (1901), pp. 3–4; Cochran, *Railroad Leaders*, pp. 291, 498. From New Bedford and to New Bedford via the New Bedford Line 108 articles moved under commodity rates. At Providence via the Providence Line 172 different articles moved under commodity rates, 100 of which were materially lower than the all-rail scale of commodity and class rates out of Providence (ICC, *Docket 6469*, 6:5239, 5181–82).

49. ICC, *Docket 6469*, 4:2365–67.

50. Ibid., 4:2279–80; ibid., vol. 9, BE 65, copy of D. F. de Young to N. A. Wilcox, 23 May 1900.

51. Ibid., 3:2018–20; ICC, *Docket 4845*, 8:3361–63.

52. Industrial Commission, *Final Report*, p. 350; *Financial Transactions*, 1:947; ICC, *Docket 6469*, 4:2283.

53. ICC, "Report of the Commission on New England Dry Goods," *ICC Reports* 49 (1919):149–50.

54. ICC, "Report of the Commission on Boston–New York Proportional Rates (No. 2)," *ICC Reports* 43 (1917):204–5; Industrial Commission, *Final Report*, pp. 279–81.

55. Industrial Commission, *Final Report*, pp. 279–80; New York,

New Haven & Hartford Railroad, *Annual Report* (1903), p. 5. The New Haven Railroad raised some of its local tariffs because of wage increases and new per diem charges on freight cars (ibid.).

56. See Industrial Commission, *Final Report*, pp. 285–86; CFT, 1902–7.

57. *Senate Hearings on the Panama Canal*, pp. 763–64.

58. ICC, *Docket 6469*, vol. 7, Petitioner's Exhibit 2.

59. Canal Investigation, file 4953/B–I–41–2–3, Metropolitan Steamship Co., Tariffs between New York and Portland, Me.; Maine Central Railroad, ICC No. C–1266, effective 20 June 1912, box 1599–2, CFT. See also Canal Investigation, file 4953/B–I–30–2–1, Eastern Steamship Co., Freight Tariffs between Boston, Mass., and Portland, Me.

60. ICC, *Docket 6469*, 3:2100–2101, 4:2312. See also ibid., vol. 11, BE 135, BE 149, BE 150.

61. Way Bills, 21 January–20 September 1875, Old Colony Steamboat Co., vol. 282 of Old Colony Railroad Collection; ICC, *Docket 6469*, vol. 8, BE 43 (app. A), pp. 6–9, 27–30, 30–35; ibid., 23:2007–8.

62. See ICC, *Docket 6469*, 6:5176.

63. See ibid., Correspondence and Testimony, passim; ibid., vol. 17, Brief of Petitioner, pp. 30–32. See also Appendix A, table 12. Maine Steamship Co. also had a heavier flow of freight traffic westbound. During 1904 and 1905 it carried more traffic to New York City than it carried to Portland. See Canal Investigation, file 4953/B–I–11–1, Maine Steamship Co., Correspondence, etc.

64. The Portland, Mt. Desert & Machias Steamboat Co. carried primarily grain, flour, provisions, tin plate, oil, sardines, and machinery. Other important items were lumber, potatoes, cement, and livestock. None in this latter group totaled more than 500 tons each in 1904. See Canal Investigation, file 4953/B–VII–29, Portland, Mt. Desert & Machias Steamboat Co. Most of the tonnage carried by the Eastern Steamship Corporation consisted of the following types of articles:

To Boston	*From Boston*
PORTLAND DIVISION	
Canned goods	Sugar
Shoes	Molasses
Cotton piece goods	General merchandise
Printing paper	Groceries
Woolen goods	Canned goods
Fresh fish	Fresh fish
	Cotton
KENNEBEC DIVISION	
Hay	Sugar
Shoes	Molasses
Apples	General merchandise

Potatoes	Groceries
Vegetables	Canned goods
Fish	Fresh fish
Canned goods	Cotton

BANGOR DIVISION

Fish—all kinds	Sugar
Sardines	General merchandise
Apples	
Potatoes	
Shoes	

INTERNATIONAL DIVISION

Sardines	Tin plate
Fish—all kinds	Cotton seed oil
	Cement
	General merchandise
	Cotton

See Canal Investigation, file 4953/B–I–30–1–2, Eastern Steamship Corp., Correspondence, etc. The Maine Steamship Co. handled westbound to New York City principally paper and wool products, plus potatoes during December and January; eastbound it handled principally supplies in quantity for merchants, mills, and farmers (Canal Investigation, file 4953/B–I–11–1, Maine Steamship Co., Correspondence, etc.). For similar data on the Metropolitan Steamship Co. see Appendix A, table 11.

65. Industrial Commission, *Final Report*, p. 365. See also testimony of many shippers in ICC, *Docket 6469;* U.S., Congress, Senate, Committee on Interstate Commerce, *Hearings before the Committee on Interstate Commerce on the Court of Commerce, Railroad Rates, etc.* (Washington, D.C., 1910), pp. 78–79.

66. ICC, *Docket 6469*, 2:398, 405.

67. Ibid., 2:161; ibid., vol. 17, Brief of Petitioner, pp. 24–26.

68. See ICC, "Report of the Commission on Steamer Lines on Long Island Sound; Application of the New York, New Haven & Hartford Railroad Company for Permission to Continue Certain Service by Water after July 1, 1914," *ICC Reports* 50 (1918):640; "Fast Freight Route," *MJ*, 24 August 1889, p. 10; New York & New England Railroad, ICC No. 6018, effective 1 January 1891, box 131, CFT.

69. ICC, *Docket 4845*, 8:3389, 3392, 3375–76; ICC, *Docket 6469*, 15:6171–74, 6267–69; ibid., vol. 8, BE 39, L. H. Kentfield to T. E. Byrnes, 22 August 1905.

70. ICC, *Docket 6469*, 15:6277–78.

71. Ibid., vol. 8, BE 39, Kentfield to Byrnes, 22 August 1905; ibid., 15:6345, 4:2473–75; ibid., vol. 1B, Benjamin I. Spock to George B. McGinty, 7 October 1916, ICC No. 92595. In practice no freight was

diverted from the Norwich Line to the New Bedford Line. During January 1916 a total of 399 cars was diverted from the Providence Line to the Fall River Line. From 1 February to 19 February, during 15 days, a total of 450 cars was diverted from the Providence Line to the Fall River Line. This tonnage resulted from the increasing demands of World War I and was not representative of prewar diversions. It does, however, show the value of the diversion plan. See ibid., 15: 5830, 5834–38.

72. See, for example, ibid., 3:1653–54.

73. Ibid., 2:160–61.

74. For figures on Massachusetts boot and shoe production see U.S., Bureau of the Census, *Abstract of the Census of Manufactures, 1914* (Washington, D.C., 1917), pp. 269–70.

75. See Herbert Burgy, *The New England Cotton Textile Industry: A Study in Industrial Geography* (Baltimore, 1932), p. 67; Thomas Russell Smith, *The Cotton Textile Industry of Fall River, Massachusetts*, pp. 53–54, 62–63, 76–77; Seymour L. Wolfbein, *The Decline of a Cotton Textile City: A Study of New Bedford* (New York, 1944), pp. 67–68.

76. See data in United States censuses from 1870 through 1910, and Bureau of the Census, *Abstract of the Census of Manufactures, 1914*, pp. 269–70.

77. ICC, *Docket 6469*, 2:128, 3:2183, 6:5242. See Appendix B for a representative list of shippers routing goods via the Sound lines.

78. See Appendix B for a list of companies favoring New Haven ownership of the Sound lines. In 1926–27 a survey was conducted by the National Electric Light Association and the Metropolitan Life Insurance Co. on the reasons for relocating textile manufacturing plants. The results were published by the National Electric Light Association in *Industrial Development in the United States and Canada* (1927). In this survey of several groups of manufacturers, transportation never ranked lower than fourth out of eight categories; it was as high as second. Labor was first for all groups. See Wolfbein, *Decline of a Cotton Textile City*, p. 83.

79. See ICC, *Docket 6469*, 3:1301, 3:1325–26, 3:1642–45, 3:1655–66, 4:3054, 5:3050–52. In Providence William H. Harris, Jr., was one of the most outspoken individuals favoring divorcement of the Sound lines from New Haven control.

80. Ibid., 4:2814, 2818–19. See also ibid., 2:490–92, 2:501–4, 3:2058–63.

81. Ibid., 2:954–56, 2:965–67, 3:1275–76, 5:3285–90; ICC, *Docket 4845*, 7:2943–44.

82. ICC, *Docket 6469*, 3:1276. In 1888 or 1889 the New Haven Railroad established an all-rail movement from points in New England to New York City. The company constructed special cars with passenger

trucks for use in the express service. This service was not successful (ibid., 3:1682–83).

83. Ibid., 3:2054–63. See also ibid., 2:520–21, 3:1251–52, 5:3778, 5:3801. For a study of this problem as applied to water transportation and with conclusions supporting the positions taken by the shippers of New England see Thorburn, *Supply and Demand of Water Transport*, pp. 163–72.

84. See ICC, *Docket 6469*, 2:394–97; Richard M. Abrams, "Brandeis and the New Haven–Boston & Maine Merger Battle Revisited," *Business History Review* 36 (Winter 1962):420.

85. ICC, *Docket 6469*, 4:2261–63.

86. Of the freight handled at Piers 14 and 15, Hudson River, in 1913, 43.5 per cent moved east to New England and 56.5 per cent had moved west from New England to New York City (ICC, *Docket 6334*, vol. 3, Complainant's Exhibit 30). See also ICC, *Docket 6469*, 4:2557, 2560–62; ICC, *Docket 6334*, vol. 3, Complainant's Exhibits 35, 36; Canal Investigation, file 4953/B–I–30–1–1, Eastern Steamship Co., Correspondence, etc.

87. ICC, *Docket 6469*, 2:501–4, 1010–11; ibid., 3:1273–77, 1397–1405, 1944–45.

88. See ibid., 2:755–56. For comments on the precarious nature of the New England textile industry after 1914 see ICC, *Investigation & Suspension Docket No. 1091, New England Dry Goods*, 2 vols., R.G. 134, National Archives, Washington, D.C., 2:623–24, 805–7, 811–12.

89. ICC, *Docket 6469*, 3:1654. See also, ibid., vols. 1A and 1B.

90. The Fall River Line had an apparent profit of $645,000; the Providence Line a profit of $130,000; the New Bedford Line $90,000; the New Haven Line $45,879; the New London (Norwich) Line $77,524; the Bridgeport Line $2,764. The operating ratios on these apparent profits for the year ending 31 December 1913 were: Fall River Line 68 per cent; Providence Line 80 per cent; New Bedford Line 80 per cent; New Haven Line 90 per cent; New London (Norwich) Line 84 per cent; Bridgeport Line 99 per cent (U.S., Congress, House, Committee on the Merchant Marine and Fisheries, *Proceedings and Report of the Committee on the Merchant Marine and Fisheries in the Investigation of Shipping Combinations under House Resolution 587*, 4 vols. [Washington, D.C., 1913–14], 2:1078).

91. Industrial Commission, *Final Report*, pp. 501–2.

92. ICC, *Docket 6469*, 2:173–74.

Chapter 6

1. ICC, *Docket No. 8994, New York Harbor Case: Committee on Ways and Means to Prosecute the Case of Alleged Railroad Rate and Service Discrimination at the Port of New York et al. v. Baltimore &*

Ohio Railroad Company et al., 14 vols., R.G. 134, National Archives, Washington, D.C., 4:1232.

2. *Transportation by Water*, 3:xix. In this report four features were held to be required in a good harbor: (1) adequate wharves; (2) warehouse space; (3) transshipping machinery; (4) belt-line railway connection between general water traffic, the adjacent railroads, and if possible, the local industries. These features should be free of adverse or exclusive private control, especially the belt railway, which should be the public servant of the whole port.

3. For an elaboration of the shortcomings of American ports see ibid., vol. 3; U.S., Rivers and Harbors Board and U.S., Shipping Board, *Port of Boston, Massachusetts*, Port Series, no. 2 (Washington, D.C., 1922), pp. 68–69; Thomas Thorburn, *Supply and Demand of Water Transport: Studies in Cost and Revenue Structures of Ships, Ports and Transport Buyers with Respect to Their Effects on Supply and Demand of Water Transport of Goods* (Stockholm, 1960), p. 141; Ernest S. Bradford, "Water Terminals in the United States and Their Control," *Annals*, American Academy of Political and Social Science, 55 (September 1914):240–41.

4. U.S., Bureau of Foreign and Domestic Commerce, *Ports of the United States: Report on Terminal Facilities, Commerce, Port Charges, and Administration at Sixty-eight Selected Ports*, Miscellaneous Series, no. 33, ed. Grosvenor H. Jones (Washington, D.C., 1916), p. 90; ICC, "Report of the Commission on The New York Harbor Case," *ICC Reports* 47 (1917):718–20, 742; "New Docks for New York," *Seaboard*, 28 August 1890, p. 8.

5. See ICC, "Report of the Commission on Lighterage and Storage Regulations at New York, N.Y.," *ICC Reports* 35 (1915):49–53; *Senate Hearings on the Panama Canal*, pp. 739–41.

6. See John A. Droege, *Passenger Terminals and Trains* (New York, 1916), pp. 159–60.

7. Ibid., p. 160; Gratz Mordecai, *A Report on the Terminal Facilities for Handling Freight of the Railroads Entering the Port of New York, Especially of Those Railroads Having Direct Western Connections* (New York, 1885), p. 60.

8. New York, New Haven & Hartford Railroad, *Annual Report* (1873), pp. 11–13; ICC, *Docket 6469*, vol. 17, Brief of Petitioner, pp. 59–60. In 1874 the railroad spent $96,887.53 on new wharves (New York, New Haven & Hartford Railroad, *Annual Report* [1874], p. 7). The following year $31,800.78 was spent on new wharves and $40,590 on new barges (*Annual Report* [1875], p. 8). In 1880 the railroad doubled its floating equipment by purchasing one new steam tug and four new ten-car barges (car floats) at a total cost of $62,000 (*Annual Report* [1880], pp. 5–6).

9. Mordecai, *Terminal Facilities of the Port of New York*, p. 60; War-

ren Jacobs, "Some Railroad Landmarks of New York City," *Railway and Locomotive Historical Society Bulletin No.* 65 (October 1944), pp. 77–78; New York, New Haven & Hartford Railroad, *Annual Report* (1886), p. 13. The pier stations centered around Pier 50, East River, were later renumbered Piers 36–42.

10. Mordecai, *Terminal Facilities of the Port of New York*, p. 23; ICC, "Report on The New York Harbor Case," p. 690; ICC, "Lighterage and Storage Regulations at New York," p. 52; "The New Haven Problem," *Railroad Gazette*, 16 October 1903, p. 740.

11. Mordecai, *Terminal Facilities of the Port of New York*, p. 60; ICC, "Report on The New York Harbor Case," pp. 689–91; ICC, "Lighterage and Storage Regulations at New York," p. 50.

12. Massachusetts General Court, Joint Standing Committee on Railroads, *Report of Hearings before the Joint Standing Committee on Railroads under the Order for Said Committee to Investigate the Conduct of the New York, New Haven and Hartford Railroad Company* [1893], pp. 110, 119.

13. Mordecai, *Terminal Facilities of the Port of New York*, pp. 64–65. See also *NG*, 12 May 1886, p. 809; "New Docks for New York," p. 8.

14. See City of New York, Department of Docks, *Reports of Board of Consulting Engineers, 1895–1897* (New York, 1897); ICC, *Docket 6334*, vol. 3, Complainant's Exhibit 38.

15. "New Docks for New York," p. 8.

16. ICC, *Docket 6334*, vol. 3, Complainant's Exhibit 38 (S. Willett Hoag, *Report Accompanying General Description of the Harbor of New York, Report No. 11* [1911], pp. 29–30).

17. ICC, *Docket 6469*, 2:68; ibid., 3:1100–1107, 2104–5; *Senate Hearings on the Panama Canal*, pp. 426–27, 739–40.

18. ICC, *Docket 6469*, 3:2121–22; ibid., vol. 17, Brief of Petitioner, p. 29. The numbering system of the piers on Manhattan is somewhat confusing because of the changes in the numbers between 1870 and 1910. For example, on 1 June 1895, Pier 28, Hudson River, terminal of the Fall River Line, was renumbered as Pier 18 ("Fall River Line Changes," *MJ*, 6 April 1895, p. 3).

19. *Transportation by Water*, 3:3–8; "Waterfront Railroads for New York City," *Railroad Gazette*, 21 May 1897, p. 347; "Wharfage Facilities in New York City," *NG*, 25 February 1904, pp. 94–95; "New York's Freight Terminal Problem," *Railway Age Gazette*, 11 April 1913, pp. 843–45.

20. See City of New York, Department of Docks, *Reports of Board of Consulting Engineers, 1895–1897*, especially p. 24; "Waterfront Railroads for New York City," p. 347; "Where Shall Sound Steamers Dock?" *MJ*, 19 November 1892, p. 9; "Railroad Aggressiveness Dangerous," *MJ*, 1 April 1899, p. 8.

21. ICC, *Docket 6334*, 2:444–48; *NG*, 25 April 1911, p. 19; "Commissioner Tomkins Home Again," *NG*, 6 October 1910, p. 160. For details of the plans advocated by Calvin Tomkins see ICC, *Docket 6334*, vol. 3, Complainant's Exhibit 38.

22. New York, New Haven & Hartford Railroad, *Annual Report* (1905), p. 9. The railroads using the route at that time were the Erie and the Delaware, Lackawanna & Western.

23. ICC, *Docket 6469*, 15:6229–30. For a map of the Providence terminal area see the *Providence Board of Trade Journal* (August 1899). See also map 2, p. 123.

24. ICC, *Docket 6469*, 15:6229–30; New York, New Haven & Hartford Railroad, *Annual Report* (1905), p. 5, and *Annual Report* (1907), pp. 5–6. Before constructing the tunnel an experiment was tried whereby the standard electric trains would reach Union Station over the tracks of the street railway. The experiment was a disaster because the electric railroad cars could not negotiate the sharp curves of the trolley tracks without derailing (New York, New Haven & Hartford Railroad, *Annual Report* [1901], p. 5; Rhode Island Railroad Commissioner, *Annual Report, 1903* [1904], pp. 26–27).

25. ICC, *Docket 6469*, 2:378–81; ibid., 6:4195, 4209, 4813; Droege, *Passenger Terminals and Trains*, pp. 74–75.

26. ICC, *Docket 6469*, 2:378–81.

27. Ibid., 6:4474, 4479–80, 4519–25, 4706–7.

28. Ibid., 6:4474, 4479–80; ICC, *Investigation & Suspension Docket No. 873, Hartford & New York Transportation Company Joint Rates*, 1 vol., R.G. 134, National Archives, Washington, D.C., pp. 60–69, 262–63. The division of the rates between trolley line and steamboat line was 50 per cent to each. Each trolley car held a maximum of 20 tons of freight. They delivered generally between one and three cars daily to the Bay State Line and received an average of two cars from the Bay State Line (ibid., pp. 33–34, 60–69, 262–63).

29. Herbert Burgy, *The New England Cotton Textile Industry: A Study in Industrial Geography* (Baltimore, 1932), p. 48. See also map 2, p. 123, for the difficulties of reaching New York City from New Bedford and the Watuppa branch.

30. ICC, *Docket 6469*, 4:2881–84; ICC, *Docket No. 952, Enterprise Transportation Company v. Pennsylvania Railroad Co., et al.*, 1 vol., R.G. 134, National Archives, Washington, D.C., pp. 66–67, 83.

31. Massachusetts State Board on Docks and Terminal Facilities, *Report of the State Board on Docks and Terminal Facilities* (Boston, 1897), pp. 79–80, 123, 126; Jones, *Ports of the United States*, p. 41; U.S., Rivers and Harbors Board, and U.S., Shipping Board, *The Port of Boston*, p. 73. The rail distance from Commonwealth Pier to the East Boston terminal of the Boston & Albany Railroad was 13 miles; the water distance was 4/5 of a mile (ibid.).

32. Edwin J. Clapp, *The Port of Boston: A Study and a Solution of*

the Traffic and Operating Problems of Boston, and Its Place in the Competition of the North Atlantic Seaports (New Haven, 1916), p. 316; ICC, *Docket 4845*, 13:6049.

33. ICC, *Docket 6469*, 2:490–92, 501–4.

34. "Portland in a Nutshell," *Portland* (Me.) *Board of Trade Journal* 3 (August 1890):107; U.S., Chief of Engineers, *Water Terminal and Transfer Facilities*, 62d Cong., 1st sess., 1913, Doc. 226, p. 63; *Fifteenth Annual Report of the Bureau of Industrial and Labor Statistics of the State of Maine* (1901), p. 81.

35. See *Transportation by Water*, vol. 3; Clapp, *The Port of Boston*, p. 159; Jones, *Ports of the United States*, especially p. 47; *Senate Hearings on the Panama Canal*, pp. 90–91, 104–5. In New York City the railroads controlled 30.8 per cent of the pier space on the west side of Manhattan (ICC, "Report on The New York Harbor Case," p. 662).

36. Rhode Island Railroad Commissioner, *Annual Report, 1903* (1904), pp. 26–27. See also map of the Providence terminal facilities in ICC, *Docket 6469*, vol. 10. For maps of other terminals serving the Sound lines see ibid., vols. 10–11.

37. ICC, *Docket 6469*, 2:114–18, 5:3904–5.

38. Ibid., 2:114–18, 122–23. In 1916 Piers 27 and 28, East River, terminal of the New Haven and Bridgeport lines, had 59 clerks and 165 longshoremen, who handled between 6,000 and 8,000 tons of freight a week; Pier 40, Hudson River, terminal of the Norwich and New Bedford lines, had 64 clerks and 240 longshoremen, who handled between 8,000 and 10,000 tons of freight a week; Pier 14, Hudson River, terminal of the Fall River and Providence lines, had 143 clerical and other workers (the commissary was located there) and 350 longshoremen who handled between 14,000 and 20,000 tons a week (ibid.). The tonnage figures include freight going in both directions; they reflect the growing congestion resulting from the demands of World War I.

39. ICC, *Investigation & Suspension Docket No. 1091, New England Dry Goods*, R.G. 134, National Archives, Washington, D.C., 2: 465–79, 491, 496–97; ICC, *Docket 6469*, 3:1487–89. The terminals used in this study were New York, Providence, Fall River, and New Bedford. The survey was made during a one-week period in August 1917.

40. ICC, *Docket 6334*, 2:627–31, 649–51, 883–84, 295–307; "Freight Congestion at New York Docks—Its Reasons, Results and Remedies," *Commercial Vehicle*, 15 July 1913, p. 15; ICC, *Docket 6469*, 2:130; ICC, *Valuation Docket 1054*, Engineering Report, p. 7. The New England Steamship Co. also tried electric trucks at its Fox Point wharf in Providence during March 1912, but decided not to adopt them (John A. Droege, *Freight Terminals and Trains* [New York, 1912], pp. 342–48).

41. "Freight Congestion at New York Docks," p. 15; "Handling

Freight with Storage Battery Trucks," *Railway Age Gazette*, 11 December 1914, p. 1094.

42. ICC, *Docket 6334*, vol. 3, Complainant's Exhibit 38 (B. F. Cresson, Jr., and H. McL. Harding, *Report on Freight Handling at Marine Terminals, Report No. 17* [1912], p. 7); ibid., Exhibit 38, passim; "Handling Freight with Storage Battery Trucks," pp. 1093–94. At Providence the electric trucks could handle eight times the amount of freight moved by two men with hand trucks (Droege, *Freight Terminals and Trains*, p. 349). For a plan of a car float of the type used at the pier stations see "A Large Harbor Car Float," *NG*, 3 March 1904, p. 108.

43. See Droege, *Freight Terminals and Trains*, pp. 342–49; "Electric Tractors at Pier 4, New York," *Railway Age Gazette*, 3 August 1917, pp. 199–200.

44. ICC, *Docket 6334*, 2:295–307, 400, 414; ibid., vol. 3, Complainant's Exhibit 44, in which there is a detailed plan of Piers 14 and 15 and diagrams of the efficient arrangement for handling incoming and outgoing freight; U.S., Congress, House, Committee on the Merchant Marine and Fisheries, *Proceedings and Report of the House Committee on the Merchant Marine and Fisheries in the Investigation of Shipping Combinations under House Resolution 587*, 4 vols. (Washington, D.C., 1913–14), 2:1088.

45. See *Investigation of Shipping Combinations*, 2:1088; "New York's Freight Terminal Problem," *Railway Age Gazette*, 11 April 1913, pp. 826, 843–45; "Handling Freight with Storage Battery Trucks," pp. 1093–94; ICC, *Docket 6334*, vol. 1, Separate Brief of the Defendant, The Central Railroad Company of New Jersey, pp. 29–30; ibid., vol. 2, Testimony, passim.

46. ICC, *Docket 4845*, vol. 2, Brief and Argument for the New York, New Haven and Hartford Railroad, Respondents, pp. 154–56. The largest tonnage was carried in fiscal year ending 30 June 1910, when the total was 1,516,089 tons. See Appendix A, table 9. It is difficult to determine a figure for an average carload of freight. The figures vary depending upon the year and the type of freight. In 1900 the average for all the freight carried by the New Haven Railroad was 10.2 tons per loaded car; in 1907 it was 13.4 tons. In 1916 it had risen to 16.27 tons. John A. Droege gave a figure of six tons per car for merchandise freight of the type carried on the Sound lines. In 1924 the Merchants & Miners Transportation Company based its capacity for each steamer in railroad carloads of 15 tons. This applied to the type of freight the company carried. See E. R. Dewsnup, "Freight Car Efficiency," *Railroad Gazette*, 22 May 1908, pp. 706–7; "New York, New Haven & Hartford," *Railway Age Gazette*, 27 October 1916, p. 732; Droege, *Freight Terminals and Trains*, p. 3; Reese D. McNeill, *Terminal Operation of Coastwise Steamers* (Paper read at the Engineering Societies

Building, New York, N.Y., 14 October 1924, mimeographed copy in ICC Library, Washington, D.C.), p. ii.

47. The Central Vermont Transportation Co. steamers during 1913 carried a total of 352,621 tons of freight; of this, 292,807 tons moved from New York to New London and points west of New London; 59,814 tons moved to New York (ICC, *Docket 6645*, BE 10). See also Appendix A, table 10. For tonnage carried by the Metropolitan Steamship Co. see Appendix A, table 11. The Maine Steamship Co. carried the following freight tonnage between New York and Portland:

YEAR	TONS
1900	178,094
1901	177,573
1902	201,681
1903	188,461
1904	191,000
1905	195,405
1906	198,071

Taken from Canal Investigation, file 4953/B–I–11–1, Maine Steamship Co., Correspondence, etc.

48. ICC, *Docket 6469*, vol. 17, Brief of Petitioner, pp. 152–53; ICC, *Docket 8994, New York Harbor Case*, 6:2648, 2667.

49. ICC, *Docket 6469*, vol. 1, Petitioner's Exhibit 1; ibid., 6:4922–23; ibid., vol. 7, Petitioner's Exhibit 1.

50. "Car Ferry Lines," *Railroad Gazette*, 24 December 1897, pp. 903–4; *Railroad Gazette*, 19 September 1913, p. 533; ICC, *Investigation & Suspension Docket No. 857, Boston–New York Proportional Rates (No. 2)*, 1 vol., R.G. 134, National Archives, Washington, D.C., pp. 67–71. In 1888 the New Haven Railroad had the following floating equipment in New York Harbor: 6 tugs, 1 transfer steamer, and 20 car floats. In 1900 it had 13 tugs, one self-propelled lighter, 2 transfer steamers, and 39 car floats. In 1914 it had 18 steam tugs and 54 car floats. See New York, New Haven & Hartford Railroad, annual reports for those years.

51. ICC, *Docket 6469*, 15:5826–27. See also *Senate Hearings on the Panama Canal*, pp. 739–40.

52. See ICC, "Report on The New York Harbor Case," pp. 670–71; ICC, "Lighterage and Storage Regulations at New York," pp. 49–53; ICC, *Docket 8994, New York Harbor Case*, vol. 12, Complainant's Exhibit 2.

53. *Transportation by Water*, 3:359–60; ICC, *Docket 6469*, vol. 17, Brief of Petitioner, pp. 14–15; *NG*, 5 August 1882, p. 131.

54. U.S., Congress, Senate, Select Committee on Interstate Commerce, *Report of the Senate Select Committee on Interstate Commerce*, 49th Cong., 1st sess., 1886, S. Rep. 46, pt. 2, 2 vols., 2:429–30;

see notes 38 and 39 above. The value of the wharves themselves at the New England ports also was high. Replacement costs ranged from $56,179 for the New London Wharf to $8,494 for Belle Dock in New Haven. At Fox Point in Providence the sea wall had a replacement value of $25,795 and the wharf a value of $41,427. These values did not include any buildings or equipment on the wharves. In 1921 Eastern Steamship Lines sold its facilities at Franklin Wharf in Portland to the state of Maine for $210,531.30 (ICC, *Valuation Docket 1054*, Engineering Report, pp. 10–26; Minute Book of Directors' Meetings [1917–21], Eastern Steamship Lines, in offices of Pierce, Atwood, Scribner, Allen & McKusick, Portland, Me.).

55. See John L. Hazard, *Crisis in Coastal Shipping: The Atlantic-Gulf Case* (Austin, Texas, 1955); John G. B. Hutchins, "The American Shipping Industry since 1914," *Business History Review* 28 (June 1954):122–25; ICC, "Report on The New York Harbor Case," pp. 734–35; *Transportation by Water*, 3:303; Merrill J. Roberts, "The Motor Transportation Revolution," *Business History Review* 30 (March 1956):57–95.

Chapter 7

1. ICC, *Docket 6469*, vol. 9, BE 57, W. L. Rice to L. H. Kentfield, 5 December 1907, memorandum enclosed dated 7 May 1897.

2. "The Joy Steamship Company," *Providence Board of Trade Journal* 11 (April 1899):55; ibid. 11 (June 1899):137; "Providence Harbor Notes," ibid. 11 (August 1899):239–41; *NG*, 15 June 1899, p. 14.

3. *MJ*, 1 July 1899, p. 4.

4. *NG*, 15 February 1900, p. 9; *Providence Board of Trade Journal* 11 (June 1899):137; "Providence Harbor Notes," ibid. 11 (August 1899):239–41; *MJ*, 3 June 1899, p. 9.

5. "Steamboat Rivalry on Long Island Sound," *NG*, 22 March 1900, p. 3.

6. "Providence Harbor Notes," *Providence Board of Trade Journal* 12 (February 1900):79; *MJ*, 17 June 1899, p. 3; Ledger, 1894–1904, New Haven Steamboat Co., G. W. Blunt White Library, Marine Historical Association, Mystic, Conn.

7. "Steamboat Rivalry on Long Island Sound," *NG*, 22 March 1900, p. 3; ICC, *Docket 6469*, vol. 8, BE 43 (app. A), A–o, John M. Hall to J. M. Williams, 26 September 1899.

8. Ibid., BE 43 (app. A), pp. 3–4; *MJ*, 10 March 1900, p. 3. Two years before the Narragansett Bay Line was started, the New Haven Steamboat Co. constructed a dock in New Haven, which it held in case the railroad decided to evict it from Belle Dock ("Steamboat Rivalry on Long Island Sound," *NG*, 22 March 1900, p. 3).

9. ICC, *Docket 6469*, vol. 8, BE 43 (app. A), pp. 3–4. For the capital

stock, which carried with it all the real estate, Hall was authorized to pay $212.50 per share (ibid.). The New Haven Railroad assumed the outstanding bonds, which totaled $364,500; the steamboat stock was placed on the New Haven books at $700,000 (New York, New Haven & Hartford Railroad, *Annual Report* [1900], p. 8).

10. New York, New Haven & Hartford Railroad, *Annual Report* (1900), p. 8.

11. ICC, *Docket 6469,* 15:6063, 6065; "Why the Chester W. Chapin Was Built," *MJ,* 19 May 1900, p. 8. The *Marine Journal* commented on the sale: "When a steamboat company gets the better of a railroad we feel like climbing to the roof and exulting in fresh air shouts loud and long" (ibid.).

12. "Bay Line Absorbed by the Consolidated," *Providence Board of Trade Journal* 12 (April 1900):165; "The New York and Boston Monopoly," *MJ,* 28 April 1900, p. 9; "The New Haven Steamboat Line Now Controlled by the Consolidated System," *NG,* 26 April 1900, p. 5.

13. "The Joy Steamship Company," *Providence Board of Trade Journal* 12 (May 1900):213.

14. ICC, *Docket 6469,* vol. 8, BE 42, Hall to Buckland, 10 July 1900. See also *Providence Board of Trade Journal* 12 (August 1900):353.

15. *Providence Board of Trade Journal* 12 (October 1900):445–46; ICC, *Docket 6469,* vol. 8, BE 42, Hall to Charles F. Brooker, 23 November 1900.

16. *Providence Journal of Commerce and Board of Trade Journal* 13 (January 1901):33; *MJ,* 10 November 1900, p. 3.

17. "Narragansett Bay Notes," *NG,* 29 August 1901, p. 7; *Providence Journal of Commerce* 13 (May 1901):200–201. The *Chester W. Chapin* later replaced the *Connecticut* (*NG,* 10 April 1902, p. 11; ibid., 2 October 1902, p. 12).

18. *NG,* 27 June 1901, p. 11; *NG,* 10 March 1904, p. iii.

19. ICC, *Docket 6469,* vol. 8, BE 44 (app. B), B–11, R. T. Haskins to Percy R. Todd, 17 September 1901; ibid., B–18, Haskins to Todd, 16 July 1901.

20. Ibid., B–14, copy of correspondence from file 307 of Percy R. Todd. For information on similar activities with grocery shippers and metal companies see ibid., B–15, B–16.

21. Ibid., vol. 10, BE 131. Total payments to Captain Dyer were $2,030 (ibid.).

22. See ICC, *Investigation & Suspension Docket No. 873, Hartford & New York Transportation Company Joint Rates,* R.G. 134, National Archives, Washington, D.C., pp. 125–26, 129. Over thirty-four special rates were in effect on items like coffee, tea, yarn, spirits, rags, leather, dry goods, molasses, salt meats, and tin plate. See also ICC, *Docket 6469,* vol. 8, BE 44 (app. B), B–20, copy of memorandum enclosed in J. H. Barrett to F. S. Holbrook, 28 January 1903.

23. Ibid., B–12, Haskins to Todd, letter marked "Personal," answered Todd's letter of 20 September 1902; ibid., B–12, Todd to Haskins, 20 September 1902, letter marked "Private." Todd enclosed the following statement of the number of passengers on the three lines serving Providence during July 1902:

	FROM NEW YORK	TO NEW YORK
Providence Line	9,120	7,638
New Line	14,584	14,986
Joy Line	9,856	11,287

See also ibid., 3:2002–6.

24. Ibid., vol. 8, BE 44 (app. B), B–20, material pertaining to the agreement; *Providence Board of Trade Journal* 14 (October 1902): 371. In 1904 the first-class fare on the Joy Line between Providence and New York was $1.25 during January, February, and March; $1.50 during April, May, October, November, and December; and $2.00 during the rest of the year (ICC, *Docket 6469*, vol. 8, BE 44 (app. B), B–22, enclosure in letter of George L. Connor to Todd, 13 January 1904).

25. *Providence Board of Trade Journal* 14 (October 1902):371. The cost of operating the New Line for two years was $320,000. By discontinuing it, the freight traffic manager of the New Haven estimated, the company during the next two years saved $157,156 (ICC, *Docket 6469*, vol. 8, BE 42, Connor to Todd, 20 June 1905).

26. Ibid., BE 44 (app. B), B–20, Buckland to Todd, 16 October 1902.

27. Ibid., 3:2002–6; ibid., vol. 8, BE 44 (app. B), B–20, F. S. Holbrook to Todd, 24 December 1904.

28. ICC, *Docket 6645*, pp. 470–73; ibid., Commission's Exhibit 3. Steamers *Mohawk* and *Mohegan* were actually owned by the Central Steamboat Co. of West Virginia, which leased them to the New London Steamboat Co. (ICC, *Docket 6469*, 6:5122–25).

29. ICC, *Docket 6645*, pp. 470–73; *Financial Transactions*, 2:2340. The New Haven paid $339,280 for the company (ibid.).

30. ICC, *Docket 6469*, 6:5124–25.

31. ICC, *Docket 6645*, pp. 141–44, 148.

32. ICC, *Docket 6469*, vol. 8, BE 43 (app. A), pp. 22–23.

33. Information taken from Charles S. Mellen Papers, New Hampshire Historical Society, Concord, N.H.

34. See "The New York, New Haven & Hartford Railroad Co.," *Providence Board of Trade Journal* 16 (January 1904):9.

35. ICC, *Docket 6469*, vol. 8, BE 17, copy of the charter of the Colonial Commercial Co. The company was organized by David McKenzie, Francis G. Way, and William S. Chappell (ibid.).

36. Ibid., BE 18, copy of New England Navigation Co. Minutes, pp.

1–7. Original directors transferred their rights to Augustus Brandegee, Frank B. Brandegee, and William J. Brennan, on 13 May 1903 (ibid.). The New Haven paid $50,000 for the capital stock and an additional $2,000 for the charter, the latter amount to F. B. Brandegee (*Financial Transactions*, 2:2342).

37. Stevenson Taylor was a consulting engineer and naval architect for the New Haven Railroad and its affiliates who took charge of completing the steamer *Providence* after George Pierce died. Formerly he had worked for W. & A. Fletcher Co. in New York, and he did much work on the installation of the machinery on steamers built for the various Sound lines. Later he worked for the Quintard Iron Works.

38. ICC, *Docket 6469*, vol. 8, BE 43 (app. A), pp. 35–42; ibid., A–16, excerpts from New Haven Railroad Directors' Minutes, 11 December 1904; ibid., BE 18, copy of New England Navigation Co. Minutes, pp. 1–7. For slightly different figures on the cost of purchasing the individual steamship companies see *Financial Transactions*, 2:2335–41.

39. ICC, *Docket 6469*, vol. 8, BE 43 (app. A), A–12, Excerpts from Stockholders Minute Book, Old Colony Steamboat Company, pp. 5–7; ibid., A–16, Excerpts from New Haven Railroad Directors' Minutes, 10 December 1904. See also ibid., A–13, pp. 21–24; ICC, *Docket 4845*, 10:4008–11, 4070–73; *Financial Transactions*, 2:2337–38.

40. ICC, *Docket 4845*, 10:4825–26, 4831–33.

41. For a description of these transactions see ICC, "Report of the Commission on The New England Investigation; in the Matter of Rates, Classifications, Regulations, and Practices of Carriers," *ICC Reports* 27 (1913):560–617; *Financial Transactions*, passim.

42. ICC, *Docket No. 952, Enterprise Transportation Company v. Pennsylvania Railroad Company*, R.G. 134, National Archives, Washington D.C., pp. 35–38, 41–45; ibid., copy of Certificate of Condition of the Enterprise Transportation Co., 16 February 1907.

43. ICC, *Docket No. 867, In the Matter of Alleged Unlawful Discrimination against the Enterprise Transportation Company by Railroad Lines Leading from New York City*, 1 vol., R.G. 134, National Archives, Washington, D.C., pp. 49–50. The *Frank Jones* and *Kennebec* could carry 150–175 tons of cotton piece goods; the *Warren* had a capacity of 200–225 tons of cotton piece goods (ibid.).

44. ICC, *Docket 6469*, vol. 8, BE 44 (app. B), B–5, Todd to Mellen, 29 May 1905; ibid., B–4, E. L. Somers to F. S. Holbrook, 31 May 1905; ibid., vol. 11, BE 132, copy of carbon of George W. Brady to George E. Beekman, 30 May 1905.

45. Ibid., vol. 8, BE 44 (app. B), B–5, clipping from *New York Times*, 13 December 1905.

46. Ibid., Second vice-president and general manager of the New England Navigation Co. to Mellen, 10 June 1905; ibid., BE 44 (app.

B), pp. 35–38; ICC, *Docket 4845*, 10:4177–80; *Financial Transactions*, 2:1448–53.

47. ICC, *Docket 6469*, vol. 8, BE 44 (app. B), B–4, E. F. DeYoung to F. S. Holbrook, 22 June 1905; ibid., F. C. Bushee to Holbrook, 22 August 1905; ibid., Bushee to Holbrook, 31 August 1905. The Fall River Line charged 12.5 cents per 100 pounds on cotton piece goods, and the Enterprise Line charged 10 cents (ICC, "Report of the Commission on In the Matter of Alleged Unlawful Discrimination against the Enterprise Transportation Company by Railroad Lines Leading from New York City," *ICC Reports* 11 [1906]:590).

48. ICC, *Docket 6469*, vol. 8, BE 44 (app. B), B–5, Mellen to W. H. Newman, 2 November 1905. In March 1906 the fare on the Fall River Line between Fall River and New York had been reduced to $1.50 to meet the competition (ICC, "Report on Discrimination against the Enterprise Transportation Co.," p. 590).

49. ICC, *Docket 6469*, vol. 8, BE 44 (app. B), B–5, clipping from the *Boston Herald*, 2 February 1906, enclosed in George L. Connor to Mellen, 15 December 1905; ibid., B–20, Holbrook to Todd, 24 December 1904; ibid. (app. B), pp. 35–38; *Financial Transactions*, 2:1448–49; Accounts Receivable Ledger, 1906–7, Joy Steamship Co., vol. 330 of New York, New Haven & Hartford Railroad Collection, in Baker Library, Harvard Business School; *NG*, 13 June 1907, p. 465.

50. See ICC, "Report on Discrimination against the Enterprise Transportation Co.," pp. 587–97; ICC, "Report of the Commission on Enterprise Transportation Company v. Pennsylvania Railroad Company and New England Navigation Company," *ICC Reports* 12 (1908):326–37.

51. ICC, *Docket 6469*, vol. 8, BE 44 (app. B), B–5, Mellen to J. A. Moore, 1 June 1906.

52. *Financial Transactions*, 1:274, 2:1464–65; ICC, *Docket 6469*, vol. 8, BE 44 (app. B), pp. 14–16; ibid., B–2, Mellen to J. C. Whitney, 30 April 1907.

53. ICC, *Docket 4845*, vol. 11, Memorandum of Conference Held in General Auditor's Office, New York, New Haven & Hartford Railroad, 28 January 1913, pp. 3–4; Accounts Receivable Ledger, 1906–1907, Joy Steamship Co., vol. 330 of New York, New Haven & Hartford Railroad Collection; ICC, *Docket 6469*, 15:5513–16; "Steamboat Competition on the Sound," *NG*, 11 April 1907, p. 322; *NG*, 13 June 1907, p. 465.

54. *NG*, 21 November 1907, p. 344; *NG*, 5 December 1907, p. 379; ICC, *Docket 6469*, vol. 8, BE 44 (app. B), B–5, Mellen to Taylor, 25 November 1907. Mellen, realizing the delicate nature of the situation, wrote Stevenson Taylor on 25 November 1907, warning him to treat the customers in Fall River carefully and not to raise rates now that the Enterprise Line had failed (*Financial Transactions*, 2:1468).

55. ICC, *Docket 6469*, 2:771–72, 15:5538. For the history of the Hartford & New York Transportation Co. see Dayton, *Steamboat Days*, and Melancthon Jacobus, *The Connecticut River Steamboat Story* (Hartford, 1956).

56. ICC, *Docket 6469*, 4:2643–44, 2655–56, 2674; ibid., 6:5090; ibid., vol. 9, BE 95; ibid., vol. 17, Brief of Petitioner, p. 51. The barge line earned between 4 and 6 per cent a year during the years after 1910 (ibid., 15:5463–68).

57. Ibid., vol. 8, BE 2, Excerpts from Minutes of New Haven Railroad Board of Directors.

58. Ibid., BE 44 (app. B), p. 8; ICC, *Docket 4845*, 10:4199–4203. The cost in dollars for the Hartford & New York Transportation Co. was $1,598,000; the New Haven Railroad paid $200 a share for the stock (ibid.).

59. Canal Investigation, file 4953/B–I–11–1, Maine Steamship Co., Correspondence, etc.; *Financial Transactions*, 2:1488–89, 1466, 1470.

60. *Financial Transactions*, 2:1459–60, 1463. In April 1907 the New England Navigation Co. disposed of 3,000 shares of Joy Line stock by receipt of $300,000 from C. W. Morse, who purchased the Boston line of the Joy Steamship Co.; the 3,000 shares were retired (ICC, *Docket 4845*, 10:4183–85). In February 1907 the Joy Line suffered a severe disaster when the steamer *Larchmont* was in collision with a schooner and over 100 lives were lost. The accident and subsequent investigation did not help the reputation of the Joy Line and probably made the New Haven even more anxious to liquidate the company.

61. ICC, *Docket 6469*, vol. 8, BE 44 (app. B), pp. 38–40; *Financial Transactions*, 2:1462.

62. ICC, *Docket 6469*, vol. 8, BE 44 (app. B), B–1; ICC, "Report of the Commission on New England Steamship Company et al.," *ICC Reports, Valuation Reports* 36:778; *NG*, 24 May 1906, p. 382.

63. ICC, *Docket 6469*, vol. 8, BE 44 (app. B), pp. 25–30; *Financial Transactions*, 2:1463–64.

64. See ICC, *Docket 6891*, pp. 58–62, 74–77; ibid., Petitioner's Exhibit 16.

Chapter 8

1. ICC, *Docket 6469*, vol. 8, BE 2, Outline of Policy Recommended for the Handling of the Steamboat Lines Controlled by the New York, New Haven & Hartford R.R. Co.

2. For details on the life of Morse see *Dictionary of American Biography*, 13:239–41.

3. *NG*, 28 March 1901, p. 7.

4. Canal Investigation, file 5365/1, Consolidated Steamship Lines

or Morse Combination, Preliminary Report, pp. 4–5; Calvin Austin to Andrew Fletcher, 15 July 1911, in miscellaneous records of Eastern Steamship Lines in possession of A. J. McLaughlin, Lauderdale-by-the-Sea, Fla. The Portland Steamship Co. and the International Steamship Co. had outstanding capital stock of $300,000 each, and the Kennebec Steamship Co. $250,000 (ibid.). Formal merger of all the companies took place between March and May 1902.

5. "New Eastern Steamboat Company," *Portland* (Me.) *Board of Trade Journal* 14 (November 1901):202. The threat of Morse's gaining control may have been the reason that the Maine Steamship Co. of New Jersey was formed. It purchased the capital stock of the Maine company in 1901.

6. Canal Investigation, file 4953/B–I–30–1–1, Eastern Steamship Co., Correspondence, etc.; *NG*, 6 August 1903, pp. xiv–xv; "Will Absorb Eastern Line," ibid., 28 December 1905, p. 468; ibid., 15 February 1906, p. 124.

7. Morse owned 10,073 shares of Eastern Steamship Co. stock out of a total of 30,000 shares; the next largest individual holding was 1,760 shares (Canal Investigation, file 4953/B–I–30–1–1, Eastern Steamship Co., Correspondence, etc.).

8. *NG*, 9 July 1903, p. 26; "Metropolitan Line Sold Out," *MJ*, 6 May 1905, p. 3; Austin to Fletcher, 15 July 1911, in miscellaneous records of Eastern Steamship Lines in possession of A. J. McLaughlin; *Morse v. Metropolitan Steamship Co.*, p. 529.

9. Morse held 13,265 shares, and the two next largest holders each had 2,000 shares; in all there were thirty-four stockholders in the new company (Canal Investigation, file 4953/B–I–41–1, Metropolitan Steamship Co., Data on Company).

10. Austin to Fletcher, 15 July 1911, in miscellaneous records of Eastern Steamship Lines in possession of A. J. McLaughlin; "The New Boston Line," *NG*, 11 May 1905, p. vii.

11. *Transportation by Water*, 4:67–70; "C. W. Morse Acquires Mallory Line," *NG*, 1 November 1906, p. 313; "New American Turbine Steamers Yale and Harvard," *NG*, 8 August 1907, pp. 88–90. For the reaction to Morse's plans see *NG*, 15 February 1906, p. 124.

12. Canal Investigation, file 5365/1, Consolidated Steamship Lines, Preliminary Report, pp. 4–5, 11, 19. For more complete explanation of the changes see *Transportation by Water*, 4:66–73.

13. See *Transportation by Water*, 4:73; Canal Investigation, file 5365/1, Consolidated Steamship Lines, p. 19; ibid., file 4953/B–I–62–1. Calvin Austin was president of all the subsidiary companies included in the Consolidated Steamship Lines.

14. Canal Investigation, file 5365/1, Consolidated Steamship Lines, p. 19; ibid., file 4953/B–I–62–1; *Transportation by Water*, 4:73. All banking transactions of the company were carried on through the National Bank of North America, a Morse bank.

15. ICC, *Docket 6469*, 15:5383–5402. The *Railroad Gazette* was convinced that the New Haven purchased the Maine Steamship Co. to check Morse. See *Railroad Gazette*, 1 February 1907, p. 164.

16. *Financial Transactions*, 1:895, 2:1471–76, 2:1619; ICC, *Docket 4845*, 10:4226–30.

17. See *Financial Transactions*, 1:834; "The New England Navigation Company," *MJ*, 16 February 1907, p. 3; *Railroad Gazette*, 15 February 1907, p. 196; "Charles W. Morse Buys New England Company's Fleet," *NG*, 7 February 1907, p. 177; "The Latest Morse Steamship Deals," *NG*, 14 February 1907, p. 193; Clarence W. Barron, *More They Told Barron: Conversations and Revelations of an American Pepys in Wall Street*, ed. Arthur Pound and Samuel Taylor Moore (New York, 1931), p. 155; ICC, *Docket 4845*, vol. 20, Commission's Exhibit 16. For Mellen's position on the offer by Morse see ibid., vol. 12, Statement Filed by C. S. Mellen, 2 May 1913.

18. Barron, *More They Told Barron*, p. 150.

19. *Financial Transactions*, 1:875; *NG*, 21 February 1907, p. 214.

20. ICC, *Investigation & Suspension Docket No. 2838* (also listed under docket 19384), *Class and Commodity Rates between New England and Eastern Trunk Line Territories via Boston (Mystic Wharf) and Merchants & Miners Transportation Company*, 3 vols., R.G. 134, National Archives, Washington, D.C., 2:566–68; "Latest Developments in Change of Ownership of Atlantic Coast Steamship Lines," *NG*, 14 March 1907, p. 254; *Financial Transactions*, 2:1617–18.

21. The *Railroad Gazette* observed that the Merchants & Miners Transportation Co. would be an effective weapon with which a combination of railroads could fight Morse should he threaten "the existing harmony," a reference to the supposed harmony between the railroads and the coastal lines ("The Coastwise Situation," *Railroad Gazette*, 23 November 1906, pp. 447–49).

22. ICC, *Docket 6469*, vol. 8, BE 44 (app. B), B–2, J. C. Whitney to C. S. Mellen, 29 April 1907, marked "Personal"; *Financial Transactions*, 1:896, 2:1475; *Senate Hearings on the Panama Canal*, pp. 740–41.

23. *Senate Hearings on the Panama Canal*, pp. 399–400. The New Haven also took $3,250,000 of new 4 per cent bonds of the company (*Financial Transactions*, 2:1625).

24. ICC, *Docket 4845*, 10:4226–30; U.S., Congress, House, Committee on the Merchant Marine and Fisheries, *Proceedings and Report of the House Committee on the Merchant Marine and Fisheries in the Investigations of Shipping Combinations under House Resolution 587*, 4 vols. (Washington, D.C., 1913–14), 2:1052–55; *Senate Hearings on the Panama Canal*, pp. 399–400.

25. "Change of Ownership of Atlantic Coast Steamship Lines," p. 255.

26. "The New Boston Line," *NG*, 11 May 1905, p. vii.

27. *NG*, 10 August 1905, p. 106; *Morse* v. *Metropolitan Steamship Co.*, pp. 605–10.

28. Canal Investigation, file 4953/B–I–62–2–6, Metropolitan Steamship Co., Petition of Charles M. Englis to Intervene in *Berwind–White Coal Mining Co.*, vs. *Metropolitan Steamship Co.*, pp. 16–17, 20, 67; *Morse* v. *Metropolitan Steamship Co.*, pp. 530–36.

29. *NG*, 15 February 1906, p. vii; *NG*, 2 May 1907, p. 378; "Routes for the New England Navigation Company's New Freighters," *NG*, 16 May 1907, p. 401; *NG*, 6 June 1907, p. 449.

30. *Financial Transactions*, 1:886, 2:1437–39, 2:1477; memorandum enclosed in Stevenson Taylor to Charles S. Mellen, 15 March 1907, in Correspondence, 1904–12, Charles S. Mellen Papers, New Hampshire Historical Society, Concord, N.H.; *NG*, 11 April 1907, p. 328; ICC, *Docket 6469*, vol. 8, BE 1, E. T. Somers to Mellen, 4 April 1907.

31. "New American Turbine Steamers Yale and Harvard," *NG*, 8 August 1907, pp. 79–81; *NG*, 11 July 1907, p. 36. The *Yale* was so speedy that she could complete the run an hour ahead of schedule using only half her boilers (ibid.).

32. *Morse* v. *Metropolitan Steamship Co.*, pp. 530–36; *NG*, 7 November 1907, p. 312; *NG*, 14 November 1907, p. 326; *Financial Transactions*, 2:1441–42.

33. *NG*, 31 October 1907, p. 296.

34. Canal Investigation, file 4953/B–I–62–1, Consolidated Steamship Lines.

35. "Consolidated Lines Default Interest," *NG*, 9 January 1908, p. 27; "Receivers for Morse Steamship Lines," *NG*, 6 February 1908, p. 101; Canal Investigation, file 4953/B–I–62–1, Consolidated Steamship Lines; ibid., file 4953/B–I–62–2–5.

36. See *Transportation by Water*, 4:74–75.

37. *NG*, 12 September 1907, p. 184; *NG*, 14 November 1907, p. 328; ICC, *Docket 6469*, vol. 8, BE 4, Campbell to F. S. Holbrook, 16 November 1907. The rates in the 1899 schedule were between one-half and two cents lower per hundred pounds than in the 1907 agreement (ibid.).

38. Ibid., Campbell to E. F. Atkins, 18 November 1907. The resolution read: "Whereas, through the efforts of a special committee of the Boston Merchants Association, the New York, New Haven & Hartford Railroad will soon establish a new outside steamship line between Boston and New York, and whereas, schedules have been made at rates satisfactory to the above Committee, it is voted that the Secretary be instructed to send notification of the proposed establishment of the new line to the shipping members of the Association, recommending the new service to their support and patronage" (ibid., BE 4, resolution, 11 December 1907).

39. Ibid., telegrams between Campbell and Atkins, 12 and 14 December 1907; ibid., letters between Campbell and Atkins, 14, 17, and 20 December 1907; ibid., letter of the Boston Merchants Association to its members, 27 December 1907.

40. Ibid., Haskins to Campbell, 26 December 1907; ibid., Campbell to Haskins, 27 December 1907. The cost of building these steamers was high: the *Bunker Hill* cost $665,543; the *Massachusetts* $671,192; the *Old Colony* $665,281 (Memoranda regarding above steamers, dated 1/8/18, initialed R. T. B., in miscellaneous records of Eastern Steamship Lines in possession of A. J. McLaughlin).

41. Brandeis had first attacked the New Haven management in a pamphlet entitled *Financial Condition of the New York, New Haven & Hartford Railroad Company and of the Boston & Maine Railroad* (Boston, 1907).

42. ICC, *Docket 6469*, vol. 8, BE 4, Campbell to Atkins, 27 January 1908. Letter was marked "Personal."

43. *Morse* v. *Metropolitan Steamship Co.*, pp. 695–97; *NG*, 16 January 1908, p. 54; Canal Investigation, file 4953/B–I–41–1, Metropolitan Steamship Co., Report 212 of special agent H. C. McCarty, January 1910. The Boston Merchants Line reduced the amount of traffic carried on the New Haven Railroad between Boston and New York. See ICC docket 6469, 6:4933–34.

44. See "The Conviction of Mr. Morse," *MJ*, 14 November 1908, p. 3; *Financial Transactions*, 1:380–82; "The Conviction of Charles W. Morse," *Outlook*, 14 November 1908, p. 558.

45. See *MJ*, 27 November 1909, p. 7.

46. *Financial Transactions*, 1:379–89; ICC, *Docket 6469*, vol. 8, BE 5½, Jacob H. Schiff to C. S. Mellen, 23 September 1910, and Mellen to Schiff, 24 September 1910; ibid., BE 4, Campbell to Haskins, 10 March 1910. The New Haven Management claimed that it was ready to re-establish the service if necessary (ibid.). Since the Merchants Line carried over 9,000 tons of freight a month, it would appear that the argument that it was not even earning its operating expenses was untrue (ibid., 6:4933–34). Steamers sold to the Metropolitan Steamship Co. of Maine were the *Jas. S. Whitney, H. M. Whitney, Herman Winter,* and *H. F. Dimock.*

47. See *NG*, 13 January 1910, p. 35.

48. Canal Investigation, file 4953/B–I–41–1, Metropolitan Steamship Co., Calvin Austin to Herbert Knox Smith, 29 August 1910; ibid., file 4953/B–I–80, Metropolitan Steamship Co. (New Jersey), Schedule-Correspondence, etc.; "Steamboat Rivalry Ends," *NG*, 24 March 1910, p. 213; *Financial Transactions*, 2:1442–44. See also "Railroad Financial News," *Railway Age Gazette*, 8 October 1909, p. 663; *Financial Transactions*, 1:379–95, 460–74, 1097–98; ibid., 2:1440–47, 2025–30; ICC, *Docket 6469*, vol. 8, BE 5½, Calvin Austin to Mellen,

7 December 1909; ibid., Mellen to Schiff, 24 September 1910; Canal Investigation, file 4953/B–I–80, Metropolitan Steamship Co. (New Jersey), Schedule-Correspondence, etc.; "Turbine Liners for Coast," NG, 29 September 1910, pp. 150–51; "New Steamer Line—Boston–New York," NG, 10 November 1910, p. 20.

49. ICC, Docket 6469, vol. 8, BE 5½, Mellen to John F. Fitzgerald, 20 October 1910; "New Steamer Line," p. 20.

50. Memoranda regarding Bunker Hill, Massachusetts, and Old Colony, dated 1/8/18, initialed R. T. B., in miscellaneous records of Eastern Steamship Lines in possession of A. J. McLaughlin; ICC, Docket 6469, vol. 8, BE 5½, copy of the Board of Directors Meeting of the New England Navigation Co., 10 December 1910; MJ, 26 November 1910, p. 6. A saloon and 225 staterooms were to be added to each freighter, with the standard of finish equal to that of the Fall River Line (ibid.).

51. Morse v. Metropolitan Steamship Co., pp. 657–58; ICC, Docket 6469, vol. 8, BE 5½, Mellen to E. G. Buckland, 12 December 1910; ibid., copy of Board of Directors Meeting of the New England Navigation Co., 20 January 1911; ibid., 15:5506–9. Calvin Austin said that he had never had any desire to operate the Harvard and the Yale after the decision had been made to send them to the Pacific coast (Morse v. Metropolitan Steamship Co., p. 577). Austin said that in 1914 it cost over $4,000, including overhead, to operate these steamers on a round trip between New York and Boston; actual steamer expenses for the Bunker Hill and the Massachusetts were about $2,200 (ibid., pp. 657–58).

52. ICC, Docket 6469, 15:5506–8; Original Capitalization of Eastern Steamship Corp., in miscellaneous records of Eastern Steamship Lines in possession of A. J. McLaughlin; Transportation by Water, 2:81–82; NG, 24 January 1912, p. 4. See also Galen L. Stone to John F. Hill, 27 September 1911, in Correspondence, 1904–12, Charles S. Mellen Papers.

53. ICC, Docket 4845, 10:4221–25; ICC, Docket 6469, vol. 19, Petitioner's Exhibit 31–A, p. 1; Original Capitalization of Eastern Steamship Corp., in miscellaneous records of Eastern Steamship Lines in possession of A. J. McLaughlin; Senate Hearings on the Panama Canal (1912), p. 758; Proceedings of the House Committee on the Merchant Marine and Fisheries in the Investigation of Shipping Combinations, 2:1050–52.

54. Boston Chamber of Commerce, Report of the Boston Chamber of Commerce for 1911 (Boston, 1912), p. 41.

55. Transportation by Water, 4:37; ICC, Docket 6645, pp. 9–10, 16–17, 83–84, 95, 98–99, 108–5; "New Transportation Line on Long Island—Central Vermont to Operate Independent Vessels between New London and New York," NG, 19 November 1908, p. 267. Original cap-

italization was $200,000 and the bonded debt was $237,000 (*Transportation by Water*, 4:37).

56. ICC, *Docket 6645*, pp. 43, 76–81, Petitioner's Exhibit AA.

57. *Providence Board of Trade Journal* 22 (February 1910):49, 58–60. See also ibid. (March 1910), passim; "The Grand Trunk and Boston," *Advance New England* 1 (May 1910):264–65. For a map showing the route of the Southern New England Railway see H. Cole Estep, "Palmer-Providence Line of Grand Trunk," *Railway Age Gazette*, 23 August 1912, pp. 338–39.

58. "The Grand Trunk's Invasion of New England," *Railway Age Gazette*, 18 March 1910, p. 718; A. W. Currie, *The Grand Trunk Railway of Canada* (Toronto, 1957), pp. 418–21.

59. *NG*, 26 March 1913, p. 9; ICC, "Report of the Commission on Central Vermont Transportation," *ICC Reports* 114 (1926):585–90; ICC, *Docket 6645*, pp. 466–67. To complete the *Narragansett* and *Manhattan* would have cost about $150,000 (ibid.). These twin-screw steel steamers had registered dimensions of 320.2' x 48.1' x 22'.

60. See "Southern New England Railway," *Providence Board of Trade Journal* 24 (November 1912):461; "The Troubles of the New York, New Haven & Hartford," *Railway Age Gazette*, 13 December 1912, pp. 1152–53. For details of the agreement and the indictment of New Haven and Grand Trunk officials see "Indictments of New England Railroad Officers," ibid., 27 December 1912, p. 1279. The agreement was never signed.

61. ICC, *Docket 6645*, pp. 375–80; ibid., Correspondence, Sullivan Machinery Co. to Central Vermont Railroad [*sic*] Co., 9 February 1916; ICC, *Docket 4845*, vol. 1, Freight Traffic Manager of the Boston & Maine Railroad to Charles A. Prouty, 15 January 1912, ICC No. 517991; ibid., Frederick H. Babbitt to Prouty, 15 April 1912, ICC No. 541132.

62. See ICC, *Docket 6645*, pp. 466–67.

63. See "Troubles of the New York, New Haven & Hartford," p. 1153; Barron, *More They Told Barron*, p. 167; Currie, *The Grand Trunk Railway*, pp. 419–21.

64. U.S. Bureau of Foreign and Domestic Commerce, *Ports of the United States: Report on Terminal Facilities, Commerce, Port Charges, and Administration at Sixty-Eight Selected Ports*, Miscellaneous Series, no. 33, ed. Grosvenor H. Jones (Washington, D.C., 1916), p. 29. For details on the complaint of the Colonial Navigation Co. see ICC, "Report of the Commission on Colonial Navigation Company v. New York, New Haven & Hartford Railroad Company," *ICC Reports* 50 (1918):625–33.

65. See "An Extraordinary Rider," *MJ*, 1 June 1912, p. 3; "The Public Benefits by Railroad-Owned Ships," *MJ*, 28 February 1914, p. 6. See also *Transportation by Water*, vol. 4.

66. ICC, "Report of the Commission on The New England Investigation," *ICC Reports* 27 (1913):586, 609–10; ICC, "Report of the Commission on In re Financial Transactions of the New York, New Haven & Hartford Railroad Company," ibid. 31 (1915):57–58.

67. ICC, "Report on The New England Investigation," pp. 578, 590–92; ICC, *Docket 4845*, 10:3841–43; ibid., vol. 20, Commission's Exhibit 16. At the hearings on these matters the accountant for the commission said that the officials of the New Haven could not explain some of the transactions. He said: ". . . the accounting officials of the company [the New Haven] are unable, that is at least one of the accounting officials is unable to explain to me the motives [for them]" (ibid., 10:4080–82). See also New York, New Haven & Hartford Railroad, annual reports (1903–12).

68. For additional information on these transactions see ICC, "Report on The New England Investigation," pp. 590–92; ICC, *Docket 4845*, 10:4008–11, 4080–82.

69. For additional information on the lease of the Boston & Maine and the New Haven monopoly in general see Richard M. Abrams, *Conservatism in a Progressive Era: Massachusetts Politics, 1900–1912* (Cambridge, Mass., 1964); Abrams, "Brandeis and the New Haven–Boston & Maine Merger Battle Revisited," *Business History Review* 36 (Winter 1962):408–30.

70. For the position of Louis D. Brandeis see Alpheus Thomas Mason, *Brandeis: A Free Man's Life* (New York, 1956); Louis D. Brandeis, *Other People's Money and How the Bankers Use It* (New York, 1932); ICC, *Docket 4845*, 7:2473–76; ibid., vol. 9, Brandeis to Prouty, ICC No. 678926, p. 19.

71. ICC, *Docket 6469*, 2:863; ICC, *Docket 4845*, 10:4106–10, 4157–65. The "good will" supposedly represented "the equity in the company as a going concern and is based upon 25 per cent of their outstanding debentures, excluding the Providence Securities Company debentures" (ibid., 10:4106–10). The Navigation Company did salvage the boilers, valued at $26,500, from the *Connecticut* for installation on company freight boats, and thus realized $44,000 from the two steamers (ibid., 10:4157–63). The *Rhode Island* was converted into a barge (*NG*, 22 May 1912, p. 15).

72. See "The Boston and Maine's Future," *Portland* (Me.) *Board of Trade Journal* 20 (May 1907):6; "The Proposed Merger," ibid. 21 (May 1908):5–6; "The New Spirit," ibid. 22 (March 1910):507; "The Outworkings of Railroad Monopoly," *Railroad Gazette*, 20 July 1906, p. 50; "The New Haven–Boston & Maine Combination," ibid., 17 May 1907, pp. 666–67; ibid., 1 May 1908, p. 624; "Railway Mergers and Their Benefits," *Outlook*, 6 July 1907, pp. 495–97; "The New Haven Road and Its Policy of Expansion," *Commercial and Financial Chronicle*, 29 June 1907, pp. 1520–22; "What New England Says on the

Proposed Railroad Merger," *New England Magazine* 38 (May 1908): 265–82.

Chapter 9

1. *Financial Transactions*, 1:867–68. For a statement made to the stockholders in 1913 regarding the acquisitions made by the New Haven and the purposes of these acquisitions see New York, New Haven & Hartford Railroad, *Annual Report* (1913), pp. 10–11.

2. For details see ICC, "Report of the Commission on The New England Investigation," *ICC Reports* 27 (1913):560–617.

3. ICC, *Docket 4845*, 2:168–70, 205–07, 215–16; ibid., 6:2163–73; ibid., 8:3382–86; ibid., vol. 2, Brief of Robert Homans, Counsel for the Boston Chamber of Commerce, pp. 50–56; ibid., vol. 15, Charles A. Prouty to Frederick H. Jackson, 24 November 1913. For the defense of the Boston and Maine Railroad see ibid., vol. 2, Brief of the Boston & Maine Railroad, p. 82. For the opinion of an influential railroad periodical see "The New Haven and New England," *Railway Age Gazette*, 20 December 1912, pp. 1171–72.

4. For a pro-Brandeis account of the affairs of the New Haven between 1913 and 1914 see Henry Lee Staples and Alpheus Thomas Mason, *The Fall of a Railroad Empire: Brandeis and the New Haven Merger Battle* (Syracuse, N.Y., 1947).

5. See ICC, *Docket 4845*, vol. 15, Prouty to Senator George W. Norris, 12 November 1913.

6. "Indicting Common Sense," *Railway Age Gazette*, 7 February 1913, pp. 235–36. See *Railway Age Gazette*, 25 July 1913, p. 133; "The New Railway Managers and the Public," ibid., 15 August 1913, p. 258. For a list of all the changes in directors and management personnel see New York, New Haven & Hartford Railroad, *Annual Report* (1913), pp. 24–25, and *Annual Report* (1914), pp. 34–35.

7. "Mr. Mellen Speaks Out," *Railway Age Gazette*, 14 November 1913, p. 918; ICC, *Docket 4845*, vol. 15, Prouty to the *Boston Post*, 10 November 1913. For Mellen's view as he stated it in 1921 see Clarence W. Barron, *They Told Barron: Conversations and Revelations of an American Pepys in Wall Street*, ed. Arthur Pound and Samuel Taylor Moore (New York, 1930), pp. 62–64.

8. For details of these transactions and investigations see ICC, "Report on The New England Investigation," pp. 560–617; ICC, "Report of the Commission on In re Financial Transactions of the New York, New Haven & Hartford Railroad," *ICC Reports* 31 (1915):32–131. See also Staples and Mason, *The Fall of a Railroad Empire*, and Robert L. Masson, *New Shares for Old: The Boston and Maine Stock Modification* (Boston, 1958).

9. "The Financial Situation," *Commercial and Financial Chronicle*,

23 May 1914, pp. 1562–63. In this article the *Chronicle* discounted Mellen's use of President Roosevelt in the dealings with Morse when Morse offered to buy the New Haven steamship lines. In July 1913 the paper had written of Mellen: "With the lapse of time his mistakes—and they were many—will dwindle into insignificance, while his achievements will loom large" ("The New Haven Railroad and Mr. Mellen," ibid., 26 July 1913, pp. 206–9).

10. Compare "Indicting Common Sense," with "Mellen, Morgan and the New Haven," *Railway Age Gazette*, 29 May 1914, pp. 1175–76. See also "A Libel on a Great Steamboat Line," *MJ*, 30 May 1914, p. 3.

11. See "The General Situation," *Commercial and Financial Chronicle*, 18 July 1914, pp. 146–48; "A Sensational Report on a Stale Scandal," *Railway Age Gazette*, 17 July 1914, p. 88.

12. See "Termination of the New Haven Trial," *Railway Age Gazette*, 14 January 1916, p. 45; "The New Haven Case and Government Prosecutions," *Commercial and Financial Chronicle*, 15 January 1916, pp. 189–90. For comments on the private litigations brought against the New Haven Railroad see ICC, "Report of the Commission on Investigation of New York, New Haven & Hartford Railroad Company," *ICC Reports* 220 (1937):606–10.

13. See ICC, "Report on The New England Investigation," pp. 560–617; ICC, "Report on In re Financial Transactions," pp. 32–131.

14. See *Original Petition for the United States of America to the Judges of the District Court of the United States for the Southern District of New York, Sitting in Equity: The United States of America, Petitioner, v. The New York, New Haven & Hartford Railroad Company and Others, Defendants* (July 1914).

15. New York, New Haven & Hartford Railroad, *Annual Report* (1914), pp. 14–18; "The New Haven Situation," *Railway Age Gazette*, 17 April 1914, pp. 883–84. For details of the ultimate disposition of these and other properties owned or controlled by the New Haven see ICC, "Report on Investigation of New York, New Haven & Hartford Railroad," pp. 505–618.

16. New York, New Haven & Hartford Railroad, *Annual Report* (1914), p. 14; ICC, *Docket 6469*, 2:9; H. E. Melzar to C. E. McGuffin, 22 April 1936, in miscellaneous records of Eastern Steamship Lines in possession of A. J. McLaughlin, Lauderdale-by-the-Sea, Fla. The deficits of the Eastern Steamship Corp. were $124,782 in 1913 and $284,173 in 1914 (*NG*, 3 March 1915, p. 7).

17. The New England Steamship Co. operated the Bridgeport Line, the New Haven Line, the New London (Norwich) Line, the Providence Line, the Fall River Line, and the New Bedford Line. It also operated a line between Newport and Wickford, R.I.; a ferry between New Bedford and Fairhaven; and a summer service between Norwich, Conn., and Block Island, R.I. The Hartford & New York Transporta-

tion Co. operated the Hartford Line, the Bay State Line, and the Merchants Line (Bridgeport to New York). The New Haven Railroad also owned the New Bedford, Martha's Vineyard & Nantucket Steamboat Co.

18. ICC, *Docket 6469*, 2:23–24, 6:5281–82, 17:5461–62; ibid., vol. 1A, Department of Justice to the Interstate Commerce Commission, 12 January 1914, ICC No. 752284.

19. *Senate Hearings on the Panama Canal*, p. 91.

20. See ICC, *Docket 6469*, 6:4915–22, 5086; ibid., 15:5615–16, 5630–36; ibid., vol. 17, Summarization of the Facts in Re Docket 6469 by Adrian H. Boole, pp. 48–49; ibid., Brief of Alexander H. Elder, pp. 43–63.

21. Ibid., vol. 17, Principals in the Hearing Representing the Commission, the Applicant, Those Favoring, and Those Opposed to the Application; ICC, "Report of the Commission on Steamer Lines on Long Island Sound," *ICC Reports* 50 (1918):634.

22. ICC, *Docket 6469*, 2:431, 823–34, 840–42, 846, 855–57; ibid., 15:5826–27, 5851–52, 5856–58; ibid., 17:5499; ibid., Brief of Petitioner, pp. 149–50.

23. For a list of many of those represented see Appendix B.

24. For a summary of this testimony see ICC, "Report on Steamer Lines," pp. 643–46.

25. See for example "Rail and Steamship Connections," *NG*, 8 October 1913, p. 12; "The New Haven Steamboat Lines," *NG*, 21 January 1914, p. 3; "Railroad Operation of Steamers," *MJ*, 4 October 1913, p. 3; "The Sound Line Hearing," *MJ*, 5 February 1916, p. 3; "Defend Railroad's Operation of Sound Steamers," *Providence Magazine* 26 (March 1914):233–36; "Public Sentiment Favorable to the New Haven," *Railway Age Gazette*, 13 March 1914, p. 545.

26. The other Providence antagonist was William H. Fiske. For their complaints see ICC, *Docket 6469*, 4:2954–59, 2973, 2992–97, 3089–3203, 3173–79; ibid., 5:3473–86, 3534, 4102–21, 4131–32, 4969. The Providence Chamber of Commerce answered Harris in "Charges That Demand Proof," *Providence Magazine* 28 (March 1916):157. More moderate criticism of the New Haven was expressed in ICC, *Docket 6469*, 3:1431–32, 1459–64 and 4:2386–90.

27. See ICC, "Report on Steamer Lines," pp. 646–47.

28. See testimony in ICC, *Docket 6645*, pp. 156–58, 310–11, 330–32, 390, 437; ICC, "Report of the Commission on Central Vermont Boat Lines," *ICC Reports* 40 (1916):589–93. As with other users of the Sound steamers, the shippers using the Central Vermont rail-water route were overwhelmingly in favor of continued operation of the water route by the railroad. The only significant difference was that most of the shippers used the differential route to the West and were not concerned with access to New York City.

29. See ICC, *Docket 6891;* ICC, "Report of the Commission on Maine Central Boat Lines," *ICC Reports* 40 (1916):272–74.

30. "Reorganization of Eastern S.S. Co.," *NG*, 14 September 1916, p. 3. The Eastern Steamship Corp. had purchased the Boston-Yarmouth line from Canadian interests. The company also began using the Cape Cod Canal as soon as it was opened, which made the Boston–New York passenger service faster and less subject to rough weather.

31. ICC, *Docket 6469*, vol. 16, Petitioner's Exhibit 40; ICC, "Report on Steamer Lines," p. 636.

32. "Eastern S.S. Co.'s Ships Sold," *NG*, 25 January 1917, p. 3; Minute Book of Directors Meetings (1917), Eastern Steamship Lines, in offices of Pierce, Atwood, Scribner, Allen & McKusick, Portland, Me. For additional details see ICC, "Report on Steamer Lines," p. 636.

33. Memorandum, dated 2/25/21, in miscellaneous records of Eastern Steamship Lines in possession of A. J. McLaughlin; *MJ*, 6 October 1917, p. 7; "Eastern Steamship Co.'s Curtailed Service," *NG*, 7 December 1918, p. 329. The profits made by selling the steamers to the government can be seen by comparing the price the company paid for them and the price the government paid Eastern Steamship Lines:

STEAMER	SALE PRICE	COST
Massachusetts	$1,350,000	$1,297,864
Bunker Hill	1,350,000	1,303,140
Old Colony	1,150,000	1,093,081
Jas. S. Whitney	380,000	299,000
H. M. Whitney	375,000	349,000
H. F. Dimock	325,000	279,000
Herman Winter	325,000	284,000

Information from memorandum dated 2/25/21, cited above.

34. Minute Book of Directors Meetings (1917–21), Eastern Steamship Lines, in offices of Pierce, Atwood, Scribner, Allen & McKusick; New Haven & Hartford Railroad, *Annual Report* (1920), p. 20.

35. See "By the Mark and by the Deep," *NG*, 27 January 1916, p. 3; *NG*, 22 February 1917, p. 3.

36. See ICC, "Report on Steamer Lines," pp. 646–47.

37. ICC, *Docket 6469*, 6:4706–7, 18:193–95, 19:417. For a general survey of the inroads made by the motor truck see Merrill J. Roberts, "The Motor Transportation Revolution," *Business History Review* 30 (March 1956):57–62.

38. For details see Roberts, "Motor Transportation Revolution," pp. 57–58; John G. B. Hutchins, "The American Shipping Industry since 1914," *Business History Review* 28 (June 1954):122–25; John L. Hazard, *Crisis in Coastal Shipping: The Atlantic-Gulf Case* (Austin, Texas, 1955), pp. 1–29; ICC, "Report of the Commission on Further Hearing of Steamer Lines on Long Island Sound," *ICC Reports* 183 (1932):323–53.

39. See Boston & Maine Railroad, *Annual Report* (1915), p. 6; *Annual Report* (1916), p. 6.

40. See ICC, *Docket 6469*, 18:193, 195; ICC, "Report on Further Hearing," p. 352.

41. ICC, *Docket 6469*, 23:2204–5, 2209–13; ibid., vol. 18, Petitioner's Exhibits 9A and 10A; ibid., vol. 22, Petitioner's Exhibits 80A–86A. ICC examiner John H. Howell observed that in 1916, during the original hearing, the burden of evidence was that the Sound lines were very useful in making deliveries in New York Harbor but not particularly useful in traffic going beyond New York by rail. In 1930 conditions had changed somewhat in that the Sound lines did constitute a bridge that was used to a considerable extent. Before World War I this practice had been considered uneconomical (ibid., 21:1192–93).

42. Ibid., 20:1029–47.

43. Ibid., 18:38–40, 200–204; ibid., Petitioner's Exhibit No. 15A. See ICC, "Report on Further Hearing," p. 353.

44. ICC, *Docket 6469*, 18:33–36, 82–83. In 1916 the New England Steamship Co. had 30 mechanical freight units, and in 1930 it had 1,904 units (ibid.).

45. Minute Book of Directors Meeting (1929–41), Eastern Steamship Lines, in offices of Pierce, Atwood, Scribner, Allen & McKusick, 6:236. See also ibid., vols. 4–5. In 1923 Eastern Steamship Lines purchased the Old Dominion Steamship Company which extended its routes into several southern ports.

46. Ibid., 6:127; Eastern Steamship Lines, *Annual Report, 1929* and *Annual Report, 1930;* ICC, "Report of the Commission on Further Hearing of Ocean Steamship Company of Savannah: Application of Central of Georgia Railway Company, under Provisions of Section 5 of Act to Regulate Commerce as Amended by Section 11 of Panama Canal Act, Relative to Ocean Steamship Company of Savannah," *ICC Reports* 203 (1934):155–64.

47. See Eastern Steamship Lines, *Annual Report, 1936*. For more detailed information on the dilemma facing the coastal lines see Hazard, *Crisis in Coastal Shipping;* Hutchins, "The American Shipping Industry since 1914," pp. 105–27.

48. See ICC, "Report on Further Hearing," pp. 324–27, 352–53; ICC, *Docket No. W–342, Common Carrier Application of the New England Steamship Company, Filed May 14, 1941*, 1 vol., Interstate Commerce Commission Building, Washington, D.C.

49. See Minute Book of Directors Meetings (1929–41), Eastern Steamship Lines, in offices of Pierce, Atwood, Scribner, Allen & McKusick, 6:165; Eastern Steamship Lines, *Annual Report, 1934, Annual Report, 1935,* and *Annual Report, 1938.*

50. As of the spring of 1966 the Central Vermont Railway had not surrendered its certificate of public convenience and necessity to the Interstate Commerce Commission. Retention of this certificate gives

it the right to re-enter the steamship business between New London and New York City. As late as 1955 the Central Vermont Transportation Co. was an active corporation in the state of Maine. See ICC, *Docket No. W–322, Central Vermont Transportation Company Common Carrier Application*, 1 vol., Interstate Commerce Commission Building, Washington, D.C.

51. Eastern Steamship Lines, *Annual Report, 1940*.

Sources

SEEKING DETAILED INFORMATION about the rail-water transportation system in New England can be frustrating. Much material of a general nature exists, but in order to provide a comprehensive account of the operation of this system many varied sources are essential.

Two quite different types of records provided the majority of information used in this work. The first includes the manuscript collections of railroad and steamship material in Baker Library of the Harvard Business School and the smaller collection of steamship material at the Marine Historical Association in Mystic, Connecticut. The second group includes the complete record of several Interstate Commerce Commission dockets that pertain to the steamship lines owned by the railroads of New England, methods of operation in New York Harbor, and individual rate and service investigations. Of less importance but quite useful for the period from about 1900 to 1912 is the Canal Investigation of the Bureau of Corporations, the complete file of which is located in the National Archives. In it may be found information on practically every water line in the United States. From the ledgers, account books, and other material at the Harvard Business School and at the Marine Historical Association the researcher can often reconstruct the way each line conducted its business and the effect of outside influences, but unfortunately these records are incomplete, and records for some lines are nonexistent.

While the account books and ledgers provide a picture of the financial side of the business, the Interstate Commerce Commission dockets give a detailed picture of the operation of the system. The single most valuable source of information for this study was *Docket No. 6469, Steamer Lines on Long Island Sound*. In it is described virtually every aspect of the history and operation of the lines controlled by the New Haven Railroad. Much of the testimony given by officials of the New Haven Railroad and the New England Steamship Company is, to the author's knowledge, unavailable elsewhere. In addition, the dockets have the advantage of giving the researcher a collection of material that he himself might take several months accumulating. A glance at the notes in chapters 4 to 6 give an indication of the information contained in the dockets, information not found in the *Interstate Commerce Commission Reports*. Thus far economic and transportation historians have made only slight use of the records of the Interstate Commerce Commission, which deserve much more attention than they have received.

For the decades between 1860 and 1890 a most worth-while source is the Dun & Bradstreet Credit Reporting Ledgers in Baker Library of the Harvard Business School. They contain references to practically every firm and important businessman throughout the eastern part of the United States. Most companies that were privately owned or that published no annual reports can be found in these ledgers. On the whole, the articles are accurate and indicate the contemporary opinion held of the individual or company. Except for New York City the volumes are well indexed and easy to use.

The records of Eastern Steamship Lines, Inc., would be very useful for a study of the coastal steamship business after World War I, but were of limited use for this work. Most of these records are now in the Maine Historical Society, Portland, Maine, but they are not yet catalogued.

The papers of Charles S. Mellen in the New Hampshire Historical Society, Concord, New Hampshire, unfortunately are not a satisfactory source for work on the New Haven after 1903. It appears that Mellen or someone else culled the papers for the years 1903–13. The material that remains is primarily of a personal nature and contains few references to the New Haven Railroad and Mellen's activities as president.

Government publications proved invaluable in this study. The investigations and hearings conducted by the Congress are often useful, especially when those testifying represented the coastal lines or the operating personnel. Reports of special commissions like the Industrial Commission should be consulted as should the published reports of the Bureau of Corporations. The reports on transportation by the Bureau of the Census are usually too general for studies such as this one, but they do provide an indication of trends within the industry. The annual reports of the Interstate Commerce Commission and the state railroad commissions sometimes contain pertinent information.

The single most valuable type of published source for this study was the annual reports of the companies themselves. Many steamship companies apparently never published annual reports, but often the connecting railroad in its annual report discussed the relations between the two companies. Excellent collections of railroad annual reports may be found in the libraries of the Harvard Business School and the Bureau of Railway Economics, which is located in Washington, D.C.

Books on the New England coastal lines, with a few exceptions, are of a popular nature and convey something of the atmosphere of the steamboat era but not much of the substance. A notable exception is Edward C. Kirkland's *Men, Cities and Transportation* (1948). Fred E.

Dayton's *Steamboat Days* (1925) is also a useful reference work. Information on the evolution of transportation in New England can be found by reading the travel guides published between 1865 and 1900. These usually include schedules and maps as well as comments on the merits of various routes. Many books dealing primarily with railroads in New England have relevant material on the steamboat lines. These include George P. Baker, *The Formation of the New England Railroad Systems* (1937); Edward Chase, *Maine Railroads* (1926); Thomas C. Cochran, *Railroad Leaders, 1845–1890* (1953); Charles E. Fisher, *The Story of the Old Colony Railroad* (1919); Alvin Harlow, *Steelways of New England* (1946); William Z. Ripley, *Railroads: Finance and Organization* (1915); and Henry L. Staples and Alpheus T. Mason, *The Fall of a Railroad Empire* (1947). Other works on terminals, rates and regulation, economic and industrial developments, politics, and prominent individuals were also used extensively. The most significant of these were Richard M. Abrams, *Conservatism in a Progressive Era* (1964); J. Herbert Burgy, *The New England Cotton Textile Industry* (1932); Benjamin Chinitz, *Freight and the Metropolis* (1960); Edwin J. Clapp, *The Port of Boston* (1916); John A. Droege, *Freight Terminals and Trains* (1912); John L. Hazard, *Crisis in Coastal Shipping* (1955); Gratz Mordecai, *A Report on the Terminal Facilities for the Port of New York* (1885); Thomas R. Smith, *The Cotton Textile Industry of Fall River* (1944); Thomas Thorburn, *Supply and Demand of Water Transport* (1960); and Seymour Wolfbein, *The Decline of a Cotton Textile City* (1944).

The *Marine Journal* and the *Nautical Gazette* are particularly valuable periodicals for their articles on all aspects of marine affairs and technology, their editorials on various subjects, and their notes on the activities in the principal harbors in the United States. With the company annual reports, the *Marine Journal* and the *Nautical Gazette* are the major published source of marine information for the years 1870 to 1900. They provide data unavailable elsewhere. The railroad periodicals like the *Railroad Gazette* also contain some material, as do financial papers like the *Commercial and Financial Chronicle*. Where available, the publications of local and state boards of trade or chambers of commerce usually contain illuminating articles on local companies and also indicate something about contemporary attitudes of the business community.

In short, the information on the coastal steamship lines in New England is widely dispersed. If one is willing to spend the time and is willing to travel, he can find much of value. But no single source exists, principally because so many of the records have been destroyed and because comprehensive statistics until well into the twentieth century are unavailable.

Index

Air Line Railroad, 55
Ames, Oakes, 9
Atkins, E. F., 193–94
Atlantic, Gulf & West Indies
  Steamship Lines, 192–93
Austin, Calvin, 44, 93, 96, 182,
  189, 193, 194, 195, 197

Babcock, D. S., 13, 26, 27, 40–41
Babcock, Samuel D., 13
Bailey, Hollis R., 173
Barnett, William E., 63
Bay State (1846), 7
Bay State (1895), 76
Bay State Line, 103, 142–43, 176,
  222
Bay State Steamboat Company,
  6–7, 10, 11
Belfast, 81, 82
Boole, Adrian H., 212–13, 215,
  216
Booth, H. P., 192
Borden, Richard, 11
Borden, Thomas, 7
Boston, 78, 85
Boston & Albany Railroad, 55,
  143, 204
Boston & Bangor Steamship Com-
  pany, 8, 44, 45–46, 72, 103,
  180–81, 233
Boston, Clinton, Fitchburg &
  New Bedford Railroad, 24–25
Boston, Clinton & Fitchburg
  Railroad, 24
Boston, Hartford & Erie Railroad,
  18, 28

Boston & Maine Railroad, 8, 33,
  45, 46, 60, 100, 122, 169, 201,
  204, 205, 206, 211, 219
Boston Merchants Line, 194, 196
Boston, Newport & New York
  Steamboat Company, 11, 14,
  15, 21, 22
Boston & Philadelphia Steamship
  Company (Winsor Line), 185,
  188
Boston & Providence Railroad, 6,
  14–15, 27, 59, 141
Boston Railroad Holding Com-
  pany, 201
Brady, George, 170
Brandeis, Louis D., 194, 205, 208,
  226, 227
Bridgeport Line, 4, 108, 119, 222
Bridgeport Steamboat Company,
  14, 29, 43–44, 116, 164, 168,
  231–32
Bristol, 11, 12, 21, 22, 74, 86, 102
Bristol Line, 12, 14, 15, 21
Brush, George J., 179
Buckland, Edward G., 63, 158,
  160, 162, 167
Bunker Hill, 79, 84, 85, 93, 96,
  190, 194, 196, 197, 217, 246,
  illus. 5
Butler, Peter, 9

Camden, 81, 82
Campbell, Benjamin, 193–94
Canadian Pacific Railway, 199
Central Railroad of New Jersey,
  150

Central Vermont Railroad, 163
Central Vermont Railway, 28, 53,
    78, 115, 163, 164, 198–99, 201,
    215
Central Vermont Transportation
    Company, 198–200, 215–16,
    220, 223, 240
Chapin, Chester W., 75, 76
Chapin, Chester W., Jr., 154–57
Chester W. Chapin, 76, 90, 154,
    155
C. H. Northam, 75
Choate, Charles F., 63, 179
Citizens Steamboat Company of
    Troy, 183
City of Augusta, 82
City of Brockton, 53, 72, illus. 3,
    illus. 9
City of Fall River, 53, 71–72, 73
City of Fitchburg, 25
City of Lawrence, 69
City of Lowell, 76, 80, 81, 85, 100
City of New Bedford, 25
City of Richmond, 44, 45
City of Taunton, 74
City of Worcester, 41–42, 51, 70–
    71, 86
Clark, Charles P., 56–57, 63, 166
Clyde Steamship Company
    (Clyde Line), 30, 183
Cocoa, 159
Colonial Commercial Company,
    167
Colonial Navigation Company
    (Colonial Line), 103, 115,
    142–43, 202–3, 223
Commodore, 12
Commonwealth (1854), 11–12
Commonwealth (1908), 78, 81,
    87, 89, 90, 92, 110, illus. 4
Connecticut, 52, 73, 82, 83, 159,
    172, 205
Connecticut River Steamboat
    Company, 5
Consolidated Railway Company,
    205

Consolidated Steamship Lines,
    82, 183–84, 192, 195
Cottage City, 77
Coyle, J. B., 8, 9, 33, 46, 53, 77
Cumberland Steam Navigation
    Company, 8

Deering, Charles, 32
Delaware, Lackawanna & West-
    ern Railroad, 150
Dunbaugh, F. M., 154, 157, 159,
    161–62, 170, 202
Dyer Transportation Company,
    160

Eastern Railroad, 7–8, 33, 46
Eastern Steamboat Company, 180
Eastern Steamship Company, 55,
    78, 81, 82, 87, 89, 96, 109, 114,
    118, 144, 159, 170, 177,
    181–82, 193, 197
Eastern Steamship Corporation,
    103–4, 115, 128, 197, 211–12,
    216–17, 226–27
Eastern Steamship Lines, Inc.,
    217, 220, 221, 223–24
Elder, Alexander H., 213
Elliott, Howard, 208, 209
Englis, Charles M., 189
Enterprise Transportation Com-
    pany (Enterprise Line), 169–
    73
Erie Railroad, 14, 22, 56, 150
European & North American
    Railroad, 32

Fall River Line, 6, 15, 21–23, 35,
    36–39, 50–51, 66, 78, 87–88,
    92, 95, 99, 102, 103, 106–10
    passim, 114, 119, 124, 126–27,
    128, 129, 137, 143, 146, 147,
    170, 206, 220, 221, 236. *See
    also* Narragansett Steamship
    Company, New England Navi-
    gation Company, New England
    Steamship Company, Old
    Colony Steamboat Company

Fall River Railroad, 7, 10
Falmouth, 33, 46
Fisk, James, Jr., 14, 21, 22
Flagler, Henry M., 159
Frank Jones, 170, 177
Fulton, Robert, 4
Furuseth, Andrew, 94

Gardner, J. Howland, 121
General Whitney, 30, 69
Goodrich, Charles C., 94, 174,
    185, 196–97
Gould, Jay, 22
Governor Cobb, 78, 81–82
Governor Dingley, 76–77, 103
Grand Trunk Railway, 8, 144,
    164, 198–202, 208

Hall, Horatio, 159–60
Hall, John M., 156, 158, 159, 165
Harlem River & Port Chester
    Railroad, 134
Harris, William H., Jr., 214
Hart, William F., 56
Hartford, 83
Hartford & New Haven Railroad,
    18, 55
Hartford & New York Transpor-
    tation Company, 83, 94, 164,
    173–75, 176, 179, 185, 196,
    203, 212, 222, 233
Harvard, 78–79, 81, 82, 84, 85,
    87, 90, 91, 93, 99, 104, 189–92,
    246
Haskins, R. T., 194
Hays, Charles M., 163–64, 198,
    200–201
H. B. Cromwell & Company, 9
Herman Winter, 53
H. F. Dimock, 53, 72
Hill, James J., 165
H. M. Whitney, 53
Horatio Hall, 77, 85
Housatonic Railroad, 4, 14
Hudson Navigation Company,
    183

International Steamship Com-
    pany, 8–9, 32, 33, 46, 47, 181,
    233
Ives, David O., 117

James, Nathaniel W., 188
John Englis, 77, 85
Joy Steamship Company (Joy
    Line), 117, 154–55, 157–62,
    169, 170–73, 175–76, 190–91,
    240

Kennebec, 170, 173
Kennebec Steamboat Company,
    180–81, 233
Knapp, Martin A., 65
Kochersperger, H. M., 167, 177

Lehigh Valley Railroad, 150
Lewiston, 45

McLeod, Archibald A., 59–61
Maine, 75, 81, 83, 91
Maine Central Railroad, 32, 44,
    45, 47, 49, 50, 99, 101, 102,
    103, 106–7, 108–9, 110–11,
    118, 129, 177, 182, 204, 211,
    215, 216, 222–23, 239
Maine Steamship Company, 31,
    32, 46, 50, 77, 78, 99, 102, 103,
    105, 128, 144, 159, 173, 175,
    182, 185, 188, 197, 238
Maine Steamship Company of
    New Jersey, 175
Mallory, H. R., 192
Mallory Steamship Company, 183
Manhattan (1891), 77, 159
Manhattan (1913), 200, 202
Martinique, 159
Massachusetts (1836), 7
Massachusetts (1877), 27, 41,
    70, 91, 158, illus. 2
Massachusetts (1907), 79, 83,
    84, 85, 93, 96, 190, 196, 197,
    217, 246
May, Augustus S., 167

Mellen, Charles S., 153–54, 165–66, 167, 172, 174, 176, 177, 179, 185–87, 188, 189, 190, 192, 193, 196, 197, 202, 207, 208–9, 210
Merchants Line, 176, 222
Merchants & Miners Transportation Company, 66, 145, 160, 185, 186–88, 211–12, 226–27, 247
Merchants' Steamship Company, 11, 12
Metis, 26
Metropolis, 84
Metropolitan Steamship Company (Metropolitan Line), 10, 29–30, 35, 39, 53, 69, 72, 78, 80, 82, 87, 96, 99, 111, 128, 144, 146, 154, 159–62, 175, 180, 182–83, 189–98, 241
Metropolitan Steamship Company of Maine, 195–96, 197
Metropolitan Steamship Company of New Jersey, 195, 196
Mohawk, 163
Mohegan, 163
Moosehead, 110–11
Morgan, J. Pierpont, 60, 165, 177, 184, 186, 188, 195, 200, 208
Morse, Charles W., 55, 78–79, 104, 175, 177–78, 180–92, 195, 226–27
Murray's Line, 183

Nantucket & Cape Cod Steamboat Company, 24
Narragansett (1866), 40–41
Narragansett (1913), 200, 202
Narragansett Bay Line, 154–57, 212
Narragansett Steamship Company, 12, 15, 21–22, 23, 34, 89
Nashua, 53, 72, 73
Naugatuck Railroad, 14
Neptune Steamship Company, 9–10, 11

New Bedford Line, 24–25, 99, 119, 122, 124, 127, 128, 137, 143, 220–21
New Bedford, Martha's Vineyard & Nantucket Steamboat Company, 50–51, 212
New Bedford & New York Steamship Company, 24–25
New Bedford Railroad, 24
New England Navigation Company, 78, 86, 88, 95–96, 104, 166–69, 170, 172, 175, 185–88, 190, 196, 197, 204–6, 216
New England Railroad, 63, 140
New England Screw Steamship Company, 9
New England Steamship Company, 88–89, 93, 104, 111, 121, 138–39, 145–51, 193, 203, 205, 212, 213, 220–21, 222, 231–32, 240, 241
New England Transfer Company, 56, 58, 135
New England Transportation Company, 220
New Hampshire, 75, 83, 91, 95
New Haven Line, 108, 119, 222
New Haven & Northampton Railroad, 55
New Haven Railroad. *See* New York, New Haven & Hartford Railroad
New Haven Steamboat Company, 4, 29, 75–76, 116–17, 154–57, 168, 231–32
New Line, 158, 161, 162
New London Northern Railroad, 14, 28, 163
New London Steamboat Company, 163, 164, 168, 198
Newport, 37
Newport Line, 15, 37
Newport & Wickford Steamboat Company, 212, 222
New York Central & Hudson River Railroad, 135

New York Central Railroad, 58,
132, 150, 204, 211
New York & Cuba Mail Steamship Company, 183
New York & Harlem Railroad, 4,
133–34
New York & New England Railroad, 18, 35, 55, 56–61, 63–64
New York, New Haven & Hartford Railroad (New Haven
Railroad), 18, 29, 35, 36, 54,
55–67, 92, 96–97, 100, 104–5,
106, 111, 116, 118–25, 127,
129, 132–36, 138–39, 140, 142,
144–45, 149, 150, 153–80,
184–215, 220, 222, 225–28
New York & New Haven Rail-
road, 18, 55
New York & Northern Railroad,
135
New York, Ontario & Western
Railroad, 200, 204
New York & Porto Rico Steamship Company, 183
New York, Providence & Boston
Railroad, 5, 11, 13, 15, 26–28,
34, 36, 44, 57, 58, 59, 61, 62,
107–8, 141
New York & Texas Steamship
Company, 183
New York, Westchester & Boston
Railroad, 209
Northern Pacific Railroad, 165
North Star, 77, 85
Norwich Line, 5, 35, 36, 38, 41,
51, 53, 60, 63, 99, 103, 106,
108, 119, 121, 122, 124, 137,
142, 221, 222
Norwich & New London Steam-
boat Company, 13
Norwich & New York Transporta-
tion Company, 13, 18, 28–29,
64, 69, 71, 76, 86, 168, 231–32,
237
Norwich & Worcester Railroad,
5, 13–14, 18, 37, 64, 106, 119

Old Colony (1865), 37
Old Colony (1907), 79, 85, 190,
196, 197, 217
Old Colony & Fall River Railway,
10
Old Colony & Newport Railway,
14–15, 22
Old Colony Railroad, 7, 11, 22–
25, 28, 34–39, 44, 50, 57, 59,
61–62, 107
Old Colony Steamboat Company,
23–24, 25, 34–39, 52–53, 54,
59, 63, 71, 73–74, 78, 86, 93,
95, 101, 119, 151, 168, 231–32,
235, 245–46, 247

Pacific Coast Navigation Com-
pany, 196
Pacific Mail Steamship Company,
40
Parker, John G., 167
Pennsylvania Railroad, 56, 58,
136, 150, 151
Penobscot, 72–73, 159, 160
Penobscot Steam Navigation
Company, 8
People's Steamboat Company,
43–44
Philadelphia, Reading & New
England Railroad, 60
Philadelphia & Reading Railroad,
59–60
Pierce, George, 71, 73, 74
Pilgrim, 51–52, 70, 71, 80, 81,
83–84, 86, 87, 92, illus. 6,
illus. 9
Plymouth, 74, 81, 84, 87, 89, 90,
102
Plymouth Rock, 12
Porter family, 8
Portland, 76, 82, 103
Portland, Bangor & Machias
Steamboat Company, 32–33,
44

Portland, Bangor, Mt. Desert & Machias Steamboat Company, 44–45, 49
Portland & Machias Steamboat Company, 32
Portland, Mt. Desert & Machias Steamboat Company, 45, 99, 107, 170, 177, 182, 216
Portland & New York Steam Packet Company, 9, 31
Portland & Rockland Steamboat Company, 182
Portland Steam Packet Company, 8, 9, 33, 34, 46, 72, 76, 77, 99, 114, 181
Portland Steamship Company, 99, 102, 181, 233
Priscilla, 70, 74, 81, 83, 84, 85, 89, 90, 248
Prouty, Charles A., 65, 209
Providence (1867), 11, 12, 21, 22, 86, 102
Providence (1905), 78, 81, 87, 89, 90, 102–3
Providence Line, 26, 27, 35–37, 39, 65–66, 93, 103, 107, 108, 119, 124, 129, 137, 141, 145, 146, 147, 155, 161–62, 234, 245
Providence & New York Steamship Company, 12, 21, 26
Providence & Stonington Steamship Company, 26, 36, 40–41, 52, 53, 59, 62–63, 70, 72, 73, 75, 82, 86, 89, 168, 231–32, 234, 245
Providence, Warren & Bristol Railroad, 14–15
Providence & Worcester Railroad, 141
Puritan, 52, 70, 73–74, 84, 85, 90, 102

Rangeley, 110–11
Rhode Island (1873), 27, 41, 52, 70, 91

Rhode Island (1882), 72, 158, 159, 172, 205
Richard Peck, 76, 81, 85, 154, 155
Roosevelt, Theodore, 186
Rosalie, 154
Rutland Railroad, 204

St. Croix, 170
Sanford, Menemon, 8
Sanford's Independent Line, 8, 44
Sanford Steamboat Company, 44
Santiago, 171
Seabury, Otis, 25
Shinnecock, 154
Shore Line Railroad, 55, 58
Smith, A. Carey, 75–76
Southern New England Railway, 198–202, 208, 216
Sprague family, 12, 26
Stearns, Onslow, 23, 36
Stonington, 40–41, 52
Stonington Line, 11, 14, 35, 37, 38, 39, 93, 103, 106, 107, 108, 114, 119, 122, 234, 245
Stonington Steamship Company, 12–13, 26, 34, 70

Taft, John B., 9
Taylor, Stevenson, 164, 168, 170, 172, 175, 176, 185
Todd, Percy R., 159–60
Tomkins, Calvin, 139
Tremont, 72, 103, 159

United States Transportation Company, 172–73, 175, 176–77, 205

Vanderbilt, Cornelius, 5, 6, 8, 22
Vermont Central Railroad, 28–29

Warren, 170
Washington County Railroad, 177

Watrous, George Henry, 39
Western Railroad, 4
Whitcomb, David, 169
Whitcomb family, 169–73
Whitney, Henry A., 27, 30
Whitney, Henry M., 182
Whitney, James S., 9–10

Whitney, Joseph C., 187–88
Winsor Line, 185, 187

Yale, 78–79, 81, 82, 84, 85, 87,
   90, 91, 93, 99, 104, 189–92,
   246